D1611778

Augusto "César"
# Sandino

*Religion and Politics*
Michael Barkun, *Series Editor*

# Augusto "César" Sandino

## Sandino

*Messiah of Light and Truth*

Marco Aurelio Navarro-Génie

 Syracuse University Press

Copyright © 2002 by Syracuse University Press
Syracuse, New York 13244-5160

*All Rights Reserved*

First Edition 2002

01  02  03  04  05  06      6  5  4  3  2  1

The paper used in this publication meets the minimum requirements
of American National Standard for Information Sciences—Permanence
of Paper for Printed Library Materials, ANSI Z39.48–1984.∞™

**Library of Congress Cataloging-in-Publication Data**

Navarro-Génie, Marco Aurelio.
    Augusto "César" Sandino : messiah of light and truth / Marco Aurelio Navarro-Génie.—
    1st ed.
    p. cm.—(Religion and politics)
    Includes bibliographical references and index.
    ISBN 0-8156-2949-4 (alk. paper)
    1.  Sandino, Augusto César, 1895–1934—Religion. 2.
Millennialism—Nicaragua—History. 3. Spiritualism—Nicaragua—History. 4.
Insurgency—Nicaragua—History. 5. Nicaragua—History—1909–1937. 6.
Revolutionaries—Nicaragua—Biography. I. Title. II. Series.
  F1526.3.S23 N38 2002
  972.8525'1'092—dc21                       2002021755

*Manufactured in the United States of America*

*To Ivania Edith Génie Valle*

*(sine qua non)*
*Requiescat in Pace*

To understand the living in Nicaragua, I found, it was necessary to begin with the dead. The country was full of ghosts. *Sandino vive,* a wall shouted at me the moment I arrived, and at once a large pinkish boulder replied, *Cristo Vive,* and what's more, *viene pronto.*

**—Salman Rushdie,** *The Jaguar Smile*

And the most glorious exploits do not always furnish us with the clearest discoveries of virtue and vice in men; sometimes a matter of less moment, an expression or a jest, informs us better of their characters and inclinations, than the most famous sieges, the greatest armaments, or the bloodiest battles whatsoever.

**—Plutarch,** *Lives*

Since virtue is concerned with passions and actions, and on voluntary passions and actions praise and blame are bestowed, on those that are involuntary pardon, and sometimes also pity, to distinguish the voluntary and the involuntary is presumably necessary for those who are studying the nature of virtue, and useful also for legislators with a view to the assigning both of honors and of punishment.

**—Aristotle,** *Nichomachean Ethics*

# Contents

# Illustrations

**Marco A. Navarro-Génie** was born in Nicaragua. He teaches political science at St. Mary's College and at Mount Royal College in Calgary, Alberta, Canada. He is author of "Augusto 'César' Sandino: Prophet of the Segovias" and of the Augusto Sandino website (http://www.sandino.org).

# Preface

MICHAEL OAKESHOTT once compared the historian's task to building
a dry stone wall. Although one may have the required number of stones and
know exactly where to build, the success or failure of the enterprise de-
pends on the builder's ability to select the stones and to place them in such
a way as to build as durable and elegant a structure as possible. Oakeshott
noted that a dry stone wall has no extraneous substances holding the pieces
together, and so even when one has done a remarkably good job of it, there
always remain gaps. When the builder is careless, however, and places the
stones in a random, unfitting, or unsightly manner, the gaps are greater, and
so is the risk of collapse.

My work on Augusto Sandino began in 1991 as an outgrowth of a study
of millenarian themes in liberation theology. Some writers I consulted for
that project repeatedly cited the Nicaraguan guerrilla leader in their work,
as though he were a prophet of sorts. Wanting to see if what they attributed
to Sandino was indeed what he had said, I started to read his own correspondence, along with some of the religious texts that his more recent editors and followers had ignored or had concealed for decades. The dry stone
wall of the history of Sandino suddenly exhibited its unsightly gaps—and
the topic captivated me. Liberation theology took a back burner.

I do not pretend to imply that this book is the full and definitive reconstruction of that wall; I merely wish to point out how I came to consider
that some of the stones needed rearrangement in order to make it more
durable. Evaluating the utility of theoretical approaches to the understanding of civilizational phenomena, Samuel Huntington (1997, 31) offers the
analogy of a map: "We need a map that both portrays reality and simplifies
reality in a way that best serves our purposes." Over a century has lapsed
since Sandino's birth, and more than a decade since he ceased to be an official state icon. It is thus time to make a fresh inquiry into his life, taking
into account those aspects that have long been ignored—especially his reli-

gious beliefs—so as to bridge the gulf between what the name "Sandino" has come to represent and who the man Sandino was in his own day.

I have based my research primarily upon published versions of Sandino's writings, along with a limited number of unpublished manuscripts. Colleagues and friends in Managua kindly supplied me with reproductions of unpublished documents as well as copies of the original publications of the reviews *Ariel* and *Amauta.* It is ironic that the single most important source of Sandino materials and documents was compiled by the tyrant who killed him: Anastasio Somoza García's *El verdadero Sandino o el calvario de las Segovias* (1936). Many readers (and not only Sandinistas) have scorned the allegedly ghostwritten book, but it remains the best single original source published; even the ideologically driven Sandinista writer Sergio Ramírez admits it to be a superlative principal source *(fuente principalísima)* (Sandino 1981, 1:21). I rely on Somoza regularly; it is particularly useful for its reproduction of many documents relating to religious beliefs that some of Sandino's other editors have concealed.

All translations from the Spanish and the French in this book are my own. In translating some of Sandino's letters and documents, I have at times consulted as reference R. E. Conrad's laundered English translation of Sandino's works (Sandino 1990). In my translation of a segment of Rubén Darío's poem "Song of Hope," I consulted Lysander Kemp's translation (Darío 1988). In order to avoid burdening the text with too many translation notes, I have thought it appropriate to clarify at the outset my translation of some common terms. Sandino occasionally used the expression *madre patria;* I translate both *madre patria* and *patria* as "motherland." I only use "country" when Sandino uses *país.* The compound word *vendepatria*—literally, someone who sells his or her motherland—will be translated as "sellout." A still more problematic word, *conciencia,* depending on the context may be translated as "conscience," "consciousness," or "awareness." Finally, the word *sandinista* poses a small problem: although it originally referred to any follower of Sandino, in the present the term typically is associated with the recent movement that appropriated his name (and which reached power in Nicaragua from 1979 to 1990); thus, I try to avoid the term as much as possible when referring to Sandino's followers in his own time. Overall, I have tried to be as accurate as possible in keeping with the original content and context of the texts. All references to the Hebrew and Christian scriptures are from the New International Version of the Bible.

·  ·  ·

**NOW,** I come to the pleasure and the duty of thanking all those who have helped in the completion of this book. I must first thank the Department of Political Science and the Faculty of Graduate Studies at the University of Calgary, whose support allowed me to conduct my research and to write. Funds from the University of Calgary Research Grants Committee enabled me to travel to Nicaragua to gather research materials.

Several people and institutions lent me their support in Nicaragua. I wish to thank the staff at the Instituto de Historia de Nicaragua (formerly the Instituto de Estudios del Sandinismo) and its director, Margarita Vannini. I also am grateful to members of the Magnetic-Spiritual School of the Universal Commune: Armejio Muñoz and his colleagues in Managua, and Pedro Sandreas in Miami. Their candid conversations, and the literature that they provided me about their school and their teachings, have helped me to understand better Sandino and his world. I thank the staff at the Hemeroteca Nacional de Nicaragua and its former director Cristina Ortega for their kind assistance. I am obliged to Vidaluz Meneses, former dean of the Faculty of Humanities at the Central American University, for suggesting venues of research. I am thankful to my dear friend Michelle Dospital for heated discussions about Sandino and the latter-day Sandinistas, for research materials, and for challenging my raw, inexperienced, "Miami-boy" skills. I am also grateful to Jorge Eduardo Arellano for his support and for the materials that he chose to share with me; may he have enjoyed lots of Concha y Toro cabernet. On my way to and from Nicaragua, Juan and Helen Fernández housed me while I sorted out lines of research and while I browsed through libraries in Miami; I thank them for harboring most of my research materials and me during the onslaught of Hurricane Andrew.

My initial enthusiasm for the study of Sandino's life and thought was fueled by the steady flow of books and articles that my brother Rigoberto kept sending me from Nicaragua. I owe much to my brother and his family for "adopting" me and for helping me to rediscover parts of Nicaragua when they occasionally thought that I had had enough exposure to the clouds of dust at the Hemeroteca Nacional. I thank my friends and former schoolmates Debala Olana, Robert Roach, John von Heyking, and Ian Brodie, who too often had the misfortune to be close to me (and to Sandino) as I conducted my research and wrote my master's thesis. Thanks for seeing me through the bumpy stretches and the smooth parts. Much gratitude is expressed to Doug McClintock, for his boundless generosity while I revised the manuscript; to Sandy Munn at the library at Mount Royal College for her assistance in the search for fresh sources on millenarianism; and to Do-

minique Navarro for compiling the index. I am very grateful to Steve
Holmes for the thoughtful and patient editing of the manuscript. I would
like to thank the anonymous reviewers for their kind reading and helpful
comments, and to Michael Barkun, from whom I have stolen the "latter-
day Sandinista" expression. I thank Professor Barry Cooper for turning me
around with his peculiar pedagogy, and for acquainting me with Alberta's
footwear and later with the art of potholing. I am especially grateful to Professor Thomas Flanagan for his guidance, patience, and consistent encouragement. Of course, my acknowledgement of the support of these
individuals and institutions in no way implies any responsibility on their
part for this book's content or for any of the infelicitous errors that it may
still contain.

Last, but most important, I am indebted to Dominique, Ivania, Gabriel,
and Diego for their loving and unfailing support.

I want to dedicate this book to the three generations that have faced
Sandino and his successors: to my grandparents, who first experienced the
chaos and adversity of the Sandino years; to my parents, their children, who
have in turn endured the magnified disorder of Sandino's children; and to
my brothers and sisters, who have paid the price of a life of exile and whose
children may never grow up in our parents' homeland. I pray that the new
generation, our children's generation, will finally become free from the re-
current fratricidal cycle.

# Abbreviations

| | |
|---|---|
| APRA | Alianza Popular Revolucionaria Americana<br>  Popular Revolutionary Alliance of the Americas |
| EDSN | Ejército Defensor de la Soberanía Nacional de Nicaragua<br>  Army in Defence of the National Sovereignty of<br>  Nicaragua |
| EMECU | Escuela Magnético-Espiritual de la Comuna Universal<br>  Magnetic-Spiritual School of the Universal Commune |
| FMLN | Frente Farabundo Martí de Liberación Nacional<br>  Farabundo Martí National Liberation Front |
| FSLN | Frente Sandinista de Liberación Nacional<br>  Sandinista National Liberation Front |
| GN | Guardia Nacional de Nicaragua<br>  National Guard of Nicaragua |
| Mafuenic | Manos Fuera de Nicaragua<br>  Hands Off Nicaragua Committee |
| PCM | Partido Comunista de México<br>  Mexican Communist Party |
| UHAO | Unión Hispano-América-Oceánica<br>  Hispano-American Oceanic Union |
| UFCO | United Fruit Company |

# Introduction

OUR PERSONAL EXPERIENCES of community and of the world affect our understandings of ourselves and of our place in them. The *mestizos* of Latin America—those of mixed European and Indian descent—have long struggled to define their identity as individuals and as a collective. Being neither Indian nor white in a rigidly delineated social context, they have lacked a predefined identity; living in a cultural vacuum, they have often felt that Europeans derided them and that Indians mistrusted them. By and large, because they have shared with the Indians the experience of oppression and suffering, they usually have chosen to ground their roots and identity in the native culture. However, existing Indian society has not proved a strong soil in which to ground those roots because the foundations of native mythical social order had collapsed with the Europeans' arrival. Thus, part of the Latin American struggle for a distinct identity has centered upon the reconstruction and cult of the past: *mestizos* and Indians alike have believed that they must establish their identity upon the recreation of the pre-Columbian cultural world, for only then, once they had grounded their origins, could they begin to interpret the meaning of their existence. In a historical irony, however, their rejection of the Iberian imperial order and their quest for independence in the nineteenth century, rather than taking them back to their desired roots, brought them forward to the worship of the modern era and of its myths.

Moreover, beyond history and sociology, these questions about the personal and collective meaning of existence have religious dimensions as well. Although political answers are sometimes attempted, they do not sufficiently articulate the full scope of the reality that human beings experience. Religions seem to provide more adequate means of explaining certain fundamental human experiences—of belonging, of beginning and end, of decay and stagnation—and the crucial issue of human purpose. Conversely, just as religion informs one's experience, so too the kind of religion that individuals choose is informed by one's experiences of community and of the world.

As one part of the broader Latin American historical and religious search—more urgently prompted in periods of crisis—the identity and self-understanding of some Nicaraguans was shaken once again when the United States Marines occupied their country from 1912 to 1933. Following their defeat of Spain at the end of the nineteenth century, the United States displaced Great Britain and expanded into the Caribbean region, ultimately bringing U.S. Marines to Nicaragua after the fall of the Liberal dictator José Santos Zelaya. Zelaya was a staunch nationalist; under his leadership, the British had been expelled from the Mosquitia (the Atlantic coast of Nicaragua) and he allegedly had resisted American plans to build an interoceanic canal through his country. Zelaya's hostility toward the United States led to his fall and to the rise of the Nicaraguan Conservatives to power, under whose rule Nicaragua lost its de facto sovereignty and became a virtual protectorate of the United States. The American government secured control of Nicaraguan customs, administered the collection of its taxes, and seized control of the National Railway Company and of the National Bank (Bolaños 1984); in addition to income and finances, the allegedly apolitical National Guard was later established and directed in its entirety by American officers. Under such pressures, Nicaragua signed the infamous Bryan-Chamorro Treaty, ceding to the United States the right to build a transoceanic route through (and military bases in) its territory for a renewable period of ninety-nine years; the treaty was signed in 1914 (the year the Panama Canal opened), and the United States Senate ratified it in 1916. In the treaty, Nicaragua also relinquished its claims to the islands of San Andrés and Providencia in favor of Colombia, from which Panama had broken away (Bethel 1991, 65–66). (The unfulfilled aspects of the treaty were finally abrogated in the 1960s, but the loss of Nicaraguan territory has never been reversed.) Moreover, the American occupation occurred at a time when Nicaragua's tenuous social order was collapsing—largely because of the power-hungry, uncompromising élite who were incapable of keeping their ambitions in check and of maintaining their house in order. For these reasons, Nicaraguans have traditionally interpreted this period as their most humiliating and darkest hour, matched only by the war against William Walker in the previous century.

In the mind of a young unknown named Augusto Sandino, the American occupation was equivalent to the domination of the Indian race by the Europeans, but with a new twist: he thought that the Anglo-Saxon conqueror wanted to destroy the newly emerging Indo-Hispanic race. Thus, between 1927 and 1933, he led a rebellious legion of peasants in a protracted guerrilla war against the U.S. Marines in the northern hills of Nicaragua, the Segovias. At the head of his ragged troops, Sandino believed himself to be the new defender of a violated and threatened race. In understanding his own and his country's historical circumstances, Sandino applied to Nicaragua political concepts and symbols drawn from socialism, anarcho-communism, and Indo-Hispanic racial rhetoric, all of which he encountered on sojourns in revolutionary Mexico. While in Mexico, he also was initiated into a variety of esoteric beliefs, and his religious quest eventually led him to the spiritist beliefs of Joaquín Trincado (1855–1935) and his Magnetic-Spiritual School of the Universal Commune (*Escuela Magnético-Espiritual de la Comuna Universal*), from whom he continued to learn about the occult, cabalistic traditions, and spiritism. In time, Sandino himself claimed divine inspiration and representation, announcing the arrival of the end of the world, final salvation, and the coming of a new era; eventually, he came to believe that he was an incarnation of the divine, a new messiah. It is the unfolding of this fascinating story that I seek to portray here.

Traditionally, Sandino's struggle against the occupying American forces and their local collaborators has been understood in strict, albeit romanticized, nationalist terms. Sandino was a heroic patriot, fighting to evict a foreign force from his motherland. One author tells us that "Sandino was a pure nationalist with no plans to transform Nicaragua after the Marines were gone" (Paige 1997, 178). Another has claimed that Sandino "never manifested a doctrinaire ideological strain of any sort" (Booth 1985, 42). In particular, Sandino's followers—including the guerrilla movement that emerged in the 1960s called the Sandinista National Liberation Front (*Frente Sandinista de Liberación Nacional*, or FSLN)—have usually concealed or downplayed evidence that he may have been motivated in his struggle by religious convictions. (Alejandro Bendaña's *La mística de Sandino* [1994], suddenly willing to look at Sandino's spiritual currents, is the exception among latter-day Sandinistas.)[1]

Conversely, some accounts appear to be interested only in showing a

---

1. "Sandino's *sandinismo*," Bendaña writes, "contains values and pivotal propositions for the contemporary search for democratic alternatives" (1994, 138). Thus, after many failed years of preaching that Sandino was the answer to Nicaragua's problems, contemporary Sandinistas are still turning to the same well for ideas. In this sense, Bendaña's book is an utilitarian refashioning of Sandino's image to be used in support of another political project; namely, making the

darker side to Sandino and to vilify the man, portraying him as a communist puppet, a bandit, and a gangster.[2] Some say that Sandino was "mentally
disturbed" (Somoza 1936, 3; see also 199, 197). Juan Matagalpa (1984, 161)
called him deluded and demented—and paid for this iconoclastic audacity
with his life, a blunt reminder that in Nicaragua, dealing with Sandino's
image (like the rest of its politics) is a game that is played for keeps. Although it may be true that Sandino had such delusions, dementia and in-
sanity are clinical diagnoses for which neither Matagalpa nor Somoza
García offered any credible evidence or analysis.

My present historiographical purpose is not to support or to attack any
of the existing views on Sandino. What is more, I refuse to enter the debate
as to whether Sandino was a bandit or a patriot, sane or insane, for these are
reductionist and convenient interpretations of who Sandino was; these pre-
fabricated conclusions have not advanced scholarship in any direction. Instead, I wish to bring Sandino's religious ideas and disposition to the
surface, to factor them into his political activities in order to give a more
complete portrait. In particular, I argue that Sandino's religion can best be
understood as a form of millenarianism—an apocalyptic tradition in which
adherents typically desire to rid the world of its imperfections, to bring redemption to a chosen few, and to create or re-create some form of heaven on
earth (referred to as "the millennium"). In order not to clutter the central
narrative with theoretical digressions, I give the case for Sandino's millenarianism (and an explanation of millenarian theories) in the last chapter;
the interested student of religion or of political ideas, or the layperson wishing a more detailed account, may choose to tackle that argument at any
point. As will soon become evident, however, the ideas, images, and emotions of the millenarian impulse form an inescapable and fundamental
component of Sandino's life and work.

In approaching Sandino in this way, I must confront an existing narra-

---

difficult transition from an armed political force to an established opposition political party in
what many hope will become a democratizing context. In Nicaragua, Sandino still is not being
studied for his own sake but with the desire to exploit an angle for political gain.

2. For example, Somoza García presented Sandino as a "bandit," a "gangster of cheap ambitions," a "man of superstition," and a "false prophet" (Somoza 1936, 3, 303, 315, 94, 175); he
argued that Sandino was an enemy of the state and "a threat to the sacred institutions upon
which rest the liberty, prosperity, and peace of the Republic" (4). He was correct about the
threat that Sandino represented to the country, and despite his overt animosity toward the guerrilla leader, Somoza's book grasped some of the essence of the real Sandino. See also Moncada
1985, 330–32; Sociedad 1947.

tive about his life that is fraught with blatant inconsistencies. Some of the factual inconsistencies in the historical evidence constitute deliberate attempts to construct new circumstances or to obscure and conceal existing ones; I will not pause to consider every one of these inconsistencies but only those that are sufficiently important to bear upon my argument about Sandino's beliefs. The relevant issues fall into two categories. The first category involves Sandino's own clever narration of specific events, designed to manipulate, to control, and to promote the specific political image that he wanted. The second category, the work of his followers, has two manifestations: the promotion of Sandino's narrations as historical facts, without critical regard or verification; and the deliberate concealment of evidence that might have brought into question the mythical figure of Sandino. Three issues of particular importance stand out: the long-standing myth that Sandino returned from exile in Mexico in 1926 exclusively to fight the political injustice of a coup and the American occupation of his country; the picture of a harmonious relationship between Sandino and Salvadoran fellow revolutionary Farabundo Martí; and the myth that once Sandino achieved his goal of removing the U.S. Marines from Nicaragua, he honorably withdrew from the battlefield and from political life with the sole objective of helping his peaceful people. In all three cases, there is sufficient historical evidence to break through the propaganda and myth to the complex human reality beneath.

Overall, this book has two objectives. The first is to place Sandino within the millenarian religious tradition; that is, to show in detail that Sandino's unfolding expectations moved toward the establishment of a real perfection on earth and that those expectations occupied a central place in his rebellion. It is not my intention to argue that all aspects of Sandino's life can be understood as millenarian; I am convinced, however, that presenting the religious underpinnings of Sandino's life and actions broadens our understanding of the rebel by accounting for rejected materials once considered marginal and by offering a framework into which to include them as well as to explain them. While I do not intend to reduce the figure of Sandino to his religion, I am persuaded that a discussion of Sandino's religious understanding expands and makes up for deficient segments in previous scholarship. The second objective of the book, closely related to the first, is to trace the development of Sandino's rebellion throughout his life. There is a close link, I argue in the subtext, between Sandino's rebellious attitude and his proclivity for millenarian scenarios.

·    ·    ·

NO man's life can be described in a single snapshot or by a single idea. Sandino's disposition was not static. It unfolded over time in a variety of circumstances and personal experiences; it possessed a dynamic character. As the significant developments in his life are presented, it will become apparent that there was not one Sandino, but many. There was, to name the most salient, Sandino the nationalist, the anarchist, the communist, the socialist, the Freemason, the spiritist, and the millenarian. Biography is therefore the best approach for tracing the development of so complex a man.

This book is divided into six chapters. The first five chapters examine Sandino's life and its developments. Chapter 1 covers Sandino's early days to the beginning of his rebellion, tracing the misery of his childhood and the suffering of his early adult life. The second chapter details his patriotic war against the American forces, his hatred for General Moncada, and the initial animus of his rebellion. Chapter 3 looks into his crucial second trip to Mexico, his disappointments in his dealings with the Mexican government and with the Mexican communists (in what amounted to a betrayal) as well as his adoption of a radical new religion. Chapter 4 examines his new set of ideas and their impact on his struggle and its means, especially his immersion in the spiritist ideas that led him to failed prophecy and to a more radically messianic path. Chapter 5 covers the peace accords between Sandino and the government of Nicaragua that came with the evacuation of the U.S. Marines, including the *Pax Sandinista* and Sandino's project of setting up a commune as a model for the perfect society, a project cut short prematurely by his death. Shifting to a more interpretive mode, chapter 6 introduces the theory of millenarianism and highlights some of its central aspects before stepping back to examine the nature and characteristics of Sandino and his beliefs, placing them within the context of millenarian theoretical prescriptions. The chapter ends with a short conclusion.

# Augusto "César"
# Sandino

Map 1. Central America

# 1

# From Misery to Rebellion

[We lived] with such low salaries and such hard tasks that our existence was painful, truly painful! Prematurely, I began to be aware
of my life as a tragedy that ate away inside me with the reality of a
terrible misery. Misery and impotence at such tender years! And
the truth is that having the opportunity to become a vagabond and
a criminal, I decided to be a person, I decided to become someone.
                    —Augusto C. Sandino, in an interview by José Román

## The Family

THE SMALL VILLAGE of Niquinohomo is located about thirty kilometers west of Managua, in the department (province) of Masaya,
Nicaragua. The village sits upon the country's southwestern plateau,
whose rich soil offers a favorable climate for the cultivation of coffee, corn,
and other local crops. In this setting, in either 1868 or 1869, Gregorio
Sandino Muñoz was born to Santiago Sandino (himself the son of Spanish
immigrant Aparicio Sandino) and Augustina Muñoz, an Indian woman (for
the uncertain dates, see Wünderich 1995, 38, and Román 1979, 36). Gregorio became a successful small merchant and coffee grower and a wealthy
and respected personality in the village, and his family occupied a house at
the heart of the town, facing the main square—a location of much prominence in the hierarchical economy of space in colonial towns. His position
was not opulent by national standards, but his plantations and business
generated employment for the surrounding area.

Although he was not himself a politician, Gregorio may have had a
strong influence in picking the village's political authorities (S. Sandino
1928). Augusto Sandino's statement that his father was a judge in the town
is sometimes repeated, but there is no evidence to that effect (see e.g. Wünderich 1995, 38). What is known is that Gregorio Sandino was a member of

4 *Augusto "César" Sandino*

the Nicaraguan Liberal Party and a supporter of the Zelaya government (1893–1909), rounded up and jailed twice during the post-Zelaya Conservative reign (S. Sandino 1928). The Nicaraguan Liberals, enamoured of French positivism since the second half of the nineteenth century, were staunchly anticlerical and embraced scientistic ideas such as Auguste Comte's "sociocracy" (an age of progress that was to follow the backwardness of theocracy); their modernizing program included grand projects of material progress and technical development, and they advocated reforms in many different areas such as labor, indigenous land tenure and general property, law, education, and suffrage (Woodward 1985, 155–56). Gregorio Sandino may have been frustrated—perhaps even embittered—by the fallen status of the Liberals after the 1911 Conservative restoration; even by the standards of the feuding Liberal and Conservative factions in the country, it was not a good time to be a Liberal in Nicaragua.

The other end of the local social spectrum was occupied by persons such as Margarita Calderón—a *campesina*, a peasant worker of the fields. She picked coffee in the fields surrounding Niquinohomo during the harvest months, and she worked as a domestic servant in the houses of the wealthier members of the village during the months of idleness on the plantations. In particular, she worked at the home and in the fields of the Sandino family.

Thus, on 18 May 1895, in Niquinohomo, from an encounter between Gregorio Sandino and his servant Margarita Calderón, Augusto Nicolás Calderón Sandino was born.[1] Augusto was raised by his mother and grew up with the moral stigma of his illegitimate birth and in the misery of her inadequate earnings—a situation soon aggravated by the arrival of more children. Margarita had difficulty making ends meet and was in debt so often that at a young age, Augusto was forced to work in the fields to help her out (something that was not uncommon at the time). For much of the year, however, he did not always have the comfort of his mother's company because he was left at home looking after his siblings when she worked as a domestic servant.

---

1. In Nicaragua, children born out of wedlock traditionally take the family name of the mother first and that of the father second, whereas the opposite is done in socially accepted circumstances. In 1920, the first national census revealed that 54 percent of births in Niquinohomo took place out of wedlock, nearly 15 percent above the national average of the time; see Dospital 1996, 197.

**Boyhood and Youth**

Augusto's relationship with his mother was shaped by their deplorable conditions. He suffered from her hardships, which were also his own, and even claimed to have stolen from time to time to feed her (Román 1979, 37). By his own account, at nine years of age he was dragged to jail with his mother when she failed to pay some of her debts; Sandino described in detail the horrifying tale of his mother's miscarriage in the detention cell right before his eyes, the product of the mistreatment she received, with no other help than his own (Román 1979, 38). To be sure, there are no means of confirming the veracity of this story (and indeed, Sandino's allegation that his father was "the judge of the pueblo" when this supposedly occurred is unconfirmed); nonetheless, whether or not the story is true, that version of events is what Sandino came to believe, and it is certainly expressive of the violence and bleakness that encircled his childhood.

Under these circumstances, Augusto's emotional relationship with his mother was ambiguous. He loved her, but at the same time he was ashamed of her social condition, and he loathed her promiscuity (he was often exposed to the many lovers she brought home to their single-room hut). To make the shame more real, Margarita was often pregnant and "she frequently gave birth," he told Román in 1933 (1979, 37); Augusto thus had several maternal siblings (although it is not clear how many), who were likely fathered by different men. As yet another source of strain between mother and child, when Augusto was only nine years old Margarita Calderón followed one of her lovers to the city of Granada, leaving the boy Augusto with his maternal grandmother in Niquinohomo.

Thus, in addition to bearing the burden of his illegitimacy in a tiny village, Augusto likely was exposed to scathing rumors and comments about his mother. As a result, the young boy not only suffered with his mother but also because of her. He described his childhood as lacking not only "in the most elemental things for bodily comfort, but also in what is most essential: the warmth of a home for spiritual tranquillity, and the formation of character and personality." It is no surprise that in hindsight, he understood his young years as "a ferocious struggle against a cruel and pitiless life, and against the designs of fatality" (Román 1979, 37). As he grew older, this basic story became the way in which Sandino interpreted his entire life.

Not surprisingly, given the conditions of his early rearing, Augusto developed social resentments. Although he boasted of being a hard-working person, he detested having to work and resented the fact that his half-brother Sócrates, the legitimate son of Gregorio, did not (Román 1979, 36). He was envious of Sócrates and would have liked to have had what he perceived to be the latter's problem-free childhood in their father's household. Envy did not make him dislike his brother, however, to whom he grew very close and for whom he developed much affection. Instead, Augusto recalled directing the bitterness of his childhood toward Providence. He cursed his own fortune and complained that God was unfair to him: "Why is God this way? . . . If the Law is the voice of God intended to protect the people, as the priest says, the Authority, why instead of helping us the poor does it favor the crooks? Why does God love Sócrates more than He loves me, since I have to work and he doesn't? God damn it! God and life are pure shit. It's only us poor people who get screwed" (Román 1979, 38). Although these are not the words of a child but those of an adult (indeed, a revolutionary leader), the statement does reflect the way in which his childhood experiences shaped the mature Sandino's interpretation of his existence and of his personal place in the social structure, showing his early bitterness, his anticlerical sentiment, his contempt for traditional authority and his hatred for conventional religion. Seeing himself as downtrodden and as on the lower end of the family-based, rigorously structured society of early-twentieth-century Nicaragua, he preferred a God who intervened on behalf of the suffering and who made all things right in the world.

Augusto's relationship with his father began after his mother's departure for Granada—a departure that was difficult for Augusto not only because his mother abandoned him but also because by moving in with his grandmother he was again required to take care of someone else. It was during this period that the young boy confronted his father on the streets. According to his later story, Augusto was a proud boy, and though in rags he walked up to Don Gregorio and challenged him: "Listen Sir, am I your son or not? . . . Sir, if I am your son, why do you not treat me like you treat Sócrates?" (Román 1979, 38). After this encounter, Don Gregorio apparently brought Augusto home to his wife, Doña América, and to their three children: Zoila, Asunción, and Sócrates. This is very likely the time when Augusto dropped his mother's last name from usage, becoming Augusto C. Sandino.

Finally, the young boy had escaped misery and abandonment and now enjoyed the protection of a father and the security of a home. He was being cared for, fed regularly, clothed, and sent to school—a significant improvement from his mother's dwelling and social habits. Nonetheless, he continued to suffer from the social stigma of being an illegitimate child. Under his stepmother's instructions, he was apparently treated like a servant in the paternal home, forced to perform chores (unlike the other children) and to eat in the kitchen with the help; he even wore the old clothes of his younger brother Sócrates, a clear sign of preferential treatment. Thus, in spite of his material improvement, the net result was not joyful, for he felt scorned and out of place.

Augusto's early experiences at school were similarly conflicted. School attendance in itself made him part of a privileged class in Nicaragua; at around the time that he was born, only 3 percent of the national population had access to elementary schooling, a figure that may have improved modestly by the time he reached school (Newland 1991, 359). However, Augusto learned his first letters at an advanced age, and thus the other children at school made fun of him, at times leading to fistfights (Ibarra 1973, 26). "My ignorance was famous in the whole school," he confessed, but wounded in his pride by schoolmates' pranks, he soon caught up: "I dedicated myself to studying with resolute tenacity" (Román 1979, 40; see also Belausteguigoitia 1985, 87). He never became an exceptional student, however; like many young boys at his age, he probably preferred to play rather than to study. No records survive from the schools that the young Augusto attended, and attempts to reconstruct his educational progress are partial and contradictory: Beals tells us from his interview with Sandino (1932, 264) that young Augusto was sent to high school in Granada, where he was a below-average student, and Belausteguigoitia adds that Augusto studied commerce in high school (1985, 87); Wünderich, however, states that Augusto only finished up to the fourth grade in elementary school (1995, 40).

Whatever the exact extent of his schooling, young Augusto may have been educated in ways that went beyond letters. Zelaya's Liberal revolution wrestled away public education from the influential Roman Catholic Church; along with building many accessible schools in the country, Zelaya's nationalist agenda strongly shaped the school curriculum itself. A new *History of Nicaragua* was commissioned by his government and adopted as the standard textbook; its author, José Dolores Gámez, was a strong nationalist, a partisan Liberal, and a Freemason. Gámez divided his history into three eras, Aboriginal, Colonial, and Modern, with the Modern period possessing its own three subdivisions. His book culminates with the Central American victory over the invading forces of William Walker and Walker's eventual execution; the narrative and its analyses are permeated by assumptions of the evolutionary progress of the Nicaraguan nation

under Liberal rule. His overarching understanding of "History" was optimistic and almost mystical, falling squarely within the nineteenth-century
tradition that saw history as a process of spiritual unfolding and enlightenment: "Before [history] disappear the tomb, darkness, confusion, injustice
and preoccupations . . . [History] is the resurrection of truth and the light
that dissipates the confusion of the past" (Gámez 1889, 13). Whether or not
young Augusto read the textbook himself, he probably soaked up these or
similar ideas.

Following his years in school, Augusto went to work in his father's
grain business, in which he gained some prosperity. As middle-class merchants, they bought grains from local producers and peasants at low prices
and then sold them at higher prices to distributors in the larger urban cen-
ters nearby (Granada, Masaya, Managua, Jinotepe, and other cities). Don
Gregorio had made a modest fortune in the business, and Augusto soon
learned the trade well. He later boasted that with his entrepreneurial
prowess at his father's disposal, they had cornered the market and had increased the family fortune twofold: "With my help, my father succeeded in
controlling the bean market of the whole region and he doubled his capital"
(Román 1979, 40).

Alongside these aspects of public activity, we can also see glimpses of a
young man's private life. As one aspect of his emerging manhood, Augusto
liked firearms: he owned a .22-caliber revolver, though it is not known
when he obtained it or began constantly to carry the weapon (Ibarra 1973,
26). (Carrying a side arm in rural towns was not uncommon at the time in
Nicaragua.) Moreover, he was apparently shy around women, and his adult
recollections of his first love are as dramatic as they are pathetic, demon-
strating the compulsive and obsessive nature of the man as a youth. He fell
in love with a local girl, his cousin María Mercedes Sandino,[2] who "completely possessed me, body and soul, and in all my senses"; he "trembled
and became mute" in her presence (Sandino 1981, 1:75–76). Unable to manifest his feelings verbally, Sandino recalled having written a letter confess-
ing his love for her, in which he "threatened, if she did not accept me, with
killing her and killing myself" (Román 1979, 41). In spite of his talk, he was

2. Ramírez (1979, 41) reports her name as Mariíta S[oledad] Sandino, and Ibarra (1973,
26–27) also calls her María Soledad. Román, however, refers to her as Mercedes, and Dospital—
who has been privy to the FSLN archives—also calls her María Mercedes when citing a fragment of a letter from Sandino to her dated 25 Sept. 1921 (Dospital 1996, 200). I will refer to her
as María Mercedes as well.

apparently so afraid that he could not even hand the letter to her. The story reveals a posture of bravado similar to that which would characterize most of Sandino's private and public pronouncements. Indeed, this whole confession may have been high drama for the interview with Román; we can not verify that the event occurred as Sandino narrated it, and the letter in question has not been found.

Apparently prompted by discord with his stepmother, Augusto left home sometime between 1913 and 1916. He stopped for a while near the Costa Rican border, where he obtained work as an apprentice mechanic, but overall his whereabouts during this period are unknown. He later claimed to have taken ship at the port of San Rafael del Sur and to have traveled half the world, although there was no mention of the specific places he visited (Román 1979, 46).

His return to the family home in 1919 is equally mysterious. Nothing is said of his stepmother's nor his father's reactions at his return, but things somehow appeared to have gained a degree of normalcy when Augusto opened his own business buying and selling grains, a profitable enterprise during the boon years following World War I. From his brother Sócrates, we learn that Sandino obtained his first political experience during the elections of 1920, when he became responsible in Niquinohomo for the campaign promotion of the national Liberal presidential candidate, José Esteban González (S. Sandino 1928). It is unknown how Sandino conquered his paralyzing fear of his cousin María Mercedes, but he eventually became engaged to her. He was twenty-five years old.

The wedding, however, was not to be. In June 1921, in a fit of rage after being struck in the face, Augusto shot and wounded Dagoberto Rivas during local religious festivities in the town square. (Sandino would later boast that the shooting took place inside the church during Sunday mass.) The exact reason for the dispute between the two young men is still unclear, but it appears that Augusto was accused of being romantically involved with Rivas's widowed sister at the same time as he was engaged to marry his cousin María Mercedes. In an interview seventy years later, however, María Mercedes claimed that the altercation developed about an unsatisfactory load of beans that Augusto had purchased from Rivas, but Rivas would not reimburse him (Wünderich 1995, 41). Whatever the cause, the subsequent situation was dangerous: Dagoberto was a member of a local influential Conservative family, political rivals of Sandino's father who would likely have gone to great lengths to have Augusto jailed. Thus, accompanied by his cousin Santiago, Augusto fled Niquinohomo "to avoid a trial and other subsequent consequences" (Román 1979, 47); in essence, he fled to avoid responsibility, to elude justice, and for fear of retribution.

The shooting of Rivas was a pivotal event in Sandino's life. He himself would refer to it years later as "an incident of great importance to my life because it gave my destiny a different path" (Román 1979, 54), and he was right. In the moment when he vented his violent tendency and fired on Rivas, he became a fugitive, and he remained one for most of his life. The incident led to many years of further wandering, during which Augusto spent much effort consciously preparing a way to return in glory to wash away the shame of his flight.

## Flight and Exile

### *The Years Adrift*

Augusto first fled to the Atlantic coast of Nicaragua, but he felt insecure there and so moved North to Honduras a month later, where he worked for two years at a sugar cane processing plant, El Ingenio Montecristo, in La Ceiba. His letters that survive from this period—two to his fiancée and one to his father—deserve careful attention for the special light they shed on his inner thoughts and feelings. Augusto wrote them without the aid of secretaries or advisors and prior to his acquaintance with revolutionary ideologies. Although fleeing from the law, he was an ordinary person, not yet a public figure. Thus, these letters are not mediated by reporters or interviewers; they are neither narrated in hindsight (like most sources on his earlier life) nor intended to create and to maintain a specific political image (like most of his later pronouncements and writings). They therefore offer a more direct and reliable window into the man than do most other materials on Sandino's life.

Consider his letters to his fiancée María Mercedes. Augusto's engagement with his cousin effectively ended with his flight, but the letters he wrote to her (which received no reply) showed his continued interest in her. Augusto was worried that his cousin would interpret his flight and absence as a termination of their romance; he therefore needed to provide an explanation while at the same time sending the message that he was still interested in keeping a romantic liaison with her. Thus, in the 1921 fragment recently uncovered by Dospital (1996, 199–200), Sandino justified the shooting and his flight by claiming injury to his honor: "I was in a personally delicate situation in the moment when my honor was at stake, and if I

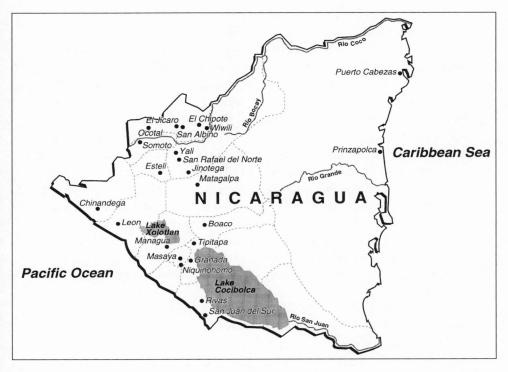

Map 2. Nicaragua

had not protested in the manner in which I did, at this time you yourself would take me for a coward." It is apparent that his personal image and honor occupied the forefront of his thoughts. In response to an anticipated complaint for his departure, he told her: "Do not confuse the love that I keep for you with the right to defend my honor." The letter suggests his emotions and his regrets for having left, without any mention of regretting the deed that led him to flee.

Another letter from his exile, written in 1922, similarly suggests his continued feelings for María Mercedes: "This year of sad absence has been nothing but a year of remorse for me; it has been a year of countless adventures. Neither you nor anyone else who has not been in adventures can understand how difficult an adventurer's life can be" (Sandino 1981, 1:75–76). However, pride quickly moved Augusto to cover his emotions and he switched to bravado, boasting how much better he was now for having endured the hardships he was enduring. "You should also understand," he wrote, "that one who has traveled such roads is four times as much a man as those who, if they have ever left their country, have done it backed by opulence." It is not clear whether Augusto was speaking in general terms or precisely alluding to people he knew when mentioning the travels of others, but in any case he was on the one hand exalting himself as a man of the world, and on the other trying to diminish the travels of others who have done so with money and comfort. Referring to those whose experiences he considered beneath his own, he continued: when one comes to meet the "little birds, who still don't know what the world is about, one feels the pride of a one hundred-dollar bill compared with a few small copper pennies." Perhaps he was only seeking the admiration of his beloved, who was not responding to his letters. He apparently attributed her lack of response to what people around her might be saying about him, and in the second half of the letter, Augusto described in detail the many ways he imagined people speaking to her about him back home. The exercise again may reveal a young man's obsessive preoccupation with other people's opinions of him.

Despite his boasting, Augusto was not prepared for the life of exile. No one ever really is. Life in a workers' camp was hard, and the heat in the coastal area was unbearable for one used to the comfortable coolness of the higher plateau; the deplorable hygienic conditions at the camps must have made matters worse. Even his days as a supposed "servant" in his father's home must have appeared sheltered to him by comparison. Many people came and went, usually destitute migrant workers, many of them outlanders looking for work in the plantations. Augusto was one of the many. Notwithstanding the relatively good earnings of the workers, he complained in a letter to his father dated 1922 (Sandino 1981, 1:73–74) that the place was a "focus of infections" and of "bohemian life." The others squandered their earnings "in their disorderly passions," whereas his own salary, he said, had to be spent "curing frequent [though unnamed] illnesses."

Augusto seemed unwilling to continue on with this kind of life and was determined to leave the plantation, but he lacked the money to do it; for his part, his father was pressuring him to pay his debts to a certain Don Florencio. In the hope of gaining his father's sympathy, Augusto described his experience of the hardship of exile and his suffering in the workers' camps with enhanced self-pity: "Everything is foreign, no one talks to you, if there is no money there is nothing. [When looking for work] one is stared at from head to toe, there are a thousand questions, among which: what do you know how to do, why did you leave the place you were before?, moreover, there are even insults most of the time." Given the highly transient nature of the work force in the Honduran plantations, cautious landowners and foremen scrutinized their hires, hoping to weed outlaws and undesirables in the process.

Augusto went on to describe for his father's benefit the corruption and the temptations that encircled him: "In these places, everywhere one goes, there is music of all kinds, frequent dances, orgies [*grandes guasas*], some today and others tomorrow, and so the only ones benefited are the owners of the countless cantinas and gambling houses," he wrote. Augusto sought to manipulate his father so that his father would add money to his sympathies; he wanted Gregorio to imagine the dreadful things to which he was exposed, but he also wanted to reassure him that he stood outside the influence and practice of these hideous activities. Augusto had every intention to leave for better places, but the message he wished to convey was that he would not be able to withstand the seduction of it all if he stayed there much longer. His point was clear:

> This life is not for a man who wishes to distinguish himself in something, and that is why I do whatever is at my reach to get out as soon as I possibly can . . . [I have] the illusion to go to more civilized countries, where I will be able, if not to make money, at least to gaze upon ample light and clear civilization from which I will gain something. . . . If I decide to settle my debts, it would mean not leaving here; you must understand that it is not very comfortable to leave a country for another with little money. . . . There are thousands of men here who wish to return to their homes but cannot, they have no money . . . you can see then the urgency that exists to arrive with money and well-groomed, rather than with nothing.

This was a far cry from the boastful letter to his fiancée. Augusto wanted his father to believe that he could not leave unless he defaulted on his debts (something his father did not wish him to do) and conversely that he could not leave if he paid his debt. Without extra money, he hints, he was condemned to stay there. For added dramatic effect, he signed off with "a strong embrace from your indefatigable, but unfortunate son."

Augusto eventually left Honduras for Guatemala the following year (1923). It is not known whether he paid his debts, and there is no indication that he succeeded in persuading his father to send him money. It seems unlikely that Augusto would have elicited great sympathy from his father, who (as a businessman himself) would have understood the purpose of the process of interviewing workers as well as knowing the tendencies and weaknesses of his son. Over a decade later, Augusto Sandino admitted to Román the true circumstances that compelled him to leave: "Once again," he said, "[it was] because of something to do with skirts [that] I had to leave the northern coast of Honduras" (Román 1979, 55).

In Quiragua, Guatemala, Sandino encountered for the first time the American presence that for years had been transforming Central America, as he worked briefly for the United Fruit Company (UFCO). The United Fruit Company was incorporated in New Jersey in March 1899 with $11 million in capital; by 1930, it controlled $215 million and owned close to one-half million acres of land in Latin America, controlling 63 percent of the Central American banana trade (Bethell 1991, 52). (By comparison, the total national income of Nicaragua in 1930 was $2.8 million [Velásquez 1992, 144].) The volume of the UFCO's business, its capital, its resources, and the number of people it employed made it extremely influential in the region, including Nicaragua; even after the UFCO sold its properties in Nicaragua in 1930, it continued to do business under a subsidiary (Bethell 1991, 52). In many respects, the UFCO operated as a relatively sovereign entity (Pérez-Brignoli 1989, 103), but it was also instrumental in setting up inoculation campaigns and in raising the relative state of health (Woodward 1985, 181, 214). Although it had not yet reached the apex of its political influence, by the time Sandino arrived in Guatemala in the early 1920s the UFCO already represented a symbol of United States intervention (Garraty 1979, 649–52). Sandino did not work for the company for long, however, and later that year (1923) he continued on to Mexico.

In Mexico, he wandered aimlessly for some time, working at several different jobs before finally stopping in Cerro Azul, near the port of Tampico. According to his job application for the Huasteca Petroleum Company in Cerro Azul, by then Augusto had a "wife" and a daughter (Macaulay 1985, 51). However, Sandino never mentioned the existence of this family to anyone else, and it is possible that he may have embellished his employment application in order to increase his chances of obtaining a job; as a foreigner in highly nationalist Mexico, he may have needed all possible advantages to get employed, including a Mexican wife and child. At the same time, his developing record with female companions makes the information on the application seem quite plausible.

In Cerro Azul, Augusto worked in American-owned oil fields as a mechanic and later gained a position as stock-keeper; later still, he may have even been manager and lessee of a gas station concession that sold by bulk

(Román 1979, 55). Whatever the case, his new position offered a significant improvement compared to the squalid conditions of the camps in Honduras. Still, it was not enough for him. He was troubled and had fantasies about looking for and finding the perfect place to live; he always wanted to reach "more civilized" places, but was never content once he reached them. Nicaraguan writer Pablo Antonio Cuadra, author of the classic *El nicaragüense*, tells us that "Nicaraguans are an errant people, a people that leave easily; at the slightest vital or political discomfort, they go into exile or think about exile. They always dream about seeking fortune and a better life in a place that is not where they live" (Cuadra 1978, 70). Cuadra's description resembles Sandino a great deal. A few years later, Sandino recalled his errant inclinations: "During my stay away from my motherland there was never tranquillity in my disposition [*ánimo*]. When I succeeded in getting acquainted with one place, I aspired to find myself in a better one, everywhere suffering the disappointment of imagining all places I was visiting better than they were in reality. For these same reasons, I confess that in our profane world I never encountered happiness" (A. Sandino 1928b).

The grief of exile may have added to Augusto's restless temperament. His continuous moving from place to place did not contribute to a more stable condition or to the development of a network of friends that might have made him feel less lonely and melancholic. In spite of his better job, his improved economic condition, and the company of a "wife" and child, he still felt empty and depressed. He now had more than the essentials for which he had wished as a child, but he still craved for the "warmth of a home [and] spiritual tranquillity" (Román 1979, 37). Perhaps led on by these emotional needs, during this period he experimented with several different philosophical and religious belief systems and was drawn toward spiritualist teachers and populist gurus; as he later wrote, "Looking for spiritual consolation I read mythical [i.e. mystical] books and I sought masters of religion" (A. Sandino 1928b).

*Assuagement*

Throughout his travels, Sandino had been struggling with the fact that he had shot a man; although he did not kill him, the episode must have tormented him. He could run away from Niquinohomo and from Nicaragua but not from himself, and this was probably in large part the root of his anxiety. Despite the strong Catholic tradition in his native land, his liberal background was stronger and he did not consider looking for guidance from a priest, or even undertaking confession. In his early childhood, during Zelaya's revolution and under the influence of his father's liberalism, Sandino had learned to distrust the clergy and the Catholic Church, allies of their political rivals, the Conservatives. Moreover, these were highly anticlerical times in Mexico as well; the Church was not the vogue remedy for spiritual anguish but rather was under persecution. Even if Sandino had looked to Catholicism for help, its resources were not readily available during the period he was in Mexico.

Augusto approached the question of his spirituality expecting a quick remedy, and he searched from place to place for relief. We know from the reports of American journalist Carleton Beals that one of the sects that Sandino tried out in Mexico was the Seventh Day Adventists, whose literature he carried with him back to Nicaragua (Beals 1932, 265). The Adventists had emerged in the United States toward the middle of the nineteenth century out of the millenarian religious movement gathered around New Englander William Miller's predictions that an Age of Perfection would begin in 1843; after Miller's prophecies of apocalypse failed (along with alternate dates in 1844), a faithful remnant became the Seventh Day Adventist church. (Some splinter congregations, such as the Branch Davidian group led by David Koresh, have maintained until today radical expectations of an apocalyptic millennium.)

Augusto also studied yoga and for a while practiced vegetarianism (Belausteguigoitia 1985, 170, 135; Macaulay 1985, 53; Román 1979, 82). Later, it would be no secret among members of Sandino's army that he often retired to engage in meditation, which he combined with periodic physical exercises; down to the present, Tomás Borge (former Sandinista chief of internal security) recalled his father's awe-stricken stories about Sandino's ability to stretch his legs behind his head (Borge 1989, 63). Thus, Augusto also became acquainted with the law of karma, along with other Eastern notions such as the transmigration of souls, maya (the cosmic illusion that is equivalent to being blinded by ignorance), nirvana or pure Being, the Absolute, and the mystical experience of light as a manifestation of the divine. Yogic doctrines are the techniques recommended to free one's self from profane life and to seek escape from the clutches of the cosmos in order to reach emancipation from the world, from suffering, pain, and ignorance (Eliade 1991b).

Other of the religious masters that he consulted provided the tormented Augusto with more than spiritual guidance. In particular, the Mexican spiritualists were highly politicized in the 1920s, still in effervescence under the impact of the Mexican Revolution, and in them Augusto found a compelling political discourse that diverted his attention toward a more palpable goal. Sandino would later recall how it was: "I succeeded in surrounding myself with a group of spiritualist friends with whom I discussed daily the submission of our people in Latin America, either to the hypocritical or to the violent advances of the assassin Yankee empire" (Alemán 1951, 36). Donald Hodges (1986) has carefully illustrated the climate of postrevolutionary Mexican spiritualism that Sandino encountered. The spiritualists were organized in sects that met in temples and lodges, and their membership often cut across other forms of associations (including anarchists, communists, and socialists). The spiritualists understood themselves as a prototype for the brotherhood of mankind; they believed in the power of prophecy, communication with spirits of the dead, and extrasensory communication with the living. They accepted the doctrine of reincarnation and conceived the world as the arena of the struggle between the forces of good and those of evil. Finally, in common with the Adventists and the followers of yoga, the spiritualists believed in the oneness of God and in inevitable progress toward the final redemption of humanity. These notions, as we will see, had a significant impact on Augusto Sandino.

Other, more explicitly political groups were also in abundance. Mexican anarchists, clustered around the teachings of Ricardo Flores Magón (1873–1922), believed in a struggle against all traditional forms of authority—economic, ecclesiastic, and political—which they planned to replace with small self-governing communes holding property in common. Although there is no direct evidence linking Sandino to Flores Magón, his followers were quite strong in the Tampico area in the 1920s, and it is likely that Sandino encountered a popularized version of his ideas (Hodges 1986, 24–29). The communists identified themselves as radical enemies of international capital, espousing the use of violent revolution as the means to seize power in order to carry on the task of national liberation. Furthermore, they understood themselves to be engaged in a struggle to the death with the imperialist forces of foreign capital and their local puppets. By contrast, Mexican socialists favored independent worker cooperatives, land for the landless peasants, and the nationalization of all the means of production—all of which they believed could be achieved through legislative means (Hodges 1986, 5–6; 1992).

Thus, Augusto was marked by the tail end of the Mexican Revolution's euphoria—its Comtean scientism, its dream of continuous progress and legal positivism, its populism and anarchism, its communism and socialism. During Álvaro Obregón's rule (1920–24), the dust of the revolution had began to settle, but the oil-producing areas were still plagued with radical labor and anarchist elements, many of whom had come from the United States (Macaulay 1985, 52). Anti-American feelings abounded, and memories of the Tampico incident that led to the United States military occupation of Veracruz in April 1914 still endured (Knight 1986, 150–62; Quirk 1962). Significantly, Augusto also witnessed and absorbed the manifestation of Mexican nationalism that glorified the country's Indian heritage.

During his years in Mexico, the young Sandino witnessed the change of government from Álvaro Obregón to Plutarco Elías Calles, who tolerated neither dissent nor opposition and who would rule indirectly for ten years. Calles distributed eight million acres of land to peasant cooperatives; his idea that Indians could be assimilated through education would later be reflected in Sandino's attempt to include them in a commune in northern Nicaragua. Calles also helped make labor more powerful and activated the anti-Church provisions of the Mexican Constitution, which led to a three-year strike and a vicious revolt known as the Cristero Rebellion. Although Augusto had already left Mexico by the time the rebellion began, he must have been acquainted with Archbishop Mora y del Rio's refusal to abide by the constitution in February 1926, which eventually led to the rebellion. The strike would end in July 1929, soon after Sandino arrived for his second trip (Meyer, Sherman, and Deeds 1999, 567–69; Meyer 1976).

Finally, among the radical currents to which Augusto was exposed, Freemasonry figures prominently. Many radical groups such as anarchist associations and labor movements, particularly in the Tampico area, had common membership with the Freemasons. This should not come as a surprise: the Freemasons' revolutionary antecedents go back to their participation in the French Revolution (Billington 1980, 91–93, 100–101), and the Mexican Revolution appears to have revived a latent revolutionary attitude. Freemasonry taught the young Sandino about the brotherhood of man, the esoteric tradition that teaches doctrines of illumination to a selected few through hierarchical degrees of learning, and an optimistic belief in the unfolding of destiny (Gould n.d.; Hodges 1986, 1992). On a symbolic level, the later Sandino would consistently use Masonic symbols and shapes—in the ways that he would pose for photographs and in his signature, for instance. Through Masonic lodges, he also had contact with radical anarchist trade unions, from which he took the red and black colors displaying a human skull that later became his standard.

## The Constitutionalist War

*Still Errant*

While Sandino endured his existential crisis in Mexico and explored a variety of ideas and beliefs, events of the mid-1920s in his native Nicaragua had caught the attention of the Mexican press. In January 1925, Nicaraguan Conservatives and Liberals achieved a political balance that allowed for a sharing of power, with Conservative Carlos Solórzano occupying the presidency and Liberal Juan Bautista Sacasa the vice-presidency. This entente brought about the apparent normalcy that led to the August 1925 evacuation of the U.S. Marines, who had occupied Nicaragua since August 1912. Merely a few months after the departure of the Americans, however, the intemperate Conservative *caudillo* Emiliano Chamorro ousted the Solórzano-Sacasa government step by step until he had himself declared president. (In the Spanish tradition, *caudillo* refers to a military ruler, generally a despot or a tyrant.) The Liberals resisted him, backed by the full support of Mexico's government. Fearing an expansion of Mexican radical revolutionism into Central America, the United States government pressured Chamorro to step down in October 1926 in favor of Conservative Adolfo Díaz, but that solution failed to satisfy the Liberals, who continued to fight. The episode became known as the Constitutionalist War (*La Guerra Constitucionalista*).

According to the orthodox version, Augusto responded to these events by returning to Nicaragua to do his patriotic, Liberal duty against the puppet president. He himself would later claim to have left his job and comforts in Cerro Azul in May 1926 in order "to join" the partisan rebels. Apparently, his patriotic pride was injured when Mexican revolutionaries referred to Nicaraguans as "sellouts" for their subservience to the United States, particularly after the Bryan-Chamorro Treaty: "That phrase danced in my head all night long and I thought that if he had insulted the honor of my mother, I could have freed my conscience blaming my fate. But if they call me a sellout even if it was a drunk doing it, that was my fault and that of all the Nicaraguans lacking in patriotism" (Román 1979, 50). Principally because of its ideological convenience, this story has prevailed almost exclusively in the literature and in the popular mythology surrounding Sandino, with Sandino himself as the principal propagandist: he wanted to show that from the moment he left Mexico, his original intention was to fight the Conservative usurpers and the occupying American presence in

Nicaragua. For the same ideological convenience, his followers have repeated it and pushed aside competing explanations.

However, Sandino's own version of the events also mentions other factors that motivated him to return.

> [It was] in 1926 . . . when I decided to return to Nicaragua: I was tired of
> working for others, I had already done much travelling and experienced life
> in various aspects. Moreover, because of my frugality and lack of vices, I
> had saved at that time a fair sum of money that I thought of bringing back
> with me to wed my cousin [María] Mercedes, who still waited for me, and
> to dedicate myself to commercial activity in Managua. The truth is that I
> was homesick. (Román 1979, 49)

As usual, it is difficult to tell fact from propaganda when reading Sandino,
but from this passage it is apparent that despite his improved economic
condition, Augusto continued to be unhappy with his errant life and with
his employment situation. He was a proud and ambitious man with a keen
entrepreneurial sense, who had previously owned a business; it might have
been difficult for him to settle for less, being in someone's employment and
in a foreign country. Thus, it is natural to assume that he was looking for
the opportunity to settle in Managua to do business, perhaps trading in
grains, which would enable him to set up his own distribution network and
to increase his profit margin. He might have wanted to open a mechanic's
shop; we do not know. The choice of Managua may not only have been a
business consideration, however: Dagoberto Rivas, or his relatives or
friends in Niquinohomo, would likely try to collect on Augusto's debt of
honor if he returned to the village. An internal exile to Managua was a better alternative. In addition, there was his cousin María Mercedes, whom he
claimed he was going to marry. Augusto was homesick; he missed his family, his fiancée, and his country.

Overall, then, it seems that Augusto's patriotic response to the political developments in Nicaragua was an addendum to his personal reasons to
return. Moreover, his account excludes the single most important factor
that enabled him to return home, a factor bearing directly on his escape
from Nicaragua in 1921. Carleton Beals noted that Augusto had returned
from Mexico "at the urgent pleading of his father" (1932, 264), but unfortunately he did not elaborate further. The final clue is provided by Sócrates
Sandino (1928): what Augusto Sandino deliberately failed to mention is
that Don Gregorio urged him to come back because the statute of limita-

tions on his attempted murder charge in the shooting of Rivas had expired by 1926 (see also Dospital 1996, 205).

Augusto's return from exile in Mexico is sufficiently important to deserve a careful look. He left Tampico in mid-May 1926 and arrived in Nicaragua in early June. His first plan—to go to Niquinohomo to see his family, María Mercedes, and his old business contacts before settling in Managua—was met by one important obstacle: he could not openly return to Niquinohomo because Dagoberto Rivas was now a prominent Conservative politician, hardly one of the "little birds" whom Augusto had scorned in his letter to María Mercedes (Román 1979, 50).[3] Augusto feared going back to his village and apparently dared visit only once, "under the cover of darkness" (Vayssière 1988, 59). Given his apprehensions, it was better for him to go to Managua; Don Gregorio could establish the contacts Augusto needed, and the family could come to see him there.

In fact, however, he never settled in Managua. If what Augusto wanted was to open his own grain business, there could have been no worse time to deal in grains in Nicaragua. Almost coincidental with Augusto's arrival in early June 1926, a grasshopper plague invaded Nicaragua from the northwest, working its way south and east and ravaging whatever crops, fruit, and vegetation it found in its way; within days, the prices of basic grains had risen drastically (see e.g. *La Prensa* for 3 and 6 June 1926). Had Augusto been well established in his business before the plague, he could have made great profits, but the chaotic state of the market made it virtually impossible to get started under such conditions. Rivas would also have been an obstacle to Augusto's plan to live in Managua, for as a deputy to the Assembly he would have visited the capital often.

Augusto did not want to risk meeting him. Instead, he went to León, a Liberal stronghold. He later claimed to have come from Mexico to fight in the Constitutionalist War—but why did he not immediately come in through the Atlantic coast, where the Liberal rebellion began? It may be supposed that he wished to see his family before joining the war, which explained his going to the western part of Nicaragua. Continuing with the order of events, it is often believed that he then went to León to establish the desired contacts to join the rebellion. However, that is not what happened: rather than enlisting, Augusto drifted again for some time until he

3. Sandino claimed that Rivas was the mayor of the town, but it is more likely that he was a Conservative deputy in the National Assembly; see *La Prensa* 27 Aug. 1926, 1, and 27 Sept. 1927, 1.

joined a band of unemployed laborers and fortune hunters on their way to the northern gold mines. Again, there is sufficient reason, given all the available evidence and the many inconsistencies in the guerrilla chief's various texts and interviews, to believe that Sandino's stated causes for his return to Nicaragua in 1926 obscure a great part of his actual motivations. While it is not wise to doubt wholly Augusto's political goals, his personal ambition appears as a strong complement, if not a competitor, among the motivators for his return to Nicaragua.

*The Making of Opportunity*

Upon reaching the northern mines in July, Sandino was hired and put in charge of the storeroom because of his literacy and work experience. It may seem odd that he would get himself hired at a mine, if he truly had as much desire to fight as he claimed; moreover, he was not working out of economic necessity, for he had brought plenty of money from Mexico, as he later told Belausteguigoitia (1985, 89). Rather, Sandino now had his own revolutionary agenda and he was holding to it. Once settled at the San Albino mine, he began to agitate the workers.

> I began to work on the disposition [*ánimo*] of those workers, explaining to them the systems of cooperatives of other countries, and how sadly we were exploited, and that we should find a government that would truly be interested in the people so that they did not get basely exploited by the capitalists and the great foreign companies, for the people are the Nation, and that we should demand, as in all the civilized countries in the world, that all the companies operating in Nicaragua have to provide to their workers medical attention, schools, laws, and organizations such as unions of workers, and that we had none of all that. I explained to them that I was not communist, but socialist. (Román 1979, 49)[4]

What did this have to do with the Liberal objectives against the government of Díaz? We know that Augusto was ambitious and that he was looking for happiness. One of the ways of attaining happiness, for some, is to

4. Sandino's apparently defensive insistence here that he was not a communist but a socialist seems inconsistent with other of his extant writings and interviews on the subject. More often, he claimed just the opposite: Sandino proudly boasted to Nicaraguan nationals and foreigners alike that he was indeed a communist, as he asserted to Belausteguigoitia right around the same time that Román interviewed him.

reach some form of glory; in Sandino's words (quoted in the epigraph at the start of this chapter), he wanted to be someone (Román 1979, 39). He may have identified two ways through which he could attain glory: either through fortune or through fame. When the opportunity to become rich in business vanished, he seized the opportunity to make history, to put into action his newly acquired political knowledge. Sandino's revolutionary ambition did not appear out of nothing; it emerged as an alternate plan to to his personal trajectory of settling down, getting married to his cousin, and opening a business. With those earlier goals unfulfilled, he became eager to show that he had become "four times as much a man" and to articulate the things that he had learned about justice, revolution, and social change in what he called the civilized societies. He had learned that this knowledge gave him the capacity to change the world.

Augusto now intended to launch a Mexican-style revolution: "I was in Mexico and my liberalism screamed from within my chest when I learned what was happening in Nicaragua," he declared in 1933. The kind of "liberalism" that Sandino had in mind, however, was the radicalism he had recently learned from the spiritualists, the anarchists, the communists, and the Freemasons in Mexico. It was imbued with revolutionary fervor; "I had been unionized in Mexico," he would later say, emphasizing the point about his liberalism (Arrieta 1971, 12). But what about the wedding with María Mercedes, one might ask? According to his later report, he had by then come to feel that she had "antiquated ideas, and would not have been able to survive in the bush" (Román 1979, 81). This clearly suggests a change in his plans.

Thus, while the Liberal forces were attempting to establish a foothold in the country—first at Cosigüina in the northwest at the end of August, later and more successfully on the Atlantic coast in mid-September—Sandino continued to fascinate the illiterate miners with his stories and social theories. It was then that Sandino discovered the power of his persuasive abilities (Macaulay 1985, 54). He would later describe the process of persuading the miners: "Little by little I gained popularity among and control of the men of the mine, from which some followed me loyally throughout all my troubles" (Román 1979, 49). Sandino was a one-man Trojan horse.

*Fertile Soil*

Sandino's seemingly fortuitous choice of the northern hinterlands as the place to begin his activities may not have been random, for the Indians and peasants in the area were ripe for radical political agitation. The region of the Segovias, tucked away in the northwestern part of the country, was made up of the departments of Nueva Segovia, Estelí, the western part of Jinotega, and the northwestern part of Matagalpa; extending over approximately thirty thousand square kilometers, it included nearly one-quarter of the Nicaraguan territorial extension. In 1929, it was sparsely populated area inhabited by roughly seventy-three thousand people (Schroeder 1993, 93), whose illiteracy rate was well above the national average of 72 percent (Dospital 1996, 142). The principal economic sources were coffee, cattle, and some mining. From this base, Sandino would later extend his activities toward the east coast of Nicaragua, in the northern Zelaya department, an even more remote area from the national political center and its culture. The largest of Nicaraguan departments but also the most thinly populated, Zelaya enjoyed its own political culture and was largely (and still remains) separate from the rest of the country. Inhabited primarily by Miskito Indians in confluence with Ramas, Sumos, Sambos, Caribbean blacks, and a few *mestizo* Nicaraguans and white foreigners, the region's main economic activities were bananas, fishing, and mining (see Brooks 1989).

Although Nicaragua is a small country, the Sandino theatre of operations was a very remote area. There were no roads coming into it, and the only way of reaching it was by beast of burden through tortuous mountain trails that became nearly impossible to travel during the rainy season. Moreover, along with the remoteness of the region, its history may have had an even more influential impact on its inhabitants: "The half-century before the Sandino rebellion witnessed profound social, economic and political upheavals across the Segovias, most of which were experienced by the majority of the rural poor as detrimental to their already precarious way of life" (Schroeder 1993, 103). The region's people "had little respect for boundaries or for laws. They had been alternatively neglected by the government of Honduras and Nicaragua, and their region had become a spawning ground for bandits and smugglers" (Macaulay 1985, 87).

Northern Indians and peasants felt threatened by the advance of the agricultural frontier, product of the influx of white European farmers and coffee growers to the region. In the latter part of the nineteenth century and the beginning of the twentieth, as coffee became the major export crop, the agricultural development of the Segovias undermined the Indian communities and displaced indigenous independent farmers deeper into the hills. The Indians in particular were subject to numerous forms of abuse, including forced labor and at times corporal punishment; rumors continually circulated of further mistreatment, including one that the government of Nicaragua intended to sell their children to the "yanquis" and to send five hundred women to forced labor to Managua (Gould 1998, 33; 1993, 400). In response, in March 1881 the Indians attacked the city of Matagalpa (Brockett 1990, 26). The attack was repelled with the help of reinforcements, but resistance endured in the surrounding hills for nearly nine months, which has been described by one scholar as a "nativistic millenarian revolt" (Schroeder 1993, 102). Gould (1998, 35–36), who has carefully studied the demise of Nicaraguan aboriginal communities, found that the attacking Indians had begun to develop an embryonic nationalistic identity; although vanquished, their demands did not vanish.

The thirteen thousand acres sold by the government for coffee plantations a decade after the rebellion again brought the labor-seeking coffee growers into tensions with the Indians. In particular, the system of *adelantos* (cash advances) before the harvest created a form of labor bondage; by law, the workers were obligated to remain in the employment of a lending coffee grower until the debt was repaid. The system produced greater problems than it sought to resolve, and attempts at reforming it resulted in unnecessary bureaucracy and draconian rules. Further, Liberal legislation in 1892 forbade workers from leaving a plantation before harvest, even when all debts had been paid off, at the same time as it established a system of registration that made it compulsory for all hired hands and their dependants to register with the local authorities (see *La Gaceta,* January 1892). The law was supposed to prevent abuses on both sides: laborers left their indebtedness in one plantation to obtain more *adelantos* in another; at times of high labor demand, coffee growers poached workers and encouraged them to leave their present employment and obligations to go work for them. Further restrictions appeared in 1894, forcing workers to carry a *boleta* (registration card) detailing their work obligations as well as the balance of *adelantos* and payments against them (*La Gaceta,* October 1894).

Mounting pressures from both sides of the labor divide led to a series of contradicting legislation. In some cases, more relaxed legislation brought arguments of greater abuses. In 1904, the 1899 vagrancy law was revamped; the *boleta* continued to be demanded and workers could be sentenced to fifteen days of public works for contraventions (Gould 1998, 42). The following year, imprisonment for debts was constitutionally banned. The Indian communities were abolished in 1906, distributing one-half of their land among Indians and ordering the sale of the remainder to *Ladinos,* those of European lineage (also known as *Criollos*). Some fifty thousand acres of former Indian land changed hands to the coffee growers between 1890 and 1910. Coffee and the Liberal revolution, Gould concludes, weakened the Indian communities' economic base and irreversible divided them (1988, 42–43).

Although forced labor and the system of *adelantos* were officially abolished by 1911, the old laws remained conveniently in use well into the 1930s. The displacement of Indians and the dispossession of roughly 20 percent of their land created a rich pool of cheap labor by the mid-1920s, a rural proletariat, and the tensions between labor and employers grew. Between 1919 and 1925, the production of coffee doubled in Matagalpa, while wages and the labor supply did not increase accordingly (Gould 1998, 50). As if the legal chaos did not sufficiently embitter the Indians, *Ladinos* often entangled them in their equally chaotic political schemes. Indians and peasants were expected to follow political cues from their employers, whether local *caudillos* or aspiring *políticos*, by joining wars or terrorizing peasants and workers of rivals. If they refused, terror against them would follow. Peasants who did not meet their obligations under the law or would not join armed conflicts were hunted down, jailed, and prosecuted; it was not unusual to see "a long file of Indians with their hands tied behind their backs, led by their ethnic brethren on horseback toward an army encampment or to peon's headquarters of the plantation" (Gould 1998, 55).

Thus, well into the third decade of the twentieth century, the northern peasants were still mistreated and oppressed. In a racist-oppressive system in which employers believed Indians to be incapable of toiling under free labor rules, some Indians withdrew from contact with *mestizos* or sought refuge by fleeing beyond the agricultural frontier, where they could be temporarily ensured of some freedom. It was largely in this area, around and beyond the frontier, that Sandino would operate and recruit his men.

*If at First . . .*

Having gained the miners' confidence and respect, Sandino formed a band of about two dozen men. He gave them weapons bought through gunrunners from Honduras and proceeded to rob the mine. Then, on All Souls Day (2 November) 1926, Sandino attacked the strategically insignificant government garrison at El Jícaro, a village of less than five hundred people. Although only a few badly trained and badly armed recruits manned the post, the attack was repelled, causing heavy casualties to the attackers; many members of Sandino's band abandoned the adventure at that point. In the aftermath, although he had not established contact with the Liberal command, Sandino began to use their name to "requisition" the things his men wanted: "From every pueblo we came across we took weapons, food, blankets, etc., and we invited the Liberals there to follow us" (Arrieta 1971, 13). It was perhaps the only way of keeping his men with him.

After the defeat at El Jícaro, Sandino realized that he needed better weapons and more ammunition. He traveled east, down the Coco River, to meet with the Liberal army on the Atlantic coast, but he did not take most of his men with him; instead of adding them to the Liberal forces, he left them stationed in the northern mountains. At Prinzapolka, Sandino appeared before the Liberals' military commander, General José María Moncada. Sandino asked to be given men and a field command of his own, as well as weapons and ammunition to open a front in the Segovia mountains. Hoping to impress Moncada like he had impressed the workers of the mine, Sandino showed him a pamphlet that he himself had written arguing that "property is theft" (Somoza 1936, 83). Understanding the implications of the argument, however, Moncada was alarmed and rejected the petition, refusing to give command to an unknown with no military experience and with the sort of disturbing anarchism that Sandino was displaying. From the encounter with Moncada, it became apparent that Sandino had no intent of joining the ranks like a regular soldier; from that moment onward, Moncada became not an ally but an obstacle to the rebel's designs.

The Liberal troops established themselves on the Atlantic shores in Puerto Cabezas and declared the town their provisional capital; the ousted Liberal Sacasa returned there as president, prompting Mexico to recognize his provisional government and to ship abundant weaponry to the rebels. With no experience as a political strategist, Sandino may have been confused about the goal of the Liberal rebellion in Nicaragua. The Mexican backing gave him the impression that Nicaragua was about to establish a Mexican-style revolutionary régime. Indeed, documents dated April 1926 and captured after the Liberal defeat at Cosigüina showed that the Nicaraguan Liberal organization in Mexico expressed its demands using Mexican revolutionary rhetoric; even their battle cry Liberty or Death (*Libertad o Muerte*) could have passed for an imitation of Emiliano Zapata's motto Land and Liberty (*Tierra y Libertad*) (see *La Prensa,* 8 September 1926). Given the conservative disposition of the Nicaraguan Liberals towards extreme revolutionary activity, however, the adoption of such rhetoric was likely a scheme to gain Mexican support rather than an actual expression of the rebels' aims.

Nonetheless, impressions are often the only source of political information, and Sandino was not the only one confused about the Liberals' goals. Concerned about the spread of Mexican bolshevism into the region, the United States intervened and declared Puerto Cabezas a "neutral zone" on 23 December 1926. They gave the Liberals twenty-four hours to evacuate, forcing them to leave behind all the *matériel* that they were unable to carry. Fortune smiled upon Sandino, never too shy to seize a good opportunity: with the help of some local prostitutes, he rescued about thirty abandoned rifles and some ammunition from falling into the Americans' hands. They then marched to meet the regrouped Liberal forces, expecting to win Moncada over with their precious cargo. However, Moncada too was a stubborn man and instructed Sandino to hand over the guns without a deal. After this second humiliation, Sandino waited around the Liberal camps for several days, enduring the heat of the coast, until he tired and decided to return to the Segovias.

The wait was not entirely in vain. Leaving camp, Sandino crossed paths with some of the political chiefs of the Liberal army, whose sympathy he won by narrating his epic rescue of the weapons. Enchanted with the story, they in turn persuaded Moncada to allow Sandino to keep the rescued guns and to form a column with whatever men he could recruit in the northeast. They had nothing to lose, they figured, by letting this unknown become a thorn in the side of government troops elsewhere, especially outside of the main theatre of operations. It was a decision that many of them would live to regret. Sandino headed back to the hills and by the time he returned on 2 February 1927, over forty days later, he had picked up a large number of followers. At that point, as Eduardo Crawley has pointed out, "Sandino was already a General in his own mind" (1984, 55). His successes, however, did not erase the memory of Moncada's humiliating refusals.

The return of the U.S. Marines greatly frustrated the Liberal designs. The rebellion that broke out in the city of Chinandega in February 1927 was brutally put down by American troops, and a large portion of the city was burned to the ground. Incensed, Sacasa lashed out, uttering threats at the United States. He was under the illusion that unless the American forces evacuated Nicaragua, the countries of Hispanic America would boycott American products and declare war upon the interventionist state (see *La Prensa*, 17 February 1927, 2).

Sandino had no formal military training but he promptly distinguished himself for his tactical talent. He treated his troops well and his name became popular; many in the rebel forces wanted to serve under his command. In the spring of 1927, Sandino came south from the Segovias, smashing through enemy lines that threatened Moncada's troops, and he began to dream of personally entering the capital city of Managua to deliver the last blow against the Conservatives. His hopes were foiled, however, by the declaration of two consecutive American-sponsored truces. At the first truce, Moncada noticed that Sandino's men carried "red and black banners with crossed bones and a skull"; he asked Sandino to get rid of them, fearing that such display would fuel the American perception that the rebels were "Bolsheviks." Sandino resisted the request only to meet Moncada's direct order. Sandino was unable to hide his displeasure, and as his men removed the symbols as ordered, he wept in rage (Somoza 1936, 82). Once again he was humiliated in front of his men; once again Moncada wounded his pride.[5]

Soon thereafter, the Constitutionalist War came to an end. The newly arrived American representative, Colonel Henry L. Stimson (1867–1950), arranged the Espino Negro (Black Thorn) Accords—also known as the Tipitapa Accords—between Liberals and Conservatives. Moncada represented the Liberals on his own authority; Sacasa, the former vice-president and leader of the Liberal party, was neither consulted nor included in the talks, though his representatives were consulted after the fact. Under the accords, both warring camps agreed to cease hostilities; the Liberal rebels would surrender their weapons and would be granted control of six departments by the Conservatives. The agreement also stipulated that there would be an American-supervised election in November of the following year (Stimson 1991).

Further bloodshed was one of the central things that the Espino Negro Accords sought to prevent. The agreement was largely the result of Colonel Stimson's abilities, but significant credit ought to be given to both Nicaraguan parties as well. As has been the pattern of civil wars in Nicaragua, the Constitutionalist War was unfolding into a protracted and murderous conflict. On both sides, men who understood the horrific toll that wars bring were looking for a way out. In addition, there were immediate practical concerns. The rains in May were soon to come, and this was important for two reasons: on the one hand, it would make it difficult—if

5. Sandino's own retrospective account of this incident is characteristically different: he claimed that he cried with rage because his country's honor was being betrayed by Moncada and Díaz and was being trampled upon by an invading force (see Sandino 1981, 1:98). The claim does not make sense, however, since the peace accords in which (according to Sandino) Moncada would sell out his country had not yet been discussed.

not in some cases impossible—to get around anywhere, especially in the battlefields; on the other hand, and more important, there was a small window of opportunity in which peasants could return to their agricultural fields in time to take advantage of the rains for seeding and avoid missing another harvest. Thus, there was some urgency to end the conflict—not just to bring peace and to prevent the further loss of life, but to get on with life in the country. Under these circumstances, the warring parties found reasons to agree, and in some respects both welcomed the American intervention. This was a pragmatic decision; the only dishonorable thing about it was that they had not been able to arrive at the talks on their own, that once again the Nicaraguan élites required the intervention and tutorship of the United States. Finally, the participation of the rebel troops in the peace agreement was not the result of one man's decision, as Sandino painted it later. Being the prudent and skilful commander that he was, Moncada consulted his troops, presenting them with the contents of the deal; even Sandino agreed indirectly when he delegated his vote to Moncada, although he went on to change his mind later.

Sandino's dream of "marching victorious into Managua," initially frustrated by the cease-fires, was effectively destroyed by the accords. "The decisive moment was at hand," he later said with evident regret, "the last bell-toll had sounded for the Conservatives" (Somoza 1936, 40). Instead of glorious victory, Moncada offered him control of the remote northern department of Jinotega as well as a salary of ten dollars for each day that he had participated in the war. Sandino felt that Moncada was again standing in his way.

Sandino rejected the accords and later accused Moncada of signing a treasonous pact, selling out the honor of the motherland. Indeed, Moncada's actions amounted to a palace coup against Sacasa. Sandino later proceeded to interpret himself as Sacasa's defender and thought that this posture somehow gave him a veto over the outcome of the rebellion and the affairs of the nation, but at the moment he was more interested in outmaneuvering and discrediting Moncada than he was in upholding Sacasa's position. To be sure, by the standards of the day, the Nicaraguan Liberal Party was a forward-looking reformist party: beside their anti-clerical stance and their desire to distance church and state, they brought political reforms in the areas of education, labor and property laws, for example. Still, the Liberals (such as Sandino's father) did not endorse or pursue a policy of absolute, radical transformation of the country. In this sense, what is taken as Sandino's early revolutionary program, from the outset, had little in common with the objectives of the Liberals in the Constitutionalist War. Ramón de Belausteguigoitia partially captured the essence of Sandino's rebellious attitude: Sandino was "wounded in his pride [*amor propio*] and [was] against the military authority of his chief, General Moncada" (1985, 92).

## Soberbia

For fear of death or imprisonment, however, Sandino shrewdly acquiesced to the accords and communicated to Moncada: "I delegate my rights to you, so that you arrange things as you best see fit."[6] He also promised to gather his people's weapons and to surrender them in Jinotega, with the excuse that some of his men had already ridden north to that town—but he had no intention of honoring his word (Somoza 1936, 33). "I was doing all this for show and neither from faith nor obedience," he later wrote (Selser 1960, 1:216). Although he was clear enough in his intention to deceive Moncada, Sandino was still confused and unsure about what to do. He claimed to have "spent three days at El Común Hill, crushed, saddened, not knowing what attitude to take, whether to give up my weapons or defend the country." He cried in solitude until illumination finally came: "a strange voice said to me 'sellout' " (Belausteguigoitia 1985, 91). Surrounded by his men at the top of the mount, he proclaimed that "it is preferable to die a thousand times rather than to live as a slave." He wanted to cleanse Nicaragua, he said, in a "baptism of blood" (Román 1979, 72).

Sandino headed north to the Segovias with twenty-nine followers (Román 1979, 72; Belausteguigoitia 1985, 93). He later claimed to have made a triumphant entrance into the city of Jinotega, evoking Christ's entrance to Jerusalem: riding his mule at the head of his men, "I was received with palms, flowers and music" (Román 1979, 69). He then moved on further into the hills to San Rafael del Norte, where he married the young Blanca Aráuz, sister of the town's telegrapher, on the day of his thirty-second birthday, 18 May 1927; this may have been less a marriage of ambition (Wünderich 1995, 70) than one of convenience. Because some members of his gang began to leave, Sandino cut short his honeymoon and moved even further north to the hills near Yalí, where he could keep tighter control over his forces. However, he still was unclear about what to do, and

6. In a verbal account of this letter, Sandino claimed to have said to Moncada: "You are in command. I give you ample authorization to sign for me yourself." See Selser 1960, 1:206.

as he grappled for solutions without a clear political or a military strategy, the guiding principle of his actions was his hatred of Moncada.

Six days after his wedding, he made a desperate proposal to the U.S. Marine Corps commander in Nicaragua. Calling himself the Chief of the Mountaineers (*Jefe de los Montañeses*), Sandino suggested "as a condition *sine qua non* to surrender our weapons, that power be assumed [in Nicaragua] by a United States military governor while there can be presidential elections supervised by the Americans" (Somoza 1936, 36). The American commander rejected the offer, a rejection that remains to this day a source of embarrassment to Sandino's followers. However, given his hatred for the Americans, it is likely that Sandino did not really intend to give away his country's sovereignty; rather, the proposal seems more like an attempt to create an excuse to continue fighting under the pretence of protecting the honor of his country against a foreign military occupation. The rejection of the proposal did not dissuade Sandino from further attempts to leave Moncada and the Conservatives out of the power equation; in mid-June, he presented a new condition for the surrender of his weapons—to have an honorable Liberal government set in place—but again obtained no results (Somoza 1936, 45).

Moncada's political ambitions were also at stake; he too wanted a favorable solution, one that would afford him the image of national peacemaker and improve his chances in the upcoming election, and so he made an effort to have Sandino surrender his weapons. Through Don Gregorio, he sent Sandino a note inviting him to a meeting (Selser 1960, 1:221), but Sandino refused. Instead, Sandino complained about what he had been denied and challenged Moncada personally. He let it be known that he suspected there was a conspiracy against him and that his former commander was envious of him. His reply hardly dealt with the substance of Moncada's letter and took instead a personal dimension and tone.

> I do not know why you want to give me orders now. I remember that *you always saw me with an evil eye* when you were the General in Chief. You never wanted anything of my requests to give me troops to fight the enemy, and when Dr. Sacasa gave me forty-five men and weapons, you became upset. It would seem that *you were jealous of me.* You undoubtedly know my temperament, and you know that I am unbreakable. Now I want you to come to disarm me. I am at my post and I wait for you. I will not otherwise desist. I do not sell myself, nor do I surrender: you have to defeat me.

I believe this to be my duty, and I wish my protest written with blood will endure for the future. (Selser 1960, 1:220; emphasis added)

The passage above betrays Sandino's disposition toward Moncada. It is apparent that Sandino thought quite highly of himself, to the point of believing that the Liberal military commander would be envious of him. To him, it was a personal conflict, and as we shall see, Sandino's personal grudge toward Moncada would never abate.

In his first addresses to the civil authorities of the northern departments in May, Sandino explained and justified himself, trying to persuade them of the righteousness of his fight. A month later, however, he abandoned subtlety and gave direct orders granting recognition to some incumbent officials and appointing new ones (Somoza 1936, 45–46). At this time, Sandino's letterhead read "General Quarters of the Defenders of National Right." On 18 June, Sandino appointed Francisco Estrada as lieutenant colonel and departmental governor (*jefe político*) of Nueva Segovia. The previous day, in a letter written to the governor appointed by Moncada, Sandino wrote: "I am determined to make others respect me and that my liberty to elect authorities in that Department be respected" (Bendaña 1994, 205). He ordered that the town of El Jícaro—site of his first attack at the head of his band of discontented miners—be renamed Ciudad Sandino (Sandino City) and proclaimed it the new departmental capital, where Estrada would serve his appointment as governor (Somoza 1936, 46).

Wünderich perceives a change in Sandino in the act of reorganizing cities, seeing it as evidence for the appearance of a "messianic form" in Sandino, although he does not say what is messianic about it (1995, 139). However, Sandino's issuing of orders and proclamations as though he now was the legitimately constituted authority was indicative of a different trend. On the surface, it was the benchmark of committed personal arrogance that irreversibly marked the beginning of his political rebellion. It exposed not just a blunt thirst for personal honor and glory but also the extent of Sandino's *soberbia*—his pride, his hubris—in his willingness to bestow upon himself the honor and glory that he thought he deserved.[7]

The renaming of the town and its declaration as capital were pregnant with more public levels of meaning as well. Symbolically, Sandino's act is

7. Wünderich (1995, 77) writes that Sandino "generally exhibited a modest and sensible behavior," but there is nothing modest about naming cities after oneself.

equivalent to the religious rite of dividing sacred from profane space, which demarcates the site of a significant experience, identifies its location, and endows it with transcendental meaning; the ancient Greeks called such a place *omphalos*, the navel of the earth (see Eliade 1959; 1991a). For Sandino, the town evoked a very personal experience: the thrill and exhilaration of leading a gang of his own into battle for the first time. It was his public baptism of blood and his initiation as a fighting revolutionary. Psychologically, the new name achieved another purpose as well: in erasing the name El Jícaro, Sandino also sought to eliminate the memory of his first defeat in battle.

# 2

# In Defense of the Motherland

There may be those who think . . . that licking the Yankees' feet
will suffice to ensure the triumph of Liberalism. Those who think
so do not have the right to live. [They] desecrate the memory of
our forefathers who died to have our rights and sovereignty respected. Freedom is not conquered with flowers!
                    —Augusto C. Sandino, in a letter to Félix Zeledón

### Party, Race, and Motherland

*The Two July Manifestos*

**IN JULY 1927,** Sandino launched his first two public political manifestos. The first, dated 10 July, was addressed "to Nicaraguans, Central
Americans and the Indo-Hispanic Race" (see Selser 1960, 1:226–29 for the
full text);[1] the second, circa 14 July (Bastille Day), was written "to my
Nicaraguan Compatriots" (Sandino 1981, 1:123–26). An earlier letter, written on 17 June and addressed "to Arnoldo Ramires" (i.e. Ramírez Abaunza,
a local politician), already sketched some of the ideas in the manifestos
(Bendaña 1994, 203–5). Together, these documents outline the basis of
Sandino's early political thought and offer a glimpse into the justifications
that he presented for his rebellion. They also are a display of the rhetoric
and of the revolutionary ideas that Sandino absorbed during his first stay in
Mexico; as he wrote to Ramírez, "I bless the hour in which I migrated to a
country where I satisfied my thirst for knowledge by drinking from new
ideas."

In the first sentence of the 10 July manifesto, Sandino set out to estab-

1. The date of 10 July 1927 is given in Selser. Ramírez, however, dates this document 1 July
1927; see Sandino 1981, 1:117–20 (which also includes the full text).

lish his credibility as a patriot, asking for the right to be heard on account of his desire to die for his country: "The man who does not ask his country even for a handful of soil for his grave deserves to be heard . . . [and] to be believed." Sandino was always very adamant to present himself as a materially disinterested party; in essence, he wanted people to understand that he was not in search of money or riches like other *caudillos* but was purely motivated by love of his motherland. However, any self-professed patriot can make that claim, and so it was also imperative for Sandino to establish the source of his patriotism. To this end, Sandino evoked the racial imagery of a mystical Indian ancestry: "I am a Nicaraguan and I am proud because in my veins flows above all the blood of the Indian race, which by atavism encompasses the mystery of being patriotic, loyal and sincere." It is true that his blood was mostly Indian; he was in fact three-quarters Indian. To his mind, his patriotism was determined as a biological attribute granted by the indigenous quality of his blood. The issue was therefore race, as he wrote to Ramírez: "My blood imposes itself above all things." It was a mystery contained in the blood, and in the first manifesto he claimed his authority on the basis of that mystical connection to the ancestral nationality: "The link of nationality gives me the right to assume responsibility for my acts in the affairs of Nicaragua and, as a result, those of Central America and the entire Hispanic portion of the Continent." With this speculative maneuver, his authority gained a regional and continental dimension but also became concealed in mystery. Grounding patriotism, sincerity, and authority in mystery was an astute formulation: linking nationality to blood, as Europeans do, and then attributing a mysterious quality to it allowed Sandino to preclude any questioning or debate. Mystery, that which can not be explained, presents no room for argument.

Sandino's formulation posed an interesting problem. If one's patriotism is biologically determined, how does one race claim to be more patriotic than another? How was Sandino more patriotic than *Ladino* Nicaraguan citizens? Sandino's answer in the first manifesto required an enlargement of the basis for his ethnically justified continental authority: "My [patriotic] ideal is based upon a broad horizon of internationalism, in the right to be free and to demand justice, even if to achieve this state of perfection it may be necessary to spill one's blood and the blood of others."[2] He was not

2. Selser's and Fonseca's (1980a, 14) versions of this passage are similar, and both differ from that of Ramírez (Sandino 1981, 1:117–20), which corrupts its meaning: "My [patriotic] ideal-alism is based upon a broad horizon of internationalism, which represents the right to be free

yet explicit as to what he meant by internationalism, but the class rhetoric of the 14 July manifesto (discussed in more detail below) perhaps suggests some of its meaning: for Sandino, internationalism seems to be that which transcends nationality and ethnicity. Here we can observe another clever formulation. By evoking an internationalist dimension to his actions, in one breath he took the argument about justice and liberty out of the reach of other Nicaraguans, who claimed authority only from their own brand of narrow, local nationalism. Note also that Sandino's claim to internationalism, based on his thirst for freedom and justice, also served as the initial basis to justify killing; it is significant to remark that from the beginning of the rebellion Sandino was willing to use violent means in order to achieve the much sought-after "state of perfection" in political affairs.

In the 14 July manifesto, Sandino argued that his enemies were "disqualified to judge [his] actions" because they did not value Nicaragua's sovereignty and national honor as he did. Moncada was singled out for disqualification because he was said to lack experience in suffering, because of his membership in another social class, and because of his lack of knowledge: he "ignores the need and suffering of the working class because he does not belong to this collectivity." As a result, Moncada was "not authorized to speak as a defender of ideals unknown to him." General Moncada was deemed unfit to represent the suffering classes because he did not have the same consciousness of the governed, whereas Sandino considered himself one of them: as he claimed in the 10 July manifesto, "My greatest pride is that I come from the bosom of the oppressed, that are the nerve and soul of our race." The oppressed were the body (symbolized in the reference to a most sentient physical element, the nerve) and the soul of the race, and oppression was the prerequisite for its spiritual existence.[3]

Curiously, for Sandino, the race and the oppressed were one and the same, thereby mixing race and class as constitutive elements for common nationality. Moreover, there was yet another layer of complexity to his understanding. Claiming in the 10 July manifesto that the people of his race and the oppressed were persecuted by traitors who were "indifferent to the

---

and to do justice, even if to achieve this it may be necessary to establish it upon a foundation of blood." Selser's and Fonseca's wordings convey Sandino's desire to attain an utopian realm of perfection and are specific as to whose blood is to be shed.

3. Conrad translates the word "nerve" by "spirit" here, robbing the expression of its physical aspect (Sandino 1990, 74).

pain and misery of Liberalism," he also fused ethnicity and social class into a political party. For Sandino, to be a Liberal meant to profess many of the radical ideas of the Mexican revolution. We can gather from the contents of these two manifestos that Sandino established himself from the early part of his rebellion as the icon and measuring-rod of Nicaraguan patriotism, the oppressed Liberal of Indian blood in search of a political paradise.

Sandino continued to direct much of his attention toward General Moncada. In his attempt to demonstrate the legitimate source of his own authority, he sought through careful contortions to erode that of the man he saw as his nemesis. Sandino both claimed continuity with the Constitutionalist War and argued that he had not broken away from Moncada; rather, Moncada had split from him by not following the true premises of Liberalism. "The Liberal revolution," he said in the 10 July manifesto, "is still standing and today more than ever it is invigorated because there will only remain in it those who have displayed the valor and abnegation that Liberals should possess." The purity of his revolution, Sandino maintained, was guaranteed now that those who might soil it by betrayal and dishonesty were gone, now that he and his men were acting according to "the duties imposed by military and national honor." In effect, Sandino argued that he and his men now constituted "the [national] army, and [were] the fundamental pillar upon which rest[ed] the honor of the motherland" that others had disgraced.

Armed with this new authority, Sandino followed the logical consequences of his thought and accused Moncada of desertion. He became prosecutor in a trial where history and the motherland were the supreme magistrates, and before these magistrates Sandino took his solemn oath: "I swear that my sword will defend the national honor and will grant redemption to the oppressed." In the 14 July manifesto, Sandino again joined his professed selflessness to his desire to deliver the oppressed from suffering: "I want nothing for me . . . I aspire to nothing [*no ambiciono nada*], I only wish redemption for the working class."

Thus, Sandino divided the world into two defined factions according to race, class, and political colors, the "patriotic hearts" on one side and "the cowardly invading colossus . . . and the [Nicaraguan] traitors" on the other. In this dialectical understanding, one was the natural enemy of the other, and in the 10 July manifesto he promised to defend what he called the "Indo-Hispanic Race" against the "claws of the monstrous eagle," dripping with Nicaraguan blood, which "assassinates the weak peoples and [is the] enemy of our race."[4] "Indo-Hispanic" meant the half-breed resulting from the mixing of Spaniards and Indians. Of course, Sandino's race-symbol left out a large number of the people actually living in the region—those of African or of Portuguese descent, and the English, French, and Dutch-speaking ethnic variations of the Caribbean, including those of Nicaragua's east coast. Once again, however, Sandino painted the contest in terms not only of opposed social classes but of two contending races.

According to the same dichotomy but mixed with his understanding of Liberalism, Nicaraguans were classified into three categories. Up to this point, Sandino still viewed his position as the defender of the rights of Liberals in Nicaragua, though only two weeks earlier he had declared that the party struggles were over: "Today, starts a new era," he wrote to Ramírez. Still, he continued to use the party rhetoric, making a clear distinction between tainted and untainted Liberals and the Conservative collaborators of the force of occupation. In a letter to a certain Dr. Castillo, Sandino wrote:

> In these days when the traitors in the motherland are multiplying, it is getting hard to recognize my friends. The men of Nicaragua have divided themselves into three classes.
>
> 1. Puritanical and honorable Liberals.
> 2. Chicken Liberals (or eunuchs).
> 3. Sellouts, that is to say the Conservatives. I beg you to tell me to which of these categories you belong. (Sandino 1981, 1:137)

Later in his campaign, the world would be divided into only two categories of people: the forces of light and the forces of darkness.

*Sovereignty and Penetration*

Once he had demonstrated the legitimacy of his patriotism and had established himself as a just liberator, the incarnation of the oppressed, a true Liberal, and a redeemer, Sandino directed his rhetoric and insults toward the U.S. Marines, banking on the anti-American feeling in Latin America, especially in Nicaragua. Until June 1927, Sandino had been relatively tame

4. The notion of the people of the United States being the enemies of Latin Americans runs through both manifestos as well as through the letter to Ramírez Abaunza. Half a century later, the latter-day Sandinistas picked up on this theme and amplified it when they included in their party's anthem a line calling Americans the *"yanqui* enemy of humanity."

in his references to the Marines, but toward the end of June the insults and death threats against them began (see Sandino 1981, 1:116). Stepping up the rhetoric, the 10 July Manifesto was an effective piece of anti-American propaganda. Sandino understood all too well the suspicion that Latin Americans in the Caribbean region harbored toward United States actions and motivations. Sandino's declarations embarrassed the American government and he gained some support for his stance, first and foremost from Nicaraguans and then from Latin Americans.

To the rhetoric of an all-embracing Indo-Hispanic race, Sandino added practical geopolitical concerns. In particular, Sandino was worried on a number of levels about the possibility of the Americans building a transoceanic canal through Nicaragua.[5] On one level, his concern was simply a reaction against the United States and the Bryan-Chamorro Treaty (which authorized the canal). More important, however, he was preoccupied with and propelled by the overall significance of the canal project. For Sandino, the canal was a dream linked to a broader and greater vision for his country, a vision that echoed the speculations of Simón Bolívar in his famous "Jamaica letter." Bolívar had speculated that commercial benefits derived from canal routes would transform the Central American region into the world's trade center and political axis. The Third Rome, he dreamed, would be situated in Central America: "This magnificent location between the two great oceans could in time become the emporium of the world. Its canals will shorten the distances throughout the world, strengthen commercial ties with Europe, America and Asia, and bring that happy region tribute from the four quarters of the world. Perhaps someday the capital of the world may be located there, just as Constantine claimed Byzantium was the capital of the ancient world" (Bolívar 1976, 70).

Sandino claimed to admire Bolívar and to have read his biography; he confessed that Bolívar's life moved him to tears (Belausteguigoitia 1985, 174) and called himself a "son of Bolívar" (Sandino 1981, 1:269). However, he never specifically mentioned what he admired about his hero, nor did he refer to any particular passage of the hero's life. Rather, Sandino used Bolívar's romantic speculations and transformed them into a political plan of his own. He understood, for example, that the privileged geographical posi-

5. On Sandino's ideas about a canal through Nicaragua, see "Interview with Carleton Beals," Feb.-Mar. 1928, in Sandino 1981, 1:247; "Letter to the Heads of State of the Americas," 20 Mar. 1929, in Sandino 1981, 1:339, 340; and "Plan for the Realization of Bolívar's Supreme Dream," in Sandino 1981, 1:343, 345.

tion of Central America suggested in Bolívar's Jamaica letter might invite foreign nations to assert their control or influence over the region: "Nature has placed us at the crux of the world [*punto de reunión del mundo*] . . . [which] has made our homeland coveted to the point that our enemies would even enslave us" to gain control over it, the Nicaraguan rebel announced in the 10 July manifesto. At the same time, he also accepted Bolívar's naïve optimism. Bolívar had anticipated that the canal project would generate great wealth; according to Sandino, that wealth was now going to contribute to his own vision of national redemption for Nicaragua: "My motherland will receive the duties that are rightfully and lawfully ours and we will then have enough income to crisscross the whole national territory with railroads and to educate our peoples in the true environment of effective democracy. Then we will be respected and not looked upon with the bloody scorn [*sangriento desprecio*] we suffer today."

Sandino did not make clear what he meant by "effective democracy," but it is likely that he meant a government in which workers and peasants would be full participants. That Nicaragua is at the crossroads of the world is, of course, a chauvinistic position, but the thrust of the message had enormous appeal to Sandino and to any Nicaraguan with a minimal knowledge of their national history. Linking a canal with slavery evoked images of William Walker, the American mercenary who had subdued Nicaragua in the 1850s with the intention, among others, of controlling the transoceanic route. Walker had declared himself president of Nicaragua and had entrenched slavery; Sandino clearly had Walker in mind when he promised that this time he would "not allow the trampling of [Nicaraguan] sovereignty."

Sandino clung strongly to Nicaraguan sovereignty as though it were the virtue of a young maiden or a motherly figure in need of protection.

> Our young motherland, that olive-skinned beauty of the tropics, must be the one who proudly wears on her head the Phrygian cap of liberty bearing the magnificent slogan symbolized by our "Red and Black" banner. She should not be the victim raped by the Yankees. (Selser 1960, 1:228)
>
> [O]ur mother Nicaragua, so many times before scorned and humiliated without compassion by her bad sons who have permitted that she be raped by the Yankee invaders for a few Pesos. (Sandino 1981, 1:163)

Although one may question Pierre Vayssière's (1988) conclusions that Sandino merged his obsession with his mother into the national cause, the elements of his analysis remain. Sandino continuously referred to Nicaragua either as a virtuous young woman or as a motherly figure to be protected from the sexual abuses of an outsider and from the permissiveness of her bad children. He constantly called himself a "legitimate son of Nicaragua" in opposition to those he thought were selling her honor (see e.g. Sandino 1981, 1:125).[6] He wanted to protect his motherland against what he perceived to be foreign, imperial penetration, mostly understood in terms of the impending opening of the transoceanic canal.

Thus, in his own eyes at least, Sandino's peasant band became the protective belt of the nation. Reflecting this self-image, in September 1927 he baptized his followers as the Army in Defense of the National Sovereignty of Nicaragua (*Ejército Defensor de la Soberanía Nacional de Nicaragua*, or EDSN). Later, in a letter to Nicaraguan politician Enoc Aguado, he revealed his pedagogical reasons for choosing the name: "It was a way to explain in detail the meaning of Sovereignty to our peasants" (Alemán 1951, 103–5).

In his statement elaborating the EDSN's organizational goals and guidelines (see Sandino 1981, 1:141–43), the rebel leader spelled out regulations for all members of his force, including foreigners. These regulations contained a pledge of loyalty expressing the soldiers' desire to "defend with their blood the liberty of Nicaragua" and their willingness "to die rather than to sell themselves or to surrender." Sandino, for his part, promised to "provide to them all the necessities such as equipment and clothing" and swore to be motivated only by the "highest patriotism" and to assume all the responsibilities for his actions "before the motherland and history." In recognition of his elevated status, the soliers were to promise "only to recognize as Supreme Commander of the Revolution the patriot General Augusto César Sandino."

Thus, once again, Sandino formally transformed his name to embody a new public image. Having been born Augusto Nicolás Calderón Sandino, he had later become Augusto C. Sandino, possibly following his move into the paternal home, in order to hide his illegitimacy. Now, establishing himself as the leader of an army, he turned his middle initial "C" into "César," becoming Augusto "César" Sandino. Later, in July 1929, his name would be readapted once again to give it a more imperial sound: César Augusto Sandino. "My name is César Augusto Sandino," he said, "but I have usually

6. For more on Sandino's notions of the "legitimate" children of the motherland, see Sandino 1981, 1:129, 152, 177, 197, 231; Somoza 1936, 62; Sandino 1980, 38.

signed as A. C. Sandino" (Villanueva 1988, 81). In other contexts, Sandino tried to downplay the issue of his name, if someone noticed or asked: "I have never wanted to be called César. That some friends of mine and of the cause want to attribute the name César to me, that is something else, and it does not interest me in the least" (Gilbert 1979, 307–8). In reality, of course, he was intensely interested in the issue of his name, for he did not discourage anyone from calling him "César" and there are several of his own documents referring to him by that name, to which he affixed his signature.

Continuing his outline of the purpose of the EDSN, Sandino stated that the army's goal was to "defend the national sovereignty and the rights of the Liberal Party" so that national policies did not "emanate from a foreign nation but should be based upon the most *absolute* national spirit." Although earlier he had said that the oppressed were the soul and nerve of the nation, he now proclaimed the EDSN itself as "the soul and nerve of the motherland and the race"; his army therefore represented the essence of his struggle, the oppressed. Sandino argued that his band of peasants was the life and the untainted continuation of the Liberal Party, conducting a Mexican-style revolution in its name. Without them, he maintained, "the Nicaraguan Liberal Party would be five feet underground" (Sandino 1981, 1:199; emphasis added). His brand of Liberalism was the broader dimension added to motherland and race: "Our sacrifice is nothing, but the performance of our duty to our motherland, our race and our party" (Sandino 1981, 1:170). Motherland, race, and party, all three, were now embodied by the EDSN and linked in the struggle against traitors and American invaders.

## War and Strategy

Sandino engaged in fierce guerrilla warfare against the U.S. Marines, and he quickly learned from a few of his military blunders. On 15 July 1927, he attacked the city of Ocotal but was soundly defeated with the help of the U.S. Air Force. He lost as many as four hundred men in the Ocotal attack, which made him understand that he could not win his war in frontal conventional attacks against garrisoned, seasoned soldiers. Sandino claimed to have been in position to set the entire town on fire but magnanimously withdrew to spare the innocent, only "carrying the war booty and the pride [*soberbia*] that [moral] victory gives us" (Maraboto 1929, 14–15). Despite the military setback, he gained notoriety as the attack made news around the globe.

*Contra Moncada*

Sandino continued to indulge his hatred for Moncada and allowed his rancor toward him to determine much of his own strategy. In October 1927, hoping to influence the Liberal leadership convention, he proposed leaders from the populist branch of the party: Sofonías Salvatierra and Escolástico Lara, whom he considered "men of high intellect and capacity to direct the nation." At the same time, he resorted to hollow flattery in challenging Moncada to step aside: "If General Moncada is a real patriot, he should decline his aspiration of winning the presidency as should all those who have stained our national honor. The motherland, in these times of sorrow, does not need any *caudillos.* I implore him, as a legitimate Nicaraguan and as a man of honor, to restrain his ambition if he really wishes to stop somewhat the blood flowing from the motherland's wounds." He suspected that Moncada would be chosen but did not want to legitimize his selection by becoming too involved; thus, in order to cover all the angles, he made the distinction between election by "popular will" and by "imposition." The "popular will" would be followed, he proposed, if anyone but Moncada was selected; if Moncada won, however, it would be by the "imposition of the murderous invaders of [his] motherland" (Sandino 1980, 38–39). Sandino failed in his bid to stop Moncada's nomination.

Early in 1928, Sandino began to formulate conditions under which he might lay down his weapons, outlining three provisos: the evacuation of the American forces, the resignation of Adolfo Díaz and the appointment of an interim president without ties to any of the traditional parties, and the promise of an election supervised by the nations of Latin America (Sandino 1981, 1:229, 236–47). After Moncada's selection as party leader, however, the guerrilla chieftain reevaluated the situation and concluded that he stood to benefit from it. According to his calculations, either Moncada or a Conservative would be elected in November; whatever the outcome, he could argue that the Americans had imposed the winner, which would strengthen his position of rebellion. "If it is Moncada," he wrote, "we will fight him until we bring him down from power," and the same would apply to a Conservative winner. Sandino also anticipated that chaos would follow the election as Liberals and Conservatives would fight one another over the results, providing him with the opportunity to step in and to install order: "During this struggle between Conservatives and Moncadistas we will derive great advantage. It would be an appropriate time to proclaim and to establish a National Government, which should be led by an honest and patriotic man who is not a *caudillo*, and who has never functioned as a politician in office" (Sandino 1981, 1:274). Implicit in his reasoning was the assumption that the Americans would leave the country in the midst of such chaos; it does not seem to have occurred to him that it could have the opposite effect.

Sandino may have had in mind none other than himself as the "honest and patriotic" man who had never held office, and his description of himself in the guidelines to his troops used very similar language. Given the highly partisan nature of Nicaraguan politics, however, it did not seem probable that a nonpartisan candidate could succeed. No other solution than the one he was proposing would be satisfactory: "We will only lay down our arms before a National Government elected by all Nicaraguans," he said (Sandino 1981, 1:274). Sandino was looking for a formula that would carry him to power. Previously, he had vowed to surrender his weapons and to enter the political mainstream only if the Liberals gained power (Somoza 1936, 62).

Moncada offered two consecutive blows to Sandino's pretension of claiming the line of authority from the Liberal Party: he was successful in winning an endorsement from his former leader, Juan Bautista Sacasa (Macaulay 1985, 129), and on 4 November 1928 he won the election, which took place as scheduled and was declared fair despite a few minor interruptions and attacks by Sandino's men. Sandino's threats, attacks, and harassment did manage to produce minor irritations in the northern departments, especially to Moncada's Liberals, whose percentage of the vote dropped in the area and who lost the department of Matagalpa. On the whole, however, the fact that the percentage of spoiled ballots and vote abstention dropped by more than two-thirds from the previous election is a strong indication that Sandino's efforts did not produce the desired fruit (Vargas 1989a, 67, 105–6). The higher voter participation and Moncada's endorsement by Sacasa and ultimate victory were robust setbacks for Sandino, the self-styled defender of the constitutional rights of Sacasa and of the Liberal Party (Sandino 1980, 37–39).

Sandino, however, was prepared for this outcome. He rejected his party's victory and arranged with several marginal groups—the *Partido Liberal Republicano*, the *Partido Laborista*, and the *Grupo Solidario al Movimiento Obrero* (Group in Solidarity with the Labor Movement)—to create a junta, apparently hoping somehow to replace the newly elected Moncada. The agreement denied the elected government any recognition of legitimacy; Dr. Pedro José Zepeda, a Nicaraguan exile in Mexico, would represent the EDSN as leader of the proposed junta, while the allied parties would name the vice-president and cabinet. Zepeda was an opportunistic political weathervane. He had been Sacasa's representative in Mexico during the Constitutionalist War but then left his leader behind, publicly opposing resistance against the American intervention (see *La Prensa*, 22 February 1927, 1 and 3 May 1927, 2); he later repented on the intervention issue and organized a Sandino Committee (*Comité Pro Sandino*) in Mexico City. Sandino's control over the projected junta was secured as the pact vested in him the future government's powers to appoint "military chiefs." The agreement does not precisely define the term, but it likely meant the authority to appoint military commanders to the key posts around the country and to the departmental capitals; thus, though Sandino would occupy no political post under the agreement, he would receive sweeping and, what is more, largely undefined military powers. He had himself appointed unconditional commander of the junta's forces, "authorized to *dictate* the necessary means for the defence of the free and independent condition of the Republic against any threat coming from within or from without." In addition to these powers, he also gave himself a new title: "Generalissimo of the Army in Defence of the National Sovereignty . . . highly committed guardian of national honor" (Somoza 1936, 111; emphasis added). Caesar was eager to become dictator.

Sandino's plan to take power in Nicaragua through his junta was contingent upon a predicted set of circumstances following the election. His prediction about the election outcome was correct, but he was wrong about the anticipated fighting between partisans and the departure of the U.S. Marines. Nonetheless, Sandino kept to his plan and outlined, on Epiphany (6 January) of 1929, the fourteen conditions under which Moncada should submit to him and gain his acceptance. He declared Moncada's government unconstitutional because it had been elected under foreign occupation and argued once again that the EDSN was the sole and untainted source of legitimacy in the country. Moncada could gain the necessary legality, however, "by rendering himself accountable to the . . . Liberating Army [i.e., the EDSN] and complying with the fundamental principles that this document outlines below. [He] will be a constitutional ruler . . . for having obtained . . . the votes of a large part of the Nicaraguans who found themselves with weapons in hand at the time of the presidential election" (Sandino 1981, 1:297). Legitimacy, according to Sandino, would have to be transferred to the government from the small group of insurrected guerrillas that he led, and not from the corpus of the national electorate. These demands were consistent with the essence of the July 1927 manifestos. To one habituated to the experiences of popular sovereignty and constitutionalism, this was a bizarre conception of democracy; it has not prevented a few, however, from declaring that Sandino was a democrat.

The principles that Sandino presented to Moncada were outlined as follows. The three chief demands directly concerning Nicaragua were that the U.S. Marines withdraw from Nicaragua; that the government recognize Sandino's "founding" of and jurisdiction over a new village to be named San Juan de Segovia, whose boundaries he outlined, where his men would settle; and that the Bryan-Chamorro Treaty be abrogated. As political demands go, these were not at all unreasonable. Marine withdrawal was contingent on pacifying the Nicaraguan countryside, which would likely be achieved if Sandino gave up his fight. The difficult issue of creating a new department under Sandino's authority may not have been impossible to reconcile because it was equivalent to what the rebel *caudillo* had been offered following the Espino Negro Accords, the command of the northern department of Jinotega. The abrogation of Bryan-Chamorro was a thornier issue, but even that may not have been entirely unachievable. However, these were not the only demands that Sandino made. He also demanded that the government of Nicaragua work toward the "proclamation of the Union of Central American Republics" and called for a conference to form what he named the "Indo-Latin American Continental and Antillean Confederation" to resist American domination. Both of these were out of the scope of the initial motivation to evict the force of occupation, but in reality were strongly bound to it. In Sandino's mind, the creation of such a fantastic confederation would ensure that no further occupations of his country or of any other Latin American country would take place. Sandino also made a long list of progressive socioeconomic demands such as a national workers accident compensation law, an eight-hour workday with overtime pay, and forcing business with more than fifteen workers to provide basic schooling for the workers.

The new formula had the virtue of incorporating Latin Americans of African descent into Sandino's scheme, but most of these demands were beyond Moncada's abilities to deliver. Indeed, Sandino's intention may well have been to trick Moncada by asking what was beyond his opponent's power. Still, the net result was the unveiling of more details about Sandino's grand design for the advancement of his Latin American race and about his plan for regional revolution. His intentions to transform the region appear in three tightly related forms: at the community level, in the village he wished to found and to rule; at the national level, through legal and social reforms; and at the hemispheric level, in the founding of an all-embracing anti-imperialist alliance stretching from the Rio Grande to the Southern Cone.

### Expectations and Disappointments

Sandino expected great things to come quickly out of his struggle. He usually planned one thing and became very excited if it worked, but if it did not materialize he became angry or disappointed (or both) and then moved on to something else. In this sense, his long-term plans and expectations matched his erratic disposition. Early in 1928, Sandino thought that the nations of the world were morally bound to help and to protect him by pressuring the United States, and he called on the Latin American states to demand an American withdrawal from Nicaragua (Sandino 1981, 1:223). He considered Central America the "great motherland" (*la patria grande*) and his own cause to be "the great cause of the freedom of Central America" (Sandino 1981, 1:232); in return, he expected the neighboring nations to come to his rescue and to combat the Americans just as they had done to defeat Walker's mercenaries. Only a few weeks later, when no such help arrived, he became convinced that the Latin American nations had allied against him (Sandino 1981, 1:243).

Months later, Sandino issued another appeal to the heads of states of Latin America, urging them to become militarily involved against the United States and warning them that "the American colonization [of the subcontinent would] rapidly advance over [their] nations." If separate, he warned, "each one would have its turn" to be invaded and subjugated, for once "Central America is dominated by the blonde pirates, they will continue toward Mexico, Colombia, Venezuela, etc.," and so he pleaded with them to unite. To Sandino's mind, the landing of the Marines in Nicaragua was part of an elaborate plan to take over Latin America, and the imperialistic strategy—a simple scheme to keep the countries divided—was working in the favor of the United States. The counterstrategy that he urged was tight union: "We are ninety million Hispano-Americans and we must only think of our unification," he beseeched them. He was convinced that the United States was their "most brutal enemy" and "the only one that intend[ed] to conquer them and put an end to [their] racial honor and [their] people's freedom" (Selser 1960, 2:31).

Sandino's long-awaited moral backing from the governments of the hemisphere did not materialize, however, not even from the neighboring Central American nations, let alone any military support. To be sure, he did enjoy support from many private citizens across frontiers, but this did not translate into official state support as he had expected. Thus, despite the popularity that he commanded, the summer of 1928 was not without its troubles. In one incident, some sixteen hundred of his men surrendered and were granted amnesty (Macaulay 1985, 128); by February 1929, he had to urge his lieutenants to be patient and to adopt different tactics "while we receive more men" (Sandino 1981, 1:315). His disappointment was also manifested as he lashed out at the European nations for not coming to his aid. He accused them of collaborating with the Americans in a conspiracy of silence against poor countries and threatened also to attack European nationals in Nicaragua. A tone of desperation ran through his condemnations, as in a May 1928 letter to Froylán Turcios: "The Yankee pirates are murdering us in the full light of day and in the presence of all the nations that in every epoch have distinguished themselves as conquerors and enslavers, such as England, Germany, France and Italy. It would appear that all these nations, and Spain as well, have some secret pact to remain deaf to the lamentations of the weak countries when they find themselves under the brutal boot of one of them" (Sandino 1981, 1:262–63).

*Immortality and Glory*

Reversals notwithstanding, Sandino became increasingly confident that his cause was sanctioned by divine power and did not hesitate in communicating that certainty to those around him. Seemingly pious expressions such as "the divine providence protects us," "God will sustain us," and "God will crown our efforts" were in fact assertions of God's favoring role in his cause (Sandino 1981, 1:250; Sandino 1980, 38). He became convinced that God would protect him from his enemies and would miraculously help to defeat them.

God and the mountains of my motherland will help us convert our [patriotic] idealism to reality. Let us have faith, God protects us because until this day my army has never suffered a defeat, the best proof is that we are getting stronger with each day that passes. . . . Motherland and Liberty [*Patria y Libertad*] is my creed. . . . My army is strengthened by its faith in the cause of justice, and by its faith in God, Who will help us gain our independence from Yankee imperialism. (A. Sandino 1928a, 1096)[7]

[To his wife Blanca:] I suppose there can be no doubt about our [final] victory, because *God not only has favored our cause but has also become an interested party.* Let us hope that the greatness attained by the Yankees does not dazzle all of you because God's greatness is our protector. The pirates will leave our territory and not even they will be able to explain the reasons for their defeat. Our victory will be providential. (Sandino 1981, 1:156; emphasis added)[8]

Perhaps for the utilitarian purpose of inspiring his troops and providing them with hope and comfort in the face of a powerful enemy against enormous odds—or perhaps because he truly believed in them—exhortations and professions of faith such as these began to be more commonplace in Sandino's letters and communiqués toward the last quarter of 1927. Sandino was clear that he was fighting for what he believed to be the cause of justice, but the obvious implication of these passages is that he was also on the side of the angels.

From the early days of his struggle, Sandino resigned himself to the possibility of death, a resignation that was rooted in his strong sense of mission. In May 1927, he declared: "It does not matter if the world collapses upon me but we will comply with our sacred duty" (Selser 1960, 1:217). A few weeks later, he elaborated on his faith and mission: "We have faith that God will fortify our spirit so that we may annihilate the invaders and traitors of my motherland. The entire region of Nueva Segovia belongs to us in body and soul and this in itself assures our effectiveness in our struggle against the enemy" (Sandino 1981, 1:134–36).

It may seem rather curious that Sandino would demonstrate such ardent affection for the region of the Segovias, being an outsider and having only arrived there as an adult. The natural beauty and its wilderness (as compared to the more populated area of his youth) do not sufficiently explain his apparent spiritual attachment for the land. Here, we can only speculate that his closeness to the land may be linked to his belief that the

---

7. A different version of this document appears in Sandino 1981, 1:206–7.

8. In an earlier version of *El pensamiento vivo*, this letter was dated 6 Oct. 1928, but in the 1981 edition Ramírez changed it to 6 Oct. 1927 without much of an explanation (see Sandino 1981, 155–57). Given the unfolding of Sandino's millenarian expectations, the 1928 dating seems more likely.

Segovians were the only people in the country ready to take up arms to defend the motherland. It may also be connected to the simplicity of the people there; Sandino scorned the sophisticated political elite of the country, who were responsible, in his mind, for the precarious condition of the Nicaraguan state and its people. In this sense, his class-consciousness may also be tied to his deep sentiments for the bucolic region. Whatever the case may be, it is clear that the territory to be "defended," the "defenders," the cause, and God all seemed to have a strong connection in Sandino's mind.

Sandino constantly repeated that he did not want personal power and seldom spoke of glory for himself, but he often promised these things to his soldiers and supporters—and one cannot bestow that which one does not have. At the start of his struggle, Sandino bestowed upon his fallen comrades the status of martyrs to be revered: "Get down on your knees, all of you, because I am going to invoke the blessed names of my comrades [*compañeros*] in arms who have died in defense of the liberty of Nicaragua" (Sandino 1981, 1:135). He opened many of his war communiqués by announcing that "the defenders [had] covered themselves with glory" or by promising that the coming triumphs would cover his men with glory. "When we enter into Managua," he promised them, "we won't even be able to walk because of the many flowers that the young girls will thrust upon you" (Sandino 1981, 1:170).

There was also a darker side to the promise of glory, however: an enthralling appeal to death enveloped in revolutionist romance. "The Indo-Hispanic people have had the glory of conquering their rights with their own blood," he wrote to Berta Munguía, secretary of the Group in Solidarity with the Labor Movement (Sandino 1981, 1:167). He encouraged her to seek glory by wrestling it away from those who had it—the powerful—by killing them, and he urged her to become a "heroine . . . Nicaragua's Joan of Arc. . . . The greatest glory [is] to humble the greatness of the mighty, converting them into miserable skeletons in our bucolic mountains." This was to be accomplished in the "bloodiest fight for freedom that had ever been recorded in the history of Nicaragua" (Sandino 1981, 1:204–5).

Sandino was committed to Armageddon. The motto Victory or Death! (*¡Vencer o morir!*) that he proclaimed to Munguía illustrated his meaning. The life of revolutionary action offers two extremes, victory or death, which in reality are the same; there is no middle ground from which to choose because the revolutionary sees no possible way to lose in the quest for glory. There is glory in victory and there is glory in death. Sandino discouraged the middle ground between the extremes, prudence and reflection: "Have no fears nor reflect too much. If we should die in the struggle for our freedom, our bodies will turn with our faces toward the sun and our martyr blood will vivify [*vivificar*] the hearts of the true Nicaraguan patriots who will follow our example." Clearly, such rhetoric was both a recruitment call and an incitement to uprising, but it was also an invitation to attain immortality in revolutionary martyrdom. "Nicaragua will have the glory of displaying your names in the pages of its history," he predicted (Sandino 1981, 1:204–5). In victory or in death (provided that prudence and reflection did not cloud the passion for celebrity and the lust for blood), glory would always be ensured, according to Sandino. He had earlier given a more compact version of this view of revolutionary activity, stating succinctly that "history will immortalize your names" (Sandino 1981, 1:134).

### Froylán Turcios: Master and Traitor

*The Propaganda Machine*

Aided by poet-journalist Froylán Turcios of Honduras—named "Sandino's official representative for Latin America"—the rebel attracted world attention as many of his manifestos and communiqués were published in the review that Turcios edited, *Ariel*. Turcios was well respected in cultural circles in Latin America, and his pen commanded attention. He built a bright aura of heroism around Sandino and skillfully exploited popular sympathy for the underdog. His review was named after the book *Ariel* by the Uruguayan José Enrique Rodó (1957), who argued that the humanistic and spiritual inheritance of Latin America was superior to the rational utilitarianism, positivism, social egalitarianism, and materialism of the Anglo-Saxon world. Rodó was alarmed by the "corrupting" influence of Anglo-Saxon ideas seeping into Latin culture and proposed to resist it. In his nationalism, Turcios embraced the spirit of Rodó's work as his own, and Sandino's campaign against the U.S. Marines seem to present itself as the practical manifestation of those ideas.

Turcios became invaluable to Sandino and although they never met, there developed a great affection between the two men. Indeed, Turcios's admiration for Sandino bordered on worship: in his correspondence with Sandino he called him "hero of heroes," "the most brilliant man of modern times," and the "new Bolívar under the skies of the Americas" (Somoza 1936, 112–13). The adulation of such a respected man of letters swelled Sandino's pride, who considered the poet the "hope and the strong arm of this cause . . . the only one who has known truly how to interpret our patriotism and loyalty to our creed" (Sandino 1981, 1:263, 252). Beyond the customary but sometimes overdone exchange of compliments in Latin American culture of the day, Sandino valued the poet's loyalty and appreciated the work that the latter performed on his behalf. He called Turcios his "best friend" and "master," and he called himself the "disciple." Gregorio Gilbert, a Dominican volunteer in Sandino's army, captured the essence of their relationship when he wrote: "So fused became Turcios to [the cause] that it would have been difficult, if not impossible, to determine who felt most for it, Sandino the guerrilla or Turcios the poet" (Gilbert 1979, 114).

Turcios's pieces were often reprinted throughout Latin America, Europe, and the United States. His propagandizing work was so effective that Sandino became famous around the world and many wished to be associated with his name. The popular Chilean poet Gabriela Mistral called for the formation of a Hispanic League to fight in Nicaragua. The first Sandino Committee appeared in Costa Rica in 1928, and many similar organizations supporting him surfaced later in the United States and across Latin America. Sandino's popularity even went beyond the Western Hemisphere: in China, Chiang Kai-Shek's Kuomintang forces named a regiment after the rebellious *caudillo*, the "Sandino Division." Later, the Comintern picked up the propagandizing effort, as its New York branch paraded Sócrates Sandino from rally to rally as his brother's spokesman and fundraiser; in Moscow, the Sixth Congress of the Comintern sent Sandino a special salute. The extreme left in the United States hailed him at the First Congress of the Anti-Imperialist League, and Sandino would also be hailed as a great son of the "struggle for liberation" by the First Congress of the World Anti-Imperialist League held in Frankfurt, Germany (Macaulay 1985, 112–14; Crawley 1984, 61–62).

*The Pupil Betrays the Master*

Soon after the setback of the 1928 election, Sandino wrote Turcios a letter bringing him up to date on the new developments and instructing him to harmonize efforts with Zepeda in preparation for the implementation of the new junta strategy. Sandino included a copy of the agreement for the formation of the junta, and he proposed that Turcios be the junta's representative once it was formed. Revealing the core of the new strategy, Sandino confided that the junta was to be proclaimed only if the Americans did not withdraw. If they did, however, Turcios was to make arrangements for Sandino to regroup to a friendly country (probably Mexico) in order to achieve three objectives: to obtain badly needed weapons to continue the war, to establish a concerted plan against the government of Moncada, and to gain the ability to communicate with the people of Nicaragua, which he was unable to do from the Segovian hills. The tone of the letter betrayed concern and doubt as to the success of the projected junta, but as if to dispel these doubts Sandino asserted: "God is with us in these supreme hours, you have said, and this phrase repeated by me daily will take us to our final victory" (Somoza 1936, 110). This was a radical departure from the initially stated objectives of Sandino's rebellion.

Turcios immediately understood the implications of the shift, and he strongly opposed both the proposed junta and its civil war alternative. In a letter written on 17 December 1928, he advised Sandino not to go ahead, warning that the latter would appear like a petty *caudillo* trying to take power; he was concerned that the image of Sandino as *libertador* that he had worked so hard to propagate would be damaged. Turcios tried to explain to Sandino the basis of his opposition to the project, stating what he had understood to be the objectives of Sandino's war and that into which he did not wish to see it degenerate: "The Sandino *caudillo* in a civil war, in a miserable fratricidal quarrel, I do not know him, and I would have nothing to do with him." Attempting to soften the stiff message to the guerrilla chieftain, Turcios proposed to negotiate with the newly elected government of Nicaragua so that it would commit itself to respecting the constitution and would grant Sandino and his men a broad amnesty in exchange for the surrender of Sandino's weapons, to be kept in Costa Rica just in case the U.S. Marines returned (Somoza 1936, 112–13).

No record survives of Sandino's response to Turcios's initial objections and proposals, but Sandino cannot have received them well. Given his intense personal animosity toward Moncada, he would not have agreed to negotiate with or to surrender his weapons to his former commander. Only a few days later, Turcios offered his resignation as the guerrilla chief's personal representative, warning Sandino about walking down the path of failure. Although we do not know specifically what may have triggered the poet's resignation, his letter reveals keen insight into Sandino's disposition at the same time as it acknowledges the futility of further argument with him.

> I am completely convinced that a fatal fortune is moving right over our cause and over the new ideology that you now present me, which rapidly

marches towards sure failure. . . . I see we are no longer in agreement as to the goal of the struggle. You do not heed my recommendations about taking action against the [American] pirates only in what concerns national sovereignty. Now you pretend to find means to change a domestic political régime using civil war, but I cannot follow you on this path. If you persist with the plan that you now confirm, we will separate as two brothers unable to understand one another. . . . I was wrong to think that you would understand my point. I would achieve nothing writing pages and pages to you about this. . . . Your Master, as you call me, no longer has any influence over your soul. (Somoza 1936, 114)

The pupil did not hesitate to accept his master's resignation and lashed out at him for daring to offer advice in disagreement with his plans. Sandino wrote to accuse the poet of trying to run his affairs (Somoza 1936, 115–16). The guerrilla chief had difficulty conceiving that one loyal to him would willingly disagree with his plans, so he declared Turcios a traitor and denounced him for selling out to the enemy for $100,000. He hinted that it was a good riddance and reassured his troops that the cause of their struggle was now reinforced with Turcios's departure (Sandino 1981, 1:313–17; see also Gilbert 1979, 145; Román 1979, 127). Five years later, Sandino still called Turcios his "great traitor" and his "true Judas" (Román 1979, 127).

Gilbert (1979, 145) places the rupture between Sandino and Turcios in an interesting light by suggesting that it resulted from the work of the "communist element" in Sandino's camp, who despised Turcios and often accused him of being bourgeois. In particular, Gilbert singles out the highest-ranking communist in Sandino's camp, Farabundo Martí, as the source of the charges of misappropriation of funds against Turcios (see next chapter). He also shows that Turcios was not the only one among Sandino's followers to disagree with the new plan; indeed, Gilbert recalls voicing to Sandino his own reservations about the junta and civil war alternatives, but Sandino brushed him off by telling him that he was ignorant of the sought-after ideals and proceeded to lecture him on the parallel plan of a Latin America without frontiers (1979, 140). It is revealing to note that even after their disagreement Gilbert remained one of the most trusted of Sandino's men; sheer ignorance, it seems, was a nonthreatening, acceptable reason for disagreeing with the chief. Soon thereafter, however, Gilbert quietly departed from the rebel *caudillo*.

Sandino's "official representation" was then assigned to the Comintern-controlled Hands Off Nicaragua Committee (*Comité Manos Fuera*

*de Nicaragua,* also known as Mafuenic) in Mexico (Sandino 1981, 1:310).
With Turcios gone, Sandino lost his line of "communication with the
world"—and also his "best friend," something he later lamented. Less than
a year after the breakup, he indirectly but publicly recanted by praising
Turcios's honesty (Somoza 1936, 135–37), and in a private letter written to
Max Viana, editor of the Honduran review *Mi Revista,* Sandino openly ex-
onerated Turcios. Turcios was promoted to the same level as Gilbert when
Sandino qualified him as "sincerely misguided" (Sandino 1981, 2:49).

On Hodges's reading, the rupture between Sandino and Turcios arose
out of what he calls (borrowing from Gilbert's phrase *nuevos ideales*) a
"new ideology," manifested in Sandino's refusal to accept the candidate
nominated by his party, in his refusal of the election result, and in the proposal to form a rival government (Hodges 1986, 85; see also Gilbert 1979,
140). Contemporaries such as Turcios clearly understood Sandino's positions as a new ideology. Moreover, on a more emotional level, this change
in disposition was accompanied by a swelling in the ambition and pride of
Augusto Sandino, as suggested by a communication to French writer Max
Grillo: "My motherland, for which I struggle, has Spanish America for frontiers. At the beginning of my campaign I thought only of Nicaragua. After-
ward . . . *my ambition grew.* I thought of the Central American Republic
. . . Tell Hispano-America that as long as Sandino breathes, the independence of Central America will have a defender. I shall never betray my cause.
That is why I am the son of Bolívar" (Sandino 1981, 1:269; emphasis added).
Sandino's plan included more than Nicaraguan affairs. His ambition out-
grew Nicaragua and it would soon outgrow Central and Latin America.

After his break with Turcios, and still facing an acute shortage of men,
Sandino made promises of imminent victory: "We have arrived at the cul-
minating moment of our liberating war and history will very soon give us
the definitive triumph in the cause of our absolute autonomy" (Sandino
1981, 1:317). (He had not yet committed to a specific date.) He went on to
introduce a novel interpretation of Nicaragua's history, from which he
adopted a new calendar. His reading of national history established the
EDSN as the heir of a "tradition" of struggle against American intervention in Nicaragua that had began in 1912 with Benjamín Zeledón. Zeledón
died (at the hands of Nicaraguans) resisting the U.S. Marines' occupation
on 4 October 1912; since then, he had occupied a special place in
Nicaraguan Liberal mythology. As though to establish a connection between him and his hero, Sandino claimed to have seen in his young years

the fallen body of Zeledón as it was being carted away through Sandino's village. It is unknown whether this event actually took place; the story may be another example of Sandino's creative memory in service of revolutionary rhetoric. What is important, however, is the place of Zeledón's mythical proportion in Sandino's psyche and the interpretation of his struggle as the forerunner of Sandino's. The year of Zeledon's death became year zero for Sandino, and so 1929 appears as the "Seventeenth Year of the Anti-Imperialist Struggle in Nicaragua" (Sandino 1981, 1:310; see also 312, 359, 2:61). In Mexico on 4 October 1929, he remembered Zeledón, "our greatest hero," and celebrated the "Eighteenth Year of the Anti-Imperialist Struggle" (Villanueva 1988, 129).

Some primitive societies expelled a goat at their celebrations of the new year in order to attain purification. Similarly, the expelling of Turcios constituted a new beginning of purification and regeneration of the rebel cause, symbolized by the new calendar. In renaming El Jícaro, Sandino had achieved a new division of space; with a new calendar, he established a new division of time.[9]

### Bolívar's Dream and the Quest for Recognition

Sandino's political offensive in no way signified the slowing down of the war in the hills, as he continued to attack the U.S. Marines. Small military victories do not win wars, however, and he was aware that he also needed to win minds. He was familiar with the shrewd uses of propaganda and understood the damage that his enemies could cause him, domestically and internationally, by portraying him as a bandit instead of the liberator that he understood himself to be. He equated himself to statesmen the likes of Washington and Bolívar but complained that while they were called "founding fathers . . . [he was] only [considered] a bandit" (Selser 1960, 2:10). He worried greatly to think of all that he could lose in the war of images and words. Indeed, he could lose what he admitted to wanting most, praise and recognition: "Turcios's resignation left us in isolation. We had

---

9. On the ritual structuring of space and time, see Eliade 1959; 1991a. Other prophetic millenarian leaders have speculated about time, including elaborating their own calendar; for one uncanny resemblance to Sandino—complete with rebellion against oppression, clash of cultures at the receding frontier, new name, new calendar, theosophical ideas, etc.—see Flanagan's work on Louis Riel (1995a; 1996, 96–99).

no communication with the world. We lacked . . . the moral support and the sympathy that we have always had from all the peoples of the Americas. The silence, the isolation, and the desperation of remaining ignored burdened us. We missed the world knowing we are still in our struggle" (Villanueva 1988, 33).

He then became convinced of the necessity of going to Mexico to enhance his image and to obtain money, weapons, and the badly desired support for his cause. On 6 January 1929 (the same day that he demanded the submission of Moncada to his authority), Sandino wrote to interim Mexican president Emilio Portes Gil requesting entry and "protection" in that country so that he could come to announce in person his "far-reaching projects" for Latin America. A trip abroad was part of the envisaged plan in the event that the American troops did not abandon Nicaraguan soil after the election in the fall of 1928. The letter to Portes Gil would later become a subject of interest in the hard days that were ahead in Mexico. It was notoriously ambiguous; although its bearer, a young Mexican captain named de Paredes, was instructed to explain "Nicaragua's political situation and [Sandino's own] calculations" to the president, when read by itself it was easily construed as an asylum request (Somoza 1936, 122).

It is not clear exactly when Sandino received an answer from Portes Gil (who agreed to welcome him), but his intense writing activity addressing heads of states in early March may indicate that he received it sometime at the end of February. The Mexican president's "invitation" helped to boost Sandino's opinion of himself, and he began to write to heads of state across the hemisphere as though he were now one among them. He even wrote an open letter to American president Herbert Hoover (1874–1964) announcing that he was not willing to abandon his battle despite American might, because "there exists a divine breath of justice that sustains us, and is a tempest for those with evil intentions." Sandino worried that his absence from the battlefield would be interpreted as failure or abdication: "Upon reason, justice and right, I have reinforced my stand in opposition to the policy you pursue against my motherland" (Sandino 1981, 1: 328). To the presidents of all Central American republics, he wrote seeking support in the dramatic tone (and mixed images) that would become typical of his later letters: "At this moment Nicaragua has a lever like the one Archimedes had and is in need of a fulcrum like the one he sought. . . . Archimedes could turn the world upside down, we together could stop being humiliated by the Yankees" (Sandino 1981, 1:332). He asked Argentinean president Hipólito

Irigoyen, then in his second term, to host a conference of Latin American states in Buenos Aires—and without waiting for a reply from the would-be host, he invited the presidents of all Latin American states to attend. In his invitation, Sandino revealed that destiny had chosen Nicaragua to lead the cause of Indo-Hispanic union: "It was written in the destiny of our [Latin American] peoples that our humbled and disgraced Nicaragua was to be the one authorized to call us to unity with a brotherly embrace. She is the one who has sacrificed herself and would gladly allow her entrails to be torn if by this means she might achieve the freedom and absolute independence of our Latin American, continental and Antillean peoples" (Sandino 1981, 1:339). Sandino did not mention where it was that Nicaragua had been proclaimed the sacrificial lamb of Latin America.

The conference would address Sandino's "far-reaching project," outlined in a pompous and convoluted forty-four-point "Plan for the Realization of Bolívar's Supreme Dream" (*Plan de Realización del Supremo Sueño de Bolívar*) (Sandino 1981, 1:341–55). Sandino believed that an alliance of all of the states south of the Rio Grande would prevent the United States from ever intervening in Latin American internal politics and economy and would guarantee that the future canal built in Nicaragua remained "under Latin American sovereignty." Sovereignty and the possible canal in Nicaragua continued to be the center of his analysis. It became apparent that what Sandino meant by "sovereignty" was no longer a strictly Nicaraguan national issue, as he now gave the term wider application, thinking that the canal would turn into "a marvelous engine for the development of [Latin America's] material and spiritual progress" and would "become the world's magnet as well as its key." He also believed that the alliance would develop into a federation by "the fusion of the twenty-one states of our America into one unique Latin American nationality," which would "have the rights over the interoceanic route in Central America."

Sandino's elaborate "project" declared the Monroe Doctrine abolished and proclaimed the existence of a Latin American "nationality" with its respective "citizenship." He proposed the creation of a Latin American court of justice that would deal with regional disputes, and he called for an apolitical military force commanded by the chief justice of the proposed court, serving a six-year term by popular election. He even went so far as to design a flag for the court and to request that a statue of Bolívar be erected in the building that would house the organization. In a similar vein, Sandino also envisaged the creation of a banking cartel to buy out all North American investment in the subcontinent, including the Panama Canal.

Significantly, Sandino declared the court's new motto to be The Spirit Will Speak for My Race (*Por Mi Raza Hablará el Espíritu*),[10] a phrase borrowed from the Mexican intellectual José Vasconcelos. Vasconcelos's work *The cosmic race* (*La raza cósmica*) strongly influenced discussions of race in many Latin American nations. A noted man of letters serving as minister of education in the Mexican revolutionary government, Vasconcelos applied a tripartite Comtean understanding of history to the evolution of the races, arguing that there were three stages in the development of races: the warrior or material phase, the intellectual or political phase, and the ethical or spiritual phase (Vasconcelos 1966, 37). The *mestizo* race of Latin America, he claimed, was destined to reach the most advanced stage because it was the heir of Atlantis (15). It would surpass the preceding four races because its spiritual evolution had been accelerated by the mixture of many races in the new continent, especially the Indian and the Iberian; he thus called this fifth race "the final race, the cosmic race" (53). With the advent of this final racial synthesis, a utopia would be established: Love and beauty would reign, all ugliness and hate would cease to be (39). Vasconcelos was greatly optimistic about his racial lineage and about the accomplishments of his epoch: "All the tendencies of the future are at present intertwined: Mendelism in biology, socialism in government, soaring sympathy in the souls, generalized progress and the advent of the fifth race that will fill the planet with the triumphs of the first truly universal, truly cosmic culture" (52). Such views accorded well with the *mestizo*-centered, pan-American outlook of Sandino, and the prominence that he gave to Vasconcelos's phrase signifies another link between the Nicaraguan rebel and a wider Mexican intellectual heritage.

Revolution does not advance through ideas alone, however, no matter how audacious; while Sandino elaborated his proposals, Moncada went on a military offensive. At the beginning of February 1929, he declared a state of siege in the regions occupied by the rebels and used the opportunity to raise a force of "volunteers" to fight Sandino. One of the most notorious commanders of the volunteer force was Juan Escamilla, a ruthless merce-

---

10. Conrad translates the phrase as "let courage speak for my race," in an attempt to signify spiritedness; see Sandino 1990, 261. The expression is still the motto for Mexico's National Autonomous University (UNAM).

nary from Mexico who was relentless in his pursuit of the guerrillas but who often applied the same methods to innocent civilians as well. The wave of government repression and violence that followed did not please the American command, who forced Moncada to dissolve his volunteers by 15 June. By then, Sandino was on his way to Mexico.

# 3

# Revolutionary Triangle

We will be disciples of the Mexican Revolution, but we will not
make its mistakes. From all those things costing lives and money
with which the Mexican Revolution experimented, we will take the
practical part for the benefit of our workers and peasant masses, but
we will never try to implant exotic doctrines or stupid radicalisms.
                    —Augusto C. Sandino, quoted by Enrique Rivera Bertrán

## Excitement and Suspicion

**AS HIS CORRESPONDENCE** in the days leading up to his 1929 trip
shows, Sandino was enthusiastic about visiting Mexico once again. He was
no longer the fugitive and migrant laborer of the earlier visit, and indeed he
now saw himself as a foreign dignitary. This time, he traveled with a contingent of over forty men—personal secretaries, bookkeepers, political advisors, and bodyguards—most of whom (save for the personal bodyguards)
were polished and well-educated foreign volunteers in the EDSN, the
so-called Latin American Legion. Sandino wanted to show himself at the
head of a movement that was truly international; the Segovian peasants,
who might have made just as good if not a better public relations stunt,
were left in the hills to continue the fight under the command of Pedro Altamirano, better known as Pedrón. Sandino's journey across Central America would have been an emotional episode for anyone: in many places,
large numbers of supporters or the merely curious lined the roads or rail
lines to welcome him as a hero, making him feel revived and encouraged. It
was "evident that [Sandino] was profoundly convinced that his trip was
going to end squarely at the Presidential Palace in Mexico City, and would
bring recognition to his movement as an international force" (Wünderich
1995, 194).

The mood soon changed, however, when the rebel's arrival in Mexico did not generate the same enthusiasm with the border authorities. In the same way that it did not take much for Sandino to feel personally encouraged, it also took little to make him discouraged; he quickly became disappointed when customs officers at the Guatemalan border put him through the regular immigration protocol, asking questions and demanding passports that he and his entourage did not have. Detained for several hours, Sandino felt harassed, and he became more upset when there was no one to receive him officially in Mexican territory. No arrangements had been made about where to spend the night, he had little or no money, and he quickly became suspicious of a possible trap; returning to Guatemala, he accused Captain de Paredes of setting him up. De Paredes managed to contact the Mexican president's office and convinced Sandino to proceed into Mexico. Once out of Chiapas, the mood changed again, as he was warmly received from Tapachula to the Gulf port of Veracruz, which he reached on 28 June 1929 (Gilbert 1979, 251; Sandino 1981, 2:51).

Shortly after his triumphant arrival in Veracruz, Sandino was instructed by the Mexican government to travel away from the political center of the country to the city of Mérida, capital of the state of Yucatán, under the guise of keeping his visit secret so as not to cause undue friction between Mexico and the United States. What Sandino did not know was that Yucatán was the preferred destination for the Mexican government to send dissidents on internal exile. Ignorant of a possible slight, Sandino interpreted the seemingly cautious move as a sign that help would be forthcoming.

For the first few months, Sandino received invitations to go to parties, receptions, ribbon-cutting ceremonies, and the like. He received and entertained guests at his first-rate hotel, where he was the center of attention of Mérida's socialists and socialites. Enthusiastic still, Sandino later wrote to President Portes Gil to announce his arrival and to demonstrate his gratitude, taking the opportunity to reveal that he was being guided by the spirit of the most secularist of Mexican heroes, Benito Juárez: "I have even begun to think that the radiant spirit of Benito Juárez, the father of the Americas, has illuminated my steps through the mountains and over the rugged terrain of the Segovias and that his voice, which the free Americas one day heard clamoring for justice and freedom against the invaders, has said to me: 'Have faith and continue' " (Sandino 1981, 1:364–65). He received no response.

Sandino formally met with members of the Mexican Communist Party (*Partido Comunista de México*, or PCM) in Veracruz early in July. The details of the discussions between them are unknown, but it seems that they were trying to outline an agenda for collaboration—hardly a prudent course of action on Sandino's part, given the illegal standing of the party and its severed relations with the Mexican government. Portes Gil had assumed the Mexican presidency in December 1928 under difficult conditions, following the assassination of the popular reformer Álvaro Obregón, and he soon found himself at odds with revolutionary sectors of the country, including the PCM. The conflict with the communists escalated by early 1929, and the government declared the PCM illegal. By June of that year, having negotiated a truce with the Catholic Church, Portes Gil launched a wave of repression against the communists; in addition, he flirted with the United States and broke off diplomatic relations with the Soviet Union. Whatever Portes Gil's own sentiments, the real power in the government was still Plutarco Elías Calles; as he steered his puppet presidents to the right, the climate of revolution in Mexico came to an end (Meyer, Sherman, and Deeds 1999, 571–72).

Also in July 1929, in a letter carried by a personal envoy, Sandino addressed the Second Congress of the World Anti-Imperialist League in Frankfurt. The league, an instrument of the Comintern that had been created in Brussels following the Comintern's Fifth Congress in 1926, was intended to advance propagandistic efforts against imperialism by becoming an umbrella group to coordinate the efforts of anti-imperialist forces as a "united front" everywhere. Soon after its formation, the league established a U.S. chapter in New York, and a Latin American chapter emerged in Mexico City. In a flattering mood, Sandino called the World Anti-Imperialist League "the first moral authority of the oppressed peoples of the world," a formula that previously had been reserved for his own peasant army (Sandino 1981, 1:367). The league reciprocated the compliment and resolved to invite Sandino to take a propaganda tour throughout Europe and Latin America (Dospital 1996, 60). Sandino was dangerously playing both sides of a very bitter rivalry between the Mexican government and the communists, but he had neither the necessary skill nor sufficient political experience to succeed; the consequences would prove to be disastrous for him and for the future of revolutionary movements in Central America.

Month after long month, in exile unawares, Sandino waited for an audience with the president. For their part, while keeping him under close surveillance, the Mexican government handed him two thousand pesos a month to cover expenses for him and his large entourage (Gilbert 1979, 282). Upon arrival, Sandino had decided to stay at Mérida's Grand Hotel, the finest hotel in the city, but it soon became evident that the government's allowance was not enough for such lifestyle. At one point, a female friend paid his bill when he was unable to pay. He and his men were forced to move to the modest quarters of the local union leader Anacleto Solis (who fed them on credit) and to receive donations from sympathizers in order to make ends meet (Sandino n.d.). Five months later, worried and impatient, Sandino wrote to the president complaining that he had "not seen the smallest sign of fulfillment of the expectations that motivated us to travel to Mexico"; he was convinced that the president was "secretly denying him an interview" (Sandino 1981, 1:405). Once again, he received no response from the president, but he must have had some hope or indication of imminent change because he kept his pride in check and continued to wait. Conveniently, the rebel *caudillo* still suspected that it was Captain de Paredes who had plotted to lure him and to keep him out of Nicaragua, thus perhaps taking his attention away from the Mexican government itself.

A few years later, Somoza García (1936, 244) claimed that there was a deal between the American and Mexican governments to keep Sandino in Mexico. Indeed, a body of evidence has established the duplicity of the Mexican government and its agreement with the United States to keep Sandino in Mexico (Millett 1977, 90). According to Mexican journalist Xavier Campos Ponce (1979, 113–17), Sandino was practically a prisoner of the Mexican government (with Mérida as Sandino's St. Helena), and he insisted in laying part of the blame on Sandino's friend de Paredes. However, young Captain de Paredes always denied any treasonous involvement and swore loyalty to his chief.

### Internal Tensions

Adding to the disappointing arrival, economic hardships, and suspicions of deceit, the EDSN experienced some internal tensions as three factions competed to position themselves favorably within Sandino's movement (Macaulay 1985, 157). To be sure, these factions had coexisted in the Segovian mountains in Nicaragua, but their differences surfaced and were exaggerated by the dire conditions of their stay in Mexico. On the battlefield, military necessity and Sandino's command had taken precedent, but Sandino was now preoccupied with plotting strategy about his victorious return to Nicaragua, attending Masonic meetings, pursuing government, communist, and private aid, or engaged in "public relations work" entertaining female benefactors. Later, his spiritist studies would occupy much of his time. The long wait gave Sandino's men more than ample opportunity to stew and to find reasons to bicker.

In the moderate camp, Pedro José Zepeda (whom Sandino had earlier included in his junta project) wished Sandino to pursue the path of a broad, Mexican-style revolution by uniting all anti-imperialist groups but favoring none. The similarity of this plan to outdated communist policy was only coincidence; in Zepeda's calculations, it would win Sandino the coveted support of the Mexican government. (Indeed, because of his tight connection with the local government, the Mexican communists mistrusted Zepeda.) However, he may not have been guarding Sandino's interests alone; as long as Sandino dealt or hoped to deal with the Mexican government, Zepeda was invaluable to Sandino, and so he peddled hope to the rebel when there was none in order to secure his own position. On at least one occasion, for example, Zepeda assured Sandino that the government was prepared to give him 200,000 pesos (Gilbert 1979, 268).

Contending with Zepeda's moderates for influence in the EDSN were supporters of two larger radical groups, the Popular Revolutionary Alliance of the Americas (*Alianza Popular Revolucionaria Americana*, or APRA) and the communists. The latter were represented by Agustín Farabundo Martí (1893–1932) from El Salvador, who had arrived in the Segovias in June 1928 after joining the Comintern that spring. A persuasive law school dropout, Martí was the central communist "element" in Sandino's camp. He eventually obtained the rank of colonel in the EDSN and became the guerrilla commander's trusted advisor and personal secretary; following his appointed mission, he used this position to help develop relations between Sandino and the Comintern network. Martí was a committed communist and an articulate propagandist of his beliefs; one of his biographers described him as an "unrelenting agitator" (Arias 1972, 52), and he tried incessantly to attract Sandino to the communist cause. He was only partially successful, however. On the one hand, Sandino shared in the communist dream of world revolution for the liberation of the workers and of the small nations from exploitation from imperialism, and he did not hesitate in availing himself of any person or organization to recruit support for his cause. On the other hand, he took orders from no one, jealously maintaining his personal autonomy—a stance that would later become a factor of discord between them. From the start, the seemingly strong relationship between Sandino and the Comintern was a relationship of tenuous utility.

The other radical faction in Sandino's camp, the APRA, was represented by the Peruvian Esteban Pavletich, who also functioned as Sandino's scribe. The APRA was founded by Peruvian exile Victor Raúl Haya de la Torre (1895–1979) in May 1924 in Mexico, where he worked as personal secretary to José Vasconcelos. Haya de la Torre was influenced (in addition to Vasconcelos) by Latin America's leading nationalist revolutionary theoretician, his compatriot José Carlos Mariátegui (1894–1930).[1] The APRA's socialist objectives were similar to those of the Comintern and of Sandino, but their central concern was narrower than the theoretical universalism of workers that was preached by communists: the establishment of what Haya de la Torre called Indo-America as a homeland for the *mestizo* race (Haya 1927). Pavletich and Sandino had a good relationship, but the APRA's small organization and lack of resources left it unable to compete for Sandino's favor against the Comintern.

Given the precariousness of his situation in Mexico, Sandino could not afford to alienate any of his supporters. Thus, although the tensions within his camp tired him, he tried to keep it from breaking up, maneuvering his way around a confrontation: "Neither extreme right, nor extreme left, but United Front is our motto" (Alemán 1951, 85). Borrowed from the Fifth Congress of the Comintern, his motto was already outdated among the communists: after its Sixth Congress in 1928, the Comintern had resolved to launch a hard line of class confrontation that precluded them from forging alliances with "bourgeois nationalist" movements.

## Crossings and Double Crossings

Sandino faced many difficult challenges. At the start of his trip, he had believed that he would be back in Nicaragua by the autumn; toward the end of 1929, he was still in Mexico and the expected aid was not forthcoming. He was in dire need of money to pay for lodging and food, a situation that

1. Mariátegui was an influential Peruvian communist, considered by many to be one of the most original Marxist thinkers of Latin America and well known for his ability to inject a religious fervor into revolutionary action. Among his most significant works are *El alma matinal* and *Defensa del marxismo*, reprinted by Amauta in Lima as vols. 3 and 5 of his *Collected Works* (3rd ed., 1967). Mariátegui was a great influence on Vasconcelos, Haya de la Torre, Fidel Castro, Che Guevara, and the latter-day Sandinistas. His most infamous followers today, albeit indirectly, are the ultraradical Peruvian Maoist guerrillas of the Shining Path movement, who have embraced the most millenarian aspects of his thought in their goal of destroying the present social order and building from its ashes a just society for the peasants. Shining Path was founded in the late 1960s and takes its name from a statement by Mariátegui; they are known for their ruthless and indiscriminate violence (Strong 1992).

would only worsen with time. Moreover, the new year only brought more turbulent events, as he became enmeshed in intrigue launched by the Venezuelan communist Gustavo Machado, head and cofounder of the Mafuenic Committee in Mexico. Machado, apparently bitter at not having been appointed Sandino's general representative, launched a smear campaign against the rebel leader: he accused Sandino of taking $60,000 from the U.S. government in exchange for a comfortable life of exile while simultaneously taking money from the Mexican Communist Party to continue the struggle.[2] He also accused Sandino of betraying the cause of the oppressed (Hodges 1986, 100; Macaulay 1985, 157–58). The slanderous remarks appeared in *El Universal* of Mexico City the day after Christmas 1929. The PCM made no attempts to deny the report, to contact Sandino, or to confirm the veracity of the accusations; instead, they promptly proceeded to distribute the report within their local and overseas channels.

The relationship between the PCM and Sandino was beginning to show signs of strain. On 2 January 1930, before he became acquainted with the published accusations against him, Sandino wrote to Hernán Laborde, secretary general of the Mexican Communist Party. In a letter to Martí (the exact contents of which are unknown), the PCM seems to have questioned Sandino's plan to form a Latin American confederation and may have suggested that in the future Sandino ought to clear statements of the sort with the communist leadership. Although Sandino had written his "Plan for the Realization of Bolívar's Supreme Dream" many months before, the Mexican communists had ample reason to be surprised and to be suspicious of it. Martí (apparently deliberately) showed Sandino the critical remarks against him. In his characteristic blunt and proud manner, Sandino replied with an affirmation of his independence of thought and action: "We will never allow ourselves to be anyone's instrument because we were born manly enough and with plentiful moral courage vigorously to place the responsibility of any action with whomever it belongs, and we will be responsible for our own actions." In addition to asserting his autonomy, Sandino went on to stress that he and his organization were on equal footing with the PCM and its related organs, and he made it clear that he did not owe explanations to them: "Some within the anti-imperialist organiza-

2. Sandino did not take any money from the Mexican government with any purpose such as the one mentioned by Machado. However, Gilbert (1979, 268) mentions that the Mexican government may have offered Sandino 50,000 *pesos* to buy a farming property so that he and his men would keep occupied while in Mexico, before returning to the battlefield.

tions may think that we ought to inform them of all details of our struggle, like we do now with this letter to the Central Committee, but so ought the anti-imperialist organizations to do with us. . . . This is not a report of our activities that we present to our headquarters, but merely a courtesy to the PCM" (Sandino 1981, 2:37–39). However, he soon made an about-face in his hard-line and aggressive tone toward the PCM. Always sensitive about his image, Sandino was disturbed by the charges against him; he had always been adamant that personal gain or the acquisition of power and property were alien to the objectives of his struggle. Thus, a few days after his confrontational letter to Laborde, Sandino wrote again to deny the accusations and to maintain his innocence (Sandino 1981, 2:41–42).

Thus, Sandino faced many difficult choices at the beginning of 1930, under pressures that he was unaccustomed to handle. The situation with the PCM preoccupied him. He continued to hope for aid from his host, who was about to step down on 4 February 1930; his financial stipend would likely come to an end with Portes Gil's mandate, for he (correctly) sensed that the presidential designate Ortiz Rubio would be hostile toward him. Sandino let Zepeda know as much in a letter written at the end of January; the letter also recounted many of Sandino's points of contention with Zepeda, and in uncharacteristically prudent and careful language blamed Zepeda for his misfortunes (Sandino 1981, 2:51–56). Perhaps not coincidentally, Zepeda at last succeeded in setting up a presidential audience for Sandino four days later. It was thus in the middle of his crisis with the communists that Sandino went to Mexico City to meet with President Portes Gil, who by then was only a few days from relinquishing office; the meeting did not please the PCM, and it may have finally proved to them that Sandino was a traitor.

Sandino had anticipated getting from the Mexican government money and a shipload of weapons—such as the Nicaraguan Liberal rebels, with the intercession of Zepeda, had obtained during the Constitutionalist War—but the help that was eventually forthcoming was as humiliating as it was disappointing: a couple of pistols, a few bullets, and some extra money for expenses. Perhaps as an excuse, Portes Gil led Sandino to believe that he had been under the impression that the rebel leader wanted asylum in Mexico; in his memoirs, the president claims to have made it clear to de Paredes from the start that he was offering asylum but no military aid (Portes 1964, 597). Adding insult to injury, the president invited Sandino to remain in Mexico and offered him and his men some land in which to work. (It has long been thought that Sandino rejected the land offer, but in July 1997

Mexico's *Excelsior* reported that in fact either Calles or Portes Gil may have granted Sandino three properties.)[3]

At this juncture, Sandino had only the communist card left to play, and the bargaining started a few days later. Sandino's position was not only known but weak. Essentially, he needed to accomplish three things: to clear his name, to earn the trust of the communists again, and to get some form of aid for his rebel campaign. A meeting was called at Sandino's request; a copy of the official act taken at that meeting is dated 3 February 1930 (reproduced in Dospital 1996, 63–64). Pavletich, Martí, and Enrique Rivera Bertrán (the local representative of the EDSN in Veracruz) accompanied Sandino, but Zepeda was absent. The meeting was also attended by representatives of the three organizations under the Comintern umbrella (the Latin American chapter of the World Anti-Imperialist League, the Mafuenic Committee, and the PCM), whom Sandino suspected of being the source of the accusations launched against him. They denied their implication in the matter, quickly expressed their displeasure with the rumors, and offered their fraternal sympathies to Sandino. As Rivera Bertrán later reported to Zepeda, this part of the meeting did not last very long: "The General began to speak, stating the objective of the meeting. Everyone said that it was not true that they had pronounced such maligning calumnies and proceeded to condemn the defamations" (Rivera 1930). Laborde, the PCM boss, swiftly ordered an investigation into the matter and the meeting then moved to address other issues.

The second item on the agenda also involved Sandino, money, and improprieties. Gustavo Machado had once raised a large sum of money for Sandino before the latter's arrival to Mexico; Sandino only claimed to have received $250 from him, but the record was clear that Machado had in fact

---

3. *The Excelsior* also reported that Sandino's three surviving grandchildren—who may be unfamiliar with the first sentence of the 10 July manifesto—now seek restitution from Zepeda's heirs and from the Mexican government. According to the grandchildren, upon the rebel's hasty flight from Mexico he left the pertinent papers for these properties with Zepeda, but Zepeda allegedly appropriated them and later sold them; they point to Book 26 of the 1932 Registro de la Propiedad in the State of Morelos in claiming that the land was registered illicitly by Zepeda. However, it is not entirely believable that Sandino knowingly accepted the properties and left the papers with Zepeda; Sandino needed money and would have urged Zepeda to sell them, had he accepted them at all. If in fact Zepeda registered and sold three properties in Mexico, this in no way proves the claim of Sandino's heirs. Their claim may originate in Edelberto Torres's poorly documented and often unreliable work, which stops just short of accusing Zepeda of theft (1984, 194).

raised $1000. When the question arose during the meeting, Sandino hinted that the guilty party was Turcios (through whom the $250 had been channeled to the rebel) rather than pointing the finger at someone in the Comintern, even though Sandino knew well that Turcios was incapable of stealing. Conveniently, perhaps, the records had burned and the acting treasurer could not provide any details about the monies. Rivera Bertrán described it as follows: "The question of the funds of the Hands Off Nicaragua [Mafuenic] Committee was brought up, General Sandino said not to have received from [Froylán] Turcios, his representative in those days, but $250. Mr. Pedrueza was present, acting as treasurer, and he informed [those assembled] that the files had burned and he could not therefore render account" (Rivera 1930). The situation was further complicated when it was learned that Sandino had extended Machado a receipt for another thousand dollars that were yet to be raised (Dospital 1996, 63; see also Sandino 1981, 2:36).

At the meeting, Sandino was "invited" to go on a European and Latin American tour to campaign for the Comintern under the guise of promoting the cause of anti-imperialism—a trip that had been originally proposed by the World Anti-Imperialist League in July of the previous year. It now seemed like an excellent opportunity to increase his notoriety and to gain further recognition; moreover, the possibility of aid from the Mexican government was closed, and the tour might open new possibilities to obtain something to bring home. If nothing else, the trip would get him out of Mexico, where he felt increasingly nervous by the impending change of administration. The offer was not without strict conditions, however; as the minutes of the February meeting reveal, Sandino promised the PCM to launch several public attacks against the Mexican government's foreign policy, while still in Mexican territory. This was a foolish pact for Sandino to make (even if he never intended to honor it) in light of section 33 of the Mexican Constitution, which proscribed foreigners from meddling in its internal affairs under threat of severe penalties. Sandino, however, was desperate. Perhaps in exchange, later that year the PCM cleared Sandino of receiving money from the United States.

Sandino's eagerness to undertake the agreed-upon European tour is apparent in his surviving correspondence from the few days immediately following the deal with the PCM. Answering the official tour invitation (dated 31 January 1930) from the secretary general of the Anti-Imperialist League in Mexico, Sandino wrote a letter submissively placing himself "at the orders" of the league, "considering it [his] duty" to do so (Sandino 1930a). The same tone is evident in letters written to communist contacts in France and in Germany (Sandino 1981, 2:62–66). Sandino could no longer afford to stand on the principle of independence and equality for his peasant army. It was the last card he had available in the attempt to draw some tangible benefit out of his long stay in Mexico.

Both Sandino and the communist organizations waited for the other to make the first move, but there was no trust between the agreeing parties. The communists waited for Sandino's promised attacks on the Mexican government's foreign policy under the excuse of needing a confirming telegram from Germany before giving him the go-ahead on the European tour. Sandino tactfully held out, wishing to be out of Mexico before attacking the Mexican government. In his letter to Zepeda, Rivera Bertrán recalled the rebel's realistic analysis about the difficulty of his position: "But do you think that I am such an idiot as to set fire to the house while I am still in it? No, Sir, I will make declarations when I judge it to be opportune, but if I start to open the lid with insults, they would expel me and they would hand me over to my enemies, and so I would accomplish nothing more than to be sacrificed stupidly. . . . If I am to throw my life away it must be with a purpose, not stupidly," Sandino said (Rivera 1930). In the meantime, the Comintern kept stalling, insisting that the awaited cable from Berlin had not arrived. Attempting to buy themselves even more time, they claimed sending a man before the World Anti-Imperialist League in Berlin with special powers to deal with the issue of Sandino's trip.

The insistence of the Comintern groups that Sandino make his attacking remarks against the Mexican government as a prerequisite for their tour contribution seems to suggest that they wanted Sandino to place himself in harm's way. It was clear that making such accusations while in Mexican territory might trigger fatal consequences for Sandino, or at the very least have him removed from the country, in which case they would no longer have to meet their end of the deal. Did it not seem reasonable for Sandino to wait until he was out of Mexican jurisdiction before making his damning statements? Rivera Bertrán claims that the PCM specifically wanted trouble and was prepared to offer Sandino as a sacrificial lamb in order to attempt to destabilize the government: "It is what they wished, that the General be expelled so as to have a motive for [political] agitation" (Rivera 1930).

Toward the end of February, the central committee of the PCM increased its pressures on Sandino and passed a resolution calling on the rebel leader to denounce the Mexican government for luring him out of

Nicaragua under false promises. Sandino replied in early March, accepting the content of the resolution and saying that he was ready to make the required statements (Dospital 1996, 65–66). He also wrote to the new secretary of the Latin American chapter of the World Anti-Imperialist League to assert that he was "in the best disposition" to go through with the trip and to announce that the awaited "declarations would be made soon" (Sandino 1930b). Incessantly, Sandino and his counterparts in the Comintern continued to write promising letters to each other in the following weeks.[4] The already existing mistrust grew, and the situation rapidly deteriorated into a game of chicken.

It may have been evident to the PCM that Sandino was holding out on his promise, and this exacerbated their suspicions about his real loyalties. Trying either to force his hand (leading to a probable sacrificial arrest) or to expose him, the Comintern made it known on 9 April that Sandino was critical of his host government's policies (Villanueva 1988, 275). The die was cast.

## Martí, Rupture, and Betrayal

Around this time (April 1930), Sandino's trusted comrade Farabundo Martí left Sandino's camp for good (Villanueva 1988, 280). The rift between the two men warrants attention not only because it affected Sandino personally but also because it ultimately had serious repercussions for the development of revolutionary movements across Central America, especially in El Salvador, Martí's homeland. Unfortunately, little detailed documentary evidence exists to illumine this confusing and controversial period in

---

4. Sandino wrote to Laborde to reassure him that he intended to keep his end of the bargain: "We are preparing the declarations we must make concerning the present situation of Mexico's foreign policy" (Sandino 1981, 2:99–100). Sandino was buying time; he had no intention of fulfilling that promise while in Mexican territory, fearing that the Mexican government would at best imprison him or at worst hand him over to the Americans. He was bluffing when he said that he had in his possession "the documents to unmask with irrefutable proof the attitude of those who have sold out to imperialism." He warned Laborde, however, that he might soon have to return to Nicaragua. At the end of the month, he again wrote to Laborde: "We continue to prepare the declarations. You shall have them at an opportune time." This time, however, Sandino showed some determination and made it clear that there would be no statements unless the issue of the tour was resolved (Sandino 1981, 2:108–9). Sandino was very eager to tell the Mexican representatives of the Comintern that he was willing to make the statements while on Mexican soil—and yet after more than two months, no declarations were made.

Sandino's life, and more often than not the documents that are known offer conflicting reports. However, even though the exact circumstances surrounding Martí's departure remain unclear, Sandino's own interpretation of the events is helpful in deciphering what happened. Reflecting the complexity of the situation, he later would give three different and seemingly contradictory interpretations of his dispute with Martí; likely, it was not one but a series of events that caused the rift between them.

Evidence suggests that Martí's departure may be directly linked with Sandino's troubles with the Mexican communists. Commenting in 1933 on the several groups that had tried to influence his movement, Sandino said: "We have always held with decisive conviction that this was essentially a national struggle. Martí, the propagandist of Communism, saw that he could not impose his program and withdrew" (Belausteguigoitia 1985, 181). This statement suggests that the rift with Martí was the product of an ideological struggle over the scope of Sandino's fight and that Martí withdrew voluntarily; and there are reasons to support this reading. Decisions made half a world away may have unwittingly conspired against the friendship of the two men: following the 1924 Stalinist vision of building socialism in one country and after the Sixth Congress of the Comintern in July 1928, the notion of a united front against imperialism was abandoned in favor of a class confrontation with whoever did not fall in line with strict communist beliefs. The APRA became a target of the new vision, its national and regional goals regarded as bourgeois. Similarly, the communists increasingly viewed Sandino's struggle only as a potential contributor in the promotion of world revolution; in sharp contrast, Sandino still saw it as an end in itself, consistent with his belief in bringing about the fulfillment of God's kingdom on earth. Thus, according to scholars such as Hodges, "It is in the context of the Comintern's mistaken assessment of the world situation and its adoption of an ultra-left strategy of class confrontation that the break between Sandino and Martí must be understood" (Hodges 1986, 100).

While Sandino admitted that there were intrigues with the communists in which Martí may have tried to entangle him, in other declarations the differences appear more personal than political: "I never really had an ideological dispute with him. Because of his rebelliousness he did not understand the limitations of my mission in Mexico, or his position of subordinate" (Román 1979, 132). In this statement (also made in 1933), Sandino is categorical in his denial that there were ideological differences and points more toward tactical differences and a clash of personalities. Sandino (in his own eyes) was the supreme commander and often felt that

Martí did not properly defer to his authority and judgment; further, Sandino interpreted Martí's lack of deference and his questioning of authority as a personal issue. Even the issue of the "limitations" of Sandino's cause is not interpreted in terms of geopolitical ideology but rather in terms of Martí's "rebelliousness."

Hodges is correct in asserting that the rift between the two revolutionaries arose from their understandings of communism and was framed by the change of ideological direction of the Comintern. However, even though these larger events were a contributing factor, their unfolding was more complex. Sandino may not have understood it in that way, and although he was not oblivious to subtle differences between their strategies, to him the Comintern's action may have appeared as a mere shift of emphasis and therefore not all that crucial. As we have seen in Sandino's early manifestos, he was already committed to fighting American imperialism and its advances in Latin America and the world, as well as committed to fighting socioeconomic and racial inequality. He was perfectly comfortable, without causing him second thoughts, with emphasizing one or the other; to Sandino, they were one and the same, co-events in the struggle to defeat the United States and its supporters in the Nicaraguan dominant classes. Given this perspective, again, it is probable that Sandino attributed the rift with Martí primarily to personal discord.

It must be pointed out that Sandino's contradictory declarations to Román and to Belausteguigoitia were made, at most, a month apart—and three years after the events occurred. Because Sandino was notorious for manipulating events in hindsight (especially when he was personally concerned), these assertions ought to be taken with a grain of salt. Documents contemporary with the events may shed more trustworthy light on the issue. In a surviving fragment of a letter to Zepeda dated 11 April 1930, Sandino wrote: "Grave mistakes reported in Martí's conduct have made him unworthy of belonging to our army" (Dospital 1996, 56). The mention of "conduct" here does not allow us to distinguish whether the issues were personal or political, but Rivera Bertrán's letter to Zepeda gives credence to the hypothesis of a personal dispute: in at least two instances Martí, under the influence of alcohol, verbally assaulted Sandino—an especially egregious offense given that in his selective Puritanism, Sandino prohibited his men from drinking. On both occasions guns were drawn and either Sandino or a bodyguard were ready and willing to shoot Martí, but Sandino forgave him (Rivera 1930). These types of behaviors may betray more than just political differences.

Was this simply a clash of personalities? It seems unlikely. Why the contradicting remarks? Sandino appears to have had more public relations sense than he is credited with, and so he did not want to air details of the rift between he and Martí in order to avoid revealing information considered damaging to his cause. More ambiguous but tantalizing information can be found in a letter written by Sandino at the end of April 1930 to Francisco Vera in Progreso, Mexico, secretary of a chapter of yet another group with whom Sandino had become associated, the Magnetic-Spiritual School of the Universal Commune (*Escuela Magnético-Espiritual de la Comuna Universal*, or EMECU): "Everything took place as that *Cátedra* [chapter] instructed me in advance. This must be taken into consideration so that such an element who tried to cause me maximum grief is put in his proper place" (Sandino 1930c; see also Rius 1986, 127). There seems little doubt that the "element" in question is Martí, but what is "everything"? From this letter one might surmise that Martí did not withdraw voluntarily (as Sandino later would later affirm) but rather was expelled by Sandino and that the decision to do so was at least shared with (and may indeed have been ordered by) the EMECU chapter in Veracruz. (Such action would be consistent with the EMECU's anti-Bolshevik stand.) Sandino's brand of communism was clearly opposed to that of the Comintern: "I am a communist because I understand it will be, or is, the highest there exists but I am not in agreement with a bunch of opportunists who always engage in nothing but intemperate schemes, which profane such a high principle worthy of better fortune" (Rivera 1930). It would seem that the disagreement between Martí and Sandino went beyond strategic interpretations of the scope of Sandino's struggle into fundamental questions of vision and commitment.[5]

Both on emotional and on intellectual levels, Martí (unlike most others) did not buy into Sandino's self-image of the spiritual prophet-messiah

---

5. Among the many interesting documents that came through my hands in Nicaragua but which I was unable to photocopy or to take notes from, one stands out in my mind. At the end of one part (of three) of the original manuscript of Anastasio Somoza García's *El verdadero Sandino,* there is an unpublished letter addressed to Augusto C. Sandino and signed by Farabundo Martí. This letter was omitted from the final publication for unknown reasons. I saw the letter almost in a flash but the closing sentence is still vivid in my mind: "Your brother in Lenin." This was in stark contrast to the EMECU's practice of calling each other brother— brothers in the spirit. Martí's closing line is therefore suggestive of the tension that existed between Sandino and Martí as a result of their differences in worldviews extending beyond Comintern doctrine.

and deity-incarnate, opting for a scientistic and materialistic communism rather than the spiritual one that Sandino offered. If we believe Sandino that Martí was thrown out of the EDSN under instructions from the EMECU, then the influence of this group on the Nicaraguan rebel was far greater and more significant than has been suspected. To be sure, as Dospital (1996, 85) stresses, Sandino's letter to the EMECU's Vera is not enough to reach hardened conclusions, but it surely disproves Wünderich's assertion that "there exists no evidence that [the EMECU] had ever exerted a direct influence over the political actions of Sandino" (1995, 145). Moreover, other evidence (such as the correspondence between Zepeda and Bertrán) supports the suggestion that Sandino's whole-hearted adoption of the EMECU's philosophy and organizational structure (discussed in more detail later in this chapter) was an important factor in the breaking of the revolutionary triangle between Sandino, Martí, and the Comintern.

However, while the EMECU's opposition to Soviet-style communism may explain Sandino's comments to Vera, it does not explain his references to grief and to limitations. We thus must look for personal dimensions alongside the political. When Martí arrived in Sandino's camps in the Segovias, his mission was to draw the Nicaraguan rebel to the Comintern. To this effect, Martí worked on separating Sandino and Turcios, concocting the story that Turcios had received money to betray Sandino—the same tactic that the communists used on Sandino while in Mexico. In effect, the rupture with Turcios left Sandino more dependant on Comintern promises. Moreover, Martí was not without affection for the Nicaraguan rebel chief, and they developed what must have been for Martí an unexpected friendship.

Given the strained circumstances between Sandino and the communists, Martí may not have had any other choice but to take sides openly. Sandino had a second meeting with Portes Gil in April, at which time he obtained both permission to leave Mexican territory and some money for his departure (Hodges 1986, 103). It is highly probable that Martí alerted the PCM about Sandino's bluff and his ongoing efforts to obtain support from the Mexican government. Suspicions about Martí's loyalty already abounded. Rivera Bertrán's letter to Zepeda narrated Sandino's suspicions: that Martí while "drunk had challenged the General [by saying:] 'What is Sandino?,' " that he "did not give a shit about Nicaragua" and "was a spy of the Communist Party," that up to then he "had not betrayed Sandino even though he was there for that purpose," and that he had "insulted the General's mother." In addition to this alleged confession, Sandino claimed to have circumstantial evidence that Martí was "spying for the communists." According to Rivera Bertrán, "The General's doubts were thus partly confirmed although he was not able to obtain sufficient proof" when Martí was caught burning a pile of letters that Sandino wished to inspect (Rivera 1930).

As the arrangements between Sandino and the Comintern turned into a standoff, the rebel leader became convinced that there was an informant in his camp: the one who "betrayed" him, "causing maximum grief," and who did not understand the "limitations of [Sandino's] mission." Nearly a year after they parted in April 1930, Martí was still repeating the party line, accusing Sandino of becoming a petty bourgeois *caudillo* who had betrayed the cause against imperialism (Dospital 1996, 56–57). After their breakup, Martí left for El Salvador to found the local communist party and to carry forward the Moscow-ordained strategy of class confrontation—with fatal consequences. Arrested and tried for treason and sedition following a peasant uprising that resulted in the brutal massacre of thirty thousand peasants, he was executed in early February 1932. Like Sandino, Martí would later be hailed as a hero-martyr in his native land, when guerrillas in 1980 named their movement the Farabundo Martí National Liberation Front (*Frente Farabundo Martí de Liberación Nacional*, or FMLN).

In his capacity as Sandino's personal representative, Zepeda tried to control the damage of the league's communiqué by issuing one of his own. He rejected the league's assertions and denied the existence of any ties between Sandino and the communist organizations. Zepeda was protecting Sandino by protecting himself: the communist statements would compromise his own connections with the Mexican government, and perhaps even his personal security. His denial only confirmed in the minds of the Comintern members that Sandino was indeed a traitor.

**Roots and Consequences**

Sandino's troubles with the Comintern influenced a chain of decisions that led the guerrilla chief to plunge deeper and deeper into despair and suspicion. Unable to react well to crisis or adversity, confounded and having difficulty distinguishing friend from foe, Sandino broke off his ties with the APRA; thus, his companion and scribe Pavletich also left his ranks. The guerrilla chief had wondered earlier if there was not a treasonous plot to keep him in Mexico: "What occurred? Why so many dissimulations? Are we in effect, victims of treachery?" (Sandino 1981, 1:55). After his break with Martí and with the Comintern, he felt betrayed once again and he became more suspicious than before. Sandino had long waited to hear from the Mexican government and from the Comintern about the European and Latin American tour, but after the league's communiqué he wisely made hasty plans to leave Mexican territory.

From the PCM's perspective, their radicalized position toward the Mexican government left no room for middle ground, which lent itself to interpreting Sandino's attempt at establishing a detached position between the two rivals as nothing less than treachery. That the conditions for Sandino to fulfil his promise to the PCM were extremely delicate, they did not care. Revolutionaries rarely see the world from a vantage point other than their own, and to them the facts were clear and uncontested: the counterrevolutionary Mexican government that had outlawed them was their enemy; it had broken off relations with the mother communist state, the Soviet Union, and was now an ally of the United States; Sandino was in Mexico as a guest of the Mexican government; Sandino was taking monetary help from the Mexican government; and Sandino, despite his promise to attack the Mexican government, had not only failed to do so but continued to meet with its agents behind their back. According to these premises, the conclusion was easily drawn: Sandino was a traitor.

Thus, both inflated expectations and harsh disappointments marked Sandino's second trip to Mexico, the consequences of which were felt until his death years later. Selser (1960, 2:68) describes this as a "bitter period" in Sandino's personal life. On the battlefield it was a stalemate (Macaulay 1985, 134) because his forces were at least saved from eradication, but his absence gave his enemies in Nicaragua time to regroup—Moncada to organize his forces, and the Americans to set up the Nicaraguan National Guard. Moreover, Sandino lost in the arena of popularity and public opinion, now being at the receiving end of calumny and defamation as a political tool. The radicalization of the left left him with only a few friends, and he no longer enjoyed ample international solidarity; in fact, intellectuals aligned with the Communist International movement everywhere abandoned him, and those who were independent enough simply kept their silent distance. Sandino was to bear the label of traitor among his former friends until his death.

On an emotional level, the second trip to Mexico was characterized by suffering, as he felt great homesickness and was overwhelmed by intrigue, betrayal, and disappointment; Sandino himself would later describe the trip as a "moral battle" (Sandino 1981, 2:309). From the center of all the bitterness, however, Sandino found renewed spiritual and political meaning. From this well of suffering sprang a new hope—millenarian and eschatologically oriented—that would strongly mark the rest of his days.

**The New Religion**

While in Mexico scheming with the communists and waiting for the expected aid from the government to arrive, Sandino continued the esoteric training that he had begun during his first trip five years earlier. He rekindled his relationship with the Freemasons, quickly rising to the degree of Master Mason. More important, he became an active member the Magnetic-Spiritual School of the Universal Commune, a "spiritist" group that had many followers in Mexico after its founding in Argentina in 1911 by the Basque electrician Joaquín Trincado.[6] Sandino's association with the EMECU in particular would have a profound and lasting impact on his life, thought, and strategy, and so the history and beliefs of the group deserve detailed attention.

Trincado constructed an elaborate speculative system of "spiritual magnetism" based upon the belief that there is an omnipresent unitary substance—consubstantial with the human spirit—governing the universe and the course of human actions. He called his doctrine the "spiritism of Light and Truth" to signify what he took to be the present age of spiritual enlightenment. The school's motto Ever Further Beyond (*Siempre mas*

6. In discussing Trincado and the EMECU, we must make a subtle but important distinction between *spiritualism* and *spiritism*. Spiritualism distinguishes between matter and spirit, body and soul, whereas Trincado's spiritism holds that spirits are enveloped by a quasimaterial substance or spiritualized matter that they identify as "ether"; moreover, spiritism claims to be a science, divorced from religions, religious allegiances, rituals, and myth. Thus, EMECU followers call themselves spiritists to separate themselves from spiritualists.

To be sure, some commentators have assumed that Sandino became acquainted with the EMECU during his first trip to Mexico in the early 1920s. For example, Belausteguigoitia claims (without evidence) that when Sandino was in Tampico from 1924 to 1926, he took "advantage of his free time and immerse[d] himself in theosophical knowledge and social issues" (1985: 88). Similarly, Edelberto Torres—the intellectual mentor of an entire generation of post-Sandino Nicaraguan revolutionary youth—connects Sandino and Trincado during the first trip (1984, 29); Hodges speculates that although Sandino did not join the EMECU during the first trip, he might have encountered their ideas at that time (1986, 42). Wünderich, by contrast, asserts that Sandino became member of the EMECU in 1930 (1995, 145). In fact, all existing documentary evidence suggests that Sandino became acquainted with the EMECU during his second trip to Mexico, in 1929 and 1930.

*allá*) is indicative of its enthusiastic reverence for progress. Of course, none of these ideas was completely new with Trincado; a speculative tradition seeking to establish a universal science or system explaining all levels of reality has been traced as far back as Quirinus Kuhlmann (1651–1689) (Vondung 1992, 118–40).[7] Trincado was particularly indebted to Allan Kardec (Hippolyte Léon Denizard Rivail)(1804–1869), a French occultist and the founder of "la doctrine du spiritisme." In works such as *Le livre des esprits* (1857) and in his *Revue Spirite* (which began in 1858), Kardec examined issues such as God and His attributes, cosmology, geology, biology, human history, moral law, and his own expectation of the imminent arrival of a realm of perfection and regeneration.

Although Trincado would break away from Kardec's specifically Christian ideas, the French thinker would strongly shape the "spiritism of Light and Truth." In his own *Los cinco amores* (The five loves, 1922), which Sandino would study with special attention, Trincado argued that there were five realms of love, each more perfect than the last: love of family, civic love (friendship), love of one's region, national love, and universal love—the most perfect stage, toward which humanity is moving and which (Trincado thought) it will soon reach. At this fifth and final stage, there would emerge a universal commune wherein all things would be held in common and the hate caused by religious allegiances and all sources of discord would disappear. In preparation, Trincado had elaborated his plan for a Hispanic-American Oceanic Union (*Unión Hispano-América-Oceánica*, or UHAO), which would unite all the Spanish-speaking states; thus, the universal commune would in fact center around one race (the Hispanic race) with a single language (Spanish) in universal brotherhood. In the tradition of a long line of Western spiritual radicals (see chapter 6), Trincado called this the "Adamic race."

Trincado was ardently opposed both to conventional organized religion and to bolshevik communism in favor of his own "solidarity of the spirit," which he understood as true communism and which he thought would soon replace religions and all backward systems of ideas. In his first dogmatic book, *Filosofía austera racional* (Austere rational philosophy, 1920), he made the point directly: "We will save humanity at the cost of destroying all religions" (quoted in Hodges 1986, 41). He believed that all of the cabalistic mysteries hidden through the ages had now been revealed in view

7. A similar quest can be detected in the search for a "unified theory" by scientists from Albert Einstein to Stephen Hawkins.

of the imminence of the Last Judgment. In a classic display of millenarian speculation, he argued in *Los cinco amores* that the recent discoveries associated with electricity laid bare all of the mysteries of the natural world, and at the same time his own ideas cracked open the concealed wisdom of all of the ages of human existence. The way to God was now openly revealed: "With the laws of electricity, all the mysteries of science have been broken, with the spiritism of Light and Truth all the secrets of wisdom and creation have been broken. We have come to know continued and eternal life" (Trincado 1955, 181). Although Trincado's link between developments in the field of electricity and spiritual enlightenment may sound odd, there is a specific logic to it: in Spanish, the word *luz* is used to refer both to light and to electrical power, and thus for the Spanish-speaking consciousness a connection between electricity and enlightenment may seem natural. More generally, modern spiritual traditions have often used concepts from electricity and magnetism to explain the inexplicable before these concepts were well understood scientifically (Flanagan 1995a, 94).

Reflecting his opposition to traditional religious organizations, Trincado commemorated Victor Emmanuel's 1870 defeat of the papal armies at Castelfidardo by founding his school on 20 September 1911, which also became the year zero in his own calendar of the "New Age" (*Nueva Era*). Trincado held structure and organization in high regard, making his school follow a rigid hierarchy both at the level of individual groups and as a large-scale organ. Like the Masons, Trincado's followers reveal their teachings in stages, and full membership requires one to be well versed in all the works of the Master. The EMECU is organized into chapters called *Cátedras*; the Central *Cátedra* is located in Buenos Aires and its director holds the school's highest office, surrounded by advisers that make up the "Government of Spiritism." The leadership is further surrounded by bishoplike *Celadores* (night watchmen), who administer and direct each *Cátedra* and are answerable only to Buenos Aires. Augusto Sandino became *Celador* of the forty-ninth *Cátedra* in Nicaragua, perhaps as early as 1931.[8]

8. The image of a "night watchman" is that of one who guards vigilantly while the others sleep during the time of darkness. Since Sandino's days, the EMECU has not grown vastly but it has kept a steady membership; in 1985, 183 chapters existed around the world, almost the same number as in 1935 (Hodges 1986, 42). In August 1992, I found that the EMECU group in Managua did not exceed a dozen people and although they meet regularly (twice a week) in a private home, their small numbers prevent them from acquiring an official Cátedra status from the Buenos Aires headquarters. They enjoyed a flowering period during the first few years of revolutionary excitement in the early 1980s; at that time, they were given fair press coverage and

We may further understand Trincado's spiritism by comparing it to another modern esoteric tradition, theosophy, with which it shares many common beliefs but from which it ultimately diverges. Theosophy, well-known in the English-speaking world, was popularized by Helena Blavatsky through the Theosophical Society that she cofounded in New York City in 1875. The objective of the society was to promote the pursuit of spiritual life, the brotherhood of man, and the inculcation of moral and spiritual principles to purify the human soul; it was to be a society of high moral standards and of service, of "mutual aid and sympathy" (Blavatsky 1992, 14).[9] The spirit and spiritual life are the central aspects of human existence, theosophists argue, and they shun those who live for the world of materialism. Theosophists believe in the discovery and the promotion of ancient yet hidden wisdom, heavily laden with oriental principles; central to their teachings is the law of karma, the notion that spirits reincarnate from past existences until perfection is reached—a law that rules over individuals as well as over human history as a whole.

Along with Eastern and Gnostic influences, Blavatsky (a Russian emigrée) also absorbed some of the liberal currents of modern European thought. Beyond race and class issues, she preached universality and brotherhood among men, and she was therefore open to accepting different religions among her associates, as long as they possessed the correct theosophical disposition (Blavatsky 1992, 13). Though aware of the problems that religious differences bring, she assumed that each religion possesses an element of truth and of a legitimate experience of the divine (32). The Theosophical Society was the means through which these differences could be finally transcended toward the "wisdom of the gods." In the question-and-answer format of *The Key to Theosophy*, Blavatsky presented the three main objectives of the society:

(1) To form the nucleus of a Universal Brotherhood of humanity without distinction of race, color, or creed. (2) To promote the study of the world's

---

even had their own segment on the state-run television channel in Managua. Soon, however, the connection of their beliefs to Sandino became a source of embarrassment to orthodox latter-day Sandinista circles, and the show was halted abruptly without an explanation.

9. The expression "mutual aid and sympathy" would be echoed in Sandino's "Society of Mutual Help and Universal Fraternity," in the Segovias at the end of his armed struggle to serve as prototype for the rest of the world (see chapter 5).

religion and sciences, and to vindicate the importance of old Asiatic literature, namely the Brahmanical, Buddhist and Zoroastrian philosophies. (3)
To investigate the hidden mysteries of Nature under every aspect possible,
and the psychic and spiritual powers latent in man especially. (25)

Blavatsky also believed that during moments of ecstasy the divine essence
communicates with those who are spiritually evolved; significantly for our
discussion, this exchange may take a magnetic form (1972, 1:137).

Thus, the principal tenets and themes of Blavatsky's theosophy parallel
those of Trincado's spiritism: universal brotherhood, service, hidden
knowledge, predestination, purification through pain, psychic powers, and
magnetic communication with the deity. Both systems see themselves as
bridging the gap between ignorance and spiritual enlightenment, a necessary step to spiritual progress.[10] However, some important differences
emerge. Coming from a liberal background, Blavatsky and the theosophists
accept other religious alternatives, and although their teachings are in
some respects millenarian, they do not expect the imminent demise of the
present world. By contrast, Trincado and his followers—product of an au-
thoritarian social and political context and influenced by a powerful
Catholic presence—are antireligious and anticlerical; seeing their own
ideas as the final truth revealed for the advancement of mankind, and in expectation of a soon-to-arrive end, they find themselves in direct competi-
tion with all religions, with Catholicism as their main competitor. In
essence, in spite of his universalistic rhetoric, Trincado's ideas are more inclined toward the parochialism of his own Hispanic culture—which may
have made them particularly appealing to the self-ascribed bearer of Hispanic pride and identity, Augusto Sandino.

*Mission Confirmed*

On the one hand, the EMECU's ideas complemented Sandino's anarchist
tendencies and provided him with a spiritual framework; indeed, according
to Hodges, "it was an almost perfect fit" (1986, 14). On the other hand,
however, it is important to remember that despite (or perhaps because of)
his wide interests and connections, Sandino had never before aligned himself so closely with any single group or philosophy. What was so special

10. Trincado and Blavatsky likely bathed in the same spiritist waters, in the work of Allan
Kardec; see Flanagan 1995a.

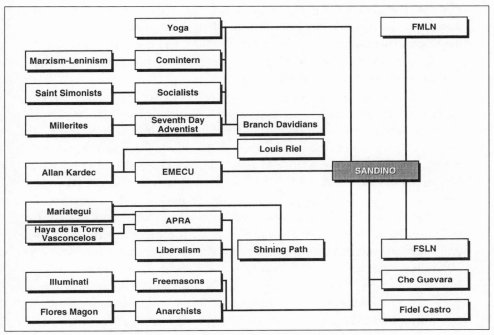

Ideas and Ideologies that Influenced Sandino

about Trincado's system of ideas that would make it so attractive to a man like Sandino, who until then had refused to embrace any single ideology? That the EMECU provided a spiritual dimension is not a sufficient explanation, because a few of the other systems with which Sandino was acquainted—socialism, Aprismo, Freemasonry, and especially the Seventh Day Adventists—also offered him spiritual support as well as plenty of fertile soil to nourish a millenarian program. Similarly, there was enough racial and spiritual content in the program promoted by the thought of Haya de la Torre and Vasconcelos. So what did Sandino find so attractive in Trincado's ideas?

Sandino's previous spiritual searching had exposed him to many of the basic elements of Trincado's thought even before he became acquainted with the EMECU: predestination, divine preference for the oppressed, brotherhood, love, freedom, justice, the transmigration of spirits, a chosen race, a kingdom of perfection, and so on. Still, Trincado's spiritism introduced to Sandino (or gave increased importance to) a number of beliefs: a final era of light that would precede the end of time, communal property, a

Creator that intervened in the lives of men to fulfill the world of freedom and justice, evolution, and a staunch anticlerical stand. Conveniently, Trincado's thoughts were presented in a tightly packaged system based on scientistic assumptions—and shrouded in secrecy and exclusivity that made it seem even more authoritative.

Sandino's choice was not solely a matter of convenience, however. He embraced spiritism at a particularly vulnerable period of his life; as we have seen, he was experiencing many disappointments during his second sojourn in Mexico, and Hodges is correct in saying that the purely spiritual aspect played a central role. In addition, a series of coincidences may have helped draw Sandino to the EMECU. Trincado believed that the Hispanic race was charged with the spiritual uplifting of the world and that Spanish was the language that would dominate the end of time; Sandino already held similar beliefs about the superiority of the *mestizo* race over the Anglo-Saxon and the European groups. Trincado believed in a federation of all of the former Latin American colonies along with their cultural progenitor, Spain, in the UHAO; Sandino too wanted a similar federation in Latin America, not including Spain (though he became more sympathetic to Spain after his EMECU experiences) but encompassing English, French, Papiamentu, and Portuguese speakers. Trincado had elaborated a new calendar that began in 1911; Sandino's own began in 1912, perhaps a negligible difference in the larger scheme of things. Given his beliefs in transmigration, Sandino likely found great significance in the fact that the first military battle of his life had been fought on All Souls Day. Finally, Sandino retrospectively interpreted Trincado's twenty-nine missionary spirits as the twenty-nine men with whom he claimed to have begun his rebellion against Moncada and the Americans after the Espino Negro Accords. As Sandino studied Trincado's spiritism and became more acquainted with it, he saw his own life reflected in the EMECU theories.

For one of Sandino's mindset—perhaps especially his affinity for predestination—these parallels between Trincado's system and his own personal experience may have constituted compelling reasons for Sandino to interpret that system as having been designed for him and to adopt it as his own. From then on, Sandino never looked back, never questioning his master in public and following most of the teachings of the EMECU with tenacity and conviction. That someone of Trincado's stature had written about the very things that he was doing and wanted to do without knowing him was for Sandino a validation of his actions and a confirmation of his own mission. This seems a plausible explanation of why a man as proud as Sandino suddenly abandoned his reluctance to be anyone's follower and enthusiastically embraced the new doctrines. After Sandino's conversion to the EMECU, his political ideas would not change; they would only gain a more radical eschatological orientation.

AS we have seen, Sandino became increasingly depressed waiting in Mérida, and even the company of his Salvadoran mistress Teresa Villatoro and of other female companions was little comfort in his rude encounter with humiliation, poverty, uncertainty, and deceit. His principal refuge became his mystical-spiritualist sessions and books, which he read avidly. The epistolary evidence shows that Sandino had contact with EMECU members in Yucatán and in Mexico City. His contact in Mexico City was the regional *Celador* and acting director, Jaime Schlittler; the most prominent one in Yucatán was Francisco Vera, secretary of the Provincial *Cátedra* No. 40 in Puerto Progreso (to whom Sandino reported Martí's dismissal). Among Trincado's works, Sandino mentions reading *Los cinco amores* and *Los extremos se tocan* (The extremes meet, 1930) (Somoza 1936, 239–40); he also read *Filosofía austera racional, El espiritismo estudiado* (Studied spiritism), and *El espiritismo en su asiento* (Spiritism in its see, 1919) (Hodges 1992, 89). Given the guerrilla's high rank and rapid ascension in the organization, he would have been familiar with all the EMECU's extant literature and rules, according to established practice. At times, he locked himself up for days to read and to meditate, giving orders not to be disturbed. However, Sandino's new religious awakening did not weaken his political convictions and resolve; neither did it abate his emptiness. His private correspondence revealed his depressed mood and frustration. He continued to think of his trip to Mexico as a mistake and to doubt that he would get any aid from the Mexican government (Alemán 1951, 71–73). However, although he thought of leaving Mexico, he was ashamed to return empty-handed: he did not have "half a penny cut in half nor a single bullet for the liberating cause of Nicaragua" (77).

Despite his depression—and perhaps reflecting his spiritual support—Sandino's setbacks and frustrations did not seem to distract him from his central goal, and he continued to address Nicaraguans in public manifestos announcing a victorious return. His tone was as strong and encouraging as it was categorical: "I will soon be with you at a time that is nearing. . . . [T]he hour of liberation is near . . . the hour to put an end to the slavery is

near. Be strong, Nicaraguans!" He assured his countrymen that his temporary absence meant that "the absolute triumph of Nicaragua's liberty" was
at hand (Alemán 1951, 78–80).

Trapped waiting in Mexico, Sandino defined his suffering in a letter to
Pedrón, his most trusted lieutenant, who had kept the war alive in the
Segovias during his chief's absence. Sandino interpreted his own suffering
as martyrdom, describing himself in terms that suggested the figure of
Jesus Christ.

> My dear brother:
> Bear in mind, you and the other brothers who find themselves in this
> struggle, that I am simply nothing but an instrument of divine justice to re-
> deem this nation. And if I need some of the miseries that exist in this earth,
> it is because I had to come before you also born of a woman and offer my-
> self to you, full of the same human miseries as we all are in this earthly
> world, because otherwise you would not have been able to believe me if I
> had not spoken and been the same as you. (Somoza 1936, 147–48)

Whereas earlier Sandino had referred to Nicaragua as the sacrificial lamb of
the Americas, by January 1930 he had transfigured the symbol—now making himself the chosen one, the incarnation of the most divine of martyrs.[11]
Sandino had once called Turcios "his Judas," but it was the humiliations
and the multiple disappointments in Mexico that led him to think of himself as a living messianic martyr.

11. See also Navarro 2000 (which is based on a conference paper originally presented in
1992). Wünderich (1995, 140, 141) agrees in interpreting this passage as Sandino referring to
himself as Christ.

# 4

# The Messianic Calling

A great flock of crows taints the heavenly blue.
A millennial blast of wind brings threat of pestilence.
Men are murdering one another in the Far East.
Has the apocalyptic anti-Christ been born?
There have been omens, there have been prodigious sights,
and it would seem the return of Christ is imminent. . . .
O Lord Jesus! Why do you delay, what do you wait for
to stretch your hand of light over the beasts
and let your divine banner shine in the sun? . . .
Come, Lord, to fulfill your glory.
Come with stellar tremor and cataclysmic horror.
Come bring love and peace over the abyss . . .
                           —Rubén Darío, "Canto de Esperanza" (Song of hope)

## Sources of Authority

**SANDINO SNEAKED OUT** of Mexico at the end of April 1930 and
was back in the Segovias by 16 May. Once in his beloved mountains, he felt
content to have fled the prison that Mexico had become for him. He was
glad to put his failed trip behind him and was pleased to hear some of the accomplishments that Pedrón reported. Under Pedrón's leadership, Sandino's
followers had carried on hostilities in the northern Nicaraguan countryside: the sacking and looting of local farms and plantations, and the harass-
ing and ambushing of U.S. Marines and National Guard patrols. While
these activities had unfolded on a smaller scale than before Sandino left, it
was enough to have kept the rebel camp fires burning; and Sandino did not
have to start the second chapter of his war of liberation from the ground up.
The scaling down of troops had been previously used as a tactic during the
months of harvest, when peasant fighters worked in the fields and then re-

joined the ranks of the guerrillas, and the system worked fairly well for them. Glad to be back, Sandino renewed hostile activities in earnest.

However, the sequence of misfortunes and disappointments also continued: a month after his arrival, Sandino was seriously wounded in battle and was bedridden for several weeks. His wife Blanca was put out of his reach, deported by the government from San Rafael to the city of León. Later that year, in August, he was further aggrieved when several members of Pedrón's family were killed in combat. After his injury, far away from both mistress (who stayed in El Salvador on the way back from Mexico) and wife, Sandino had to nurse himself back to health, and his recovery was a lengthy one. He stayed away from battle, preferring to spend his time studying his spiritist books—troubled, perhaps, by his vulnerability and by the realization of his own mortality. During his convalescence, he became significantly more mystical and he wrote numerous letters and addresses with a strong apocalyptic content.

Since Moncada had come to power, Sandino had experienced one setback after another, with only minor and often exaggerated victories in between; during the long months in Mexico, he had firmly believed that a return to the motherland would allow him to deliver the final victory that he had promised to his people. By early 1931, however, that victory had failed to materialize. In a letter to Abraham Rivera, a trusted agent, Sandino explained away his lack of success by finding new meaning in his failures and disappointments and by reasserting his prophetic authority: "There have been curious things in my life. I myself did not know that [in my travels] I was learning the secrets of human perversity, so that later I could manifest the truth to our brothers, not only in Nicaragua but in all the terrestrial globe" (Somoza 1936, 209). Reinterpreting the failed goals and promises of his trip, Sandino presented a new and broader vision of himself and of his mission: to spread his view of the world, the mystical underpinnings of his fight, his understanding of relations among men, and his eschatological vision to his troops and countrymen—and to the entire world. Failing on his promise to deliver the final blow to the occupying forces upon his return, Sandino moved toward a radically spiritual and eschatological struggle. It was now directed to more than Nicaragua, Central, and Latin America but to the entire "terrestrial globe." (For a discussion of millenarian leaders and failed prophecy, see chapter 6.)

Moreover, the shift in his self-interpretation and in his conception of his army would involve the intensification of his spiritual activity in the several months that followed his return. By February 1931, in language

similar to his self-reference of divine incarnation a year earlier, Sandino af-
firmed to Pedrón that he was the incarnation of the EDSN's authority:
"Our Supreme Command . . . that is to say, its spirit, is incarnate in matter
that we know under the name of Augusto C. Sandino, and it is necessary
that it be so, so that I may be full of the same human miseries that fill all of
the others that have to be defended from the corrosion of the Corrupting
Spirits" (Somoza 1936, 201). Looking at the first part of the statement, it
seems as though Sandino is only speaking metaphorically; however, as he
repeats that he must be incarnate in order to experience the same miseries
as other corruptible humans, the notion of his self-perception as an incarnation of the incorruptible divine substance becomes clear. The others had
to be defended from spiritual decay, but not him. Later, he would write that
he was the incarnation of God's only daughter: Divine Justice.

Significantly, the influence of EMECU ideals became more overt in
Sandino's thought. Like EMECU members, his men were called upon to address one another as "brother"; one of his guerrilla camps was named
"Joaquín Trincado." However, even as much of Sandino's new religious understanding was adopted from Trincado, the guerrilla chieftain only borrowed what conformed to his own program and what satisfied his own
needs. Among the welcomed notions of Trincado's was the pantheistic idea
of magnetic energy as a manifestation of the divine: "It is natural and logical that even in the most imperceptible atom in the universe exists an elec-
tron of love, because God is everywhere," Sandino asserted to Abraham
Rivera, wishing to attract him to his beliefs and to make him an "apostle"
(Somoza 1936, 186–88). (Sandino was persistent in his attempts to win
Rivera to his faith; Rivera was a loyal supporter and a valuable asset for the
rebel because of his command of local languages and his contacts in the
aboriginal communities along the Coco River.) Sandino also professed the
EMECU's concept of a triune constitution of man: for Trincado, "Creator,
nature and spirit" composed "the trinity of the macrocosm," which "engendered the second trinity of the microcosm or man: spirit, soul and body"
(Trincado 1955, 200). Only with the discovery of the spirit as one's third
component could one become enlightened; knowledge of one's spirit was
considered knowledge of self. Sandino embraced this belief, with his own
added twist: "If you have the fortune of having discovered your trinity, and
in your spirit there is 'the spark of love and justice,' we will find no incon-
venience in supporting your revolutionary movement," he told Nicaraguan
politician Enoc Aguado (Sandino 1981, 2:151). Similarly, in a letter addressed to Hilario Chavarría dated 12 May 1931, Sandino wrote that for as

long as one is ignorant of one's trinity, one will not accept the collective good (Somoza 1936, 228). Enlightenment and political revolution, in the guerrilla chieftain's understanding, went hand in hand.

Sandino successfully adapted ideas and beliefs from the EMECU and incorporated them into the rich body of religious symbols and imagery that already existed among the inhabitants of the Segovian region. The central place that Sandino gave to the region itself in his own thought is one example. In contrast to his earlier christening of Sandino City, Sandino renounced the idea of a departmental capital city bearing his name as the center of regional political power and came to believe that the whole region of the Segovias was a world center of spiritual activity, a more universal and spiritually oriented *omphalos* (navel of the earth). He claimed that the region's peacefulness enabled one to contact something beyond oneself, "beyond everything that is human" (Román 1979, 79). He was also convinced that the high altitude of the mountains brought him and his men physically closer to God (Belausteguigoitia 1985, 144). He considered the mountains a sacred place and wrote to Trincado that the peak of El Chipote, his favorite hideout, was an altar where a voice spoke to him (Somoza 1936, 239).

Clearly, the core of Sandino's religious doctrine was idiosyncratic, bearing the stamp of his unique personality. In practice, however, Sandino's religion was closer to that of the Segovian peasants than might be generally imagined. In Latin America, traditional Christian beliefs are often mixed with a variety of magic beliefs and pagan rituals, and these practices are often common in isolated areas. Discussing José Lezama's idea of the "culture of the Counter Conquest," Carlos Fuentes states that it is "a syncretic culture in which the naked sacrality of the Indian world could hide itself and reincarnate fully dressed in the robes of Christianity; in which African sorcerers could reappear as Catholic priests; in which idols could hide behind the altars" (Fuentes 1985, 31). Even at the dawn of the twenty-first century, similar syncretisms abound in Nicaragua: some pious people wear, in small plastic pouches hanging from their necks or concealed in their clothing, popular prayers to various saints requesting specific benefits. The Segovian people in the 1930s were in this respect no different from those of today. An anonymous prayer recorded by a U.S. Marine illustrates the practice of invoking divine favor and protection from the enemy:

> Jesus Christ, do not forget that this Divine Saint will blind eyes and tame hearts with the power of God. . . . Do not allow injustice to come, let His

sacred wounds accompany me; protect me, console me. Defend [me] with His grace and allow Saint John to defend me with all the angels of Heaven . . . Let all the powerful men fall at my feet. Oh, divine and consecrated magic, in the name of God Almighty, I believe, and I confess to the Most Sacred Sacrament of the Altar; I take to my mouth the divine chalice. Let the thirty-three angels of Heaven protect me, and I will be able to conquer all my enemies. (Bendaña 1994, 178)

In the pocket of another unknown follower of Sandino, in October 1932, was found a sixteenth-century Spanish prayer known as the "Just Judge" (*Justo Juez*), which reads in part:

There are lions and lions coming against me; they shall stop like Jesus stopped them with the Dominus Deus, and I say to the Just Judge: The fury of my enemy I see coming, and I repeat thrice: though they have eyes, let them not see me; though they have hands, let them not touch me; though they have a mouth, let them not speak to me; though they have feet, they do not catch up to me; with two I see them, with three I speak to them; their blood I drink and their hearts I crush. . . . I trust in the Virgin Mary and in the Consecrated Host, which will be celebrated with the milk of the virginal breasts of the Most Holy Mary; and through this I will be free of prisons, I will not be hurt nor wounded nor will my blood be spilled, nor shall I die a painful death. (Wünderich 1995, 135)

Such prayers indicate the popular belief in a God that will save and protect His people from being harmed by enemies or by misfortunes. In this sense, Sandino's religion was not entirely divorced from the practices of many Segovianos—suggesting some of its appeal to those dissatisfied with the Christian churches or yearning for more guidance.

Given that in Sandino's understanding the region of the Segovias was sacred, a kind of holy land—Wünderich refers to El Chipote as Sandino's "New Jerusalem" (1995, 140)—its inhabitants were called to fulfill a special mission. Expressing this, Sandino continuously repeated the phrase "God will speak for the people of the Segovias" (*Dios hablará por los segovianos*) (Belausteguigoitia 1985, 192; see also Somoza 1936, 230). To be sure, the expression preceded Sandino; it had long been common among the inhabitants of the Segovias, who used it to give themselves comfort as the more urbane and sophisticated people of León and Granada often sneered at them. In Sandino's lips, however, the expression gained broader and deeper meaning by evoking José Vasconcelos's formula "the spirit will speak for my race." Moreover, there is an added nuance in the meaning of the expression because of the preposition *por,* which has two distinct but subtle meanings that can be translated as "for" and as "through" in English. Thus, with the first meaning in mind, the expression signifies that God will speak on behalf of the people from the Segovian region; God's message speaks their experience, they are God's children and will be protected in some measure. With the second meaning in mind, however, it means that God speaks through the Segovians; they are literally God's mouthpieces, their words are those of God (and thus infallible), their voice is God's voice—*vox segoviani, vox Dei.* Either formula denotes the predilection of the deity toward the Segovian people; both interpretations are consistent with Sandino's teachings to the peasants that they are God's elect.

However, the assertion of a divine predilection for the Segovian population posed an interesting problem for Sandino. Why was Sandino, an outsider from the other end of the country, their leader? Sandino had a clever explanation: he was not originally from the Segovias "so that [he] could have knowledge of all places and in order not to be disadvantaged by people who might consider [him] a localist" (Somoza 1936, 230)—thus echoing Jesus' words that "no prophet is accepted in his hometown" (Luke 4:24). Sandino continued to interpret himself as the chosen one, leading the oppressed elect toward redemption.

Bendaña (1994, 235) reports Sandino's belief that ignorance makes people superstitious and subject to exploitation; accordingly, Bendaña asserts that "Sandino's 'religion' offered no room for rituals and superstitions" (128). However, there is copious evidence to contradict this view. In keeping with his esoteric training, Sandino was careful to reveal fully his beliefs and powers only to those toward whom he felt a "magnetic affinity"; he was convinced that he communicated through magnetic waves with those closest and most attuned to him. (Some of his most revealing correspondence was addressed to Pedrón and to Abraham Rivera, to both of whom he felt spiritually connected; see Somoza 1936, 200, 202.) He also claimed to have had experiences with supernatural forces on "various occasions": "I have felt a sort of mental trepidation and palpitations, [it was] something very strange inside me." Visions and premonitions that came to him in dreams helped to reveal the movement of the American troops; Sandino may have picked up his belief in the power of dreams from his mother, who believed that she had the gift. In Sandino's system, the receptacle of all of these magnetic powers was "the back of the head" (Belausteguigoitia 1985, 175). Similarly, upon meeting José Román, Sandino directed him to lower his head in order to inspect the protuberance of the occipital; judging from its rather large size, he concluded on the spot that Román was the reincarnation of "Thales, one of the seven wise men of ancient Greece." Fascinated, he pressed Román for his date and year of birth, upon which Sandino established that he and Román had the same zodiac signs, Taurus (in the Mesopotamian horoscope) and Horse (in the Chinese system). "Incredible!" Sandino exclaimed; "I know no one else who has my same two signs." Sandino invited Román to join him for a few days and became even more impressed when a mule that tolerated no stranger to approach it allowed the young man to caress it, even to kiss it (Román 1979, 28–31). In addition, Sandino carried in his pocket—next to his little book of Chinese horoscopes—soil from around the tombs of the young Mexican soldiers who had fought against the 1914 American landing force in Veracruz (Villanueva 1988, 26). Similar beliefs determined other serious aspects of Sandino's life; in one instance, Sandino pardoned a man who was about to be executed because the revolver misfired, leading him to conclude that the alleged traitor was innocent (Macaulay 1985, 213).

Thus, Sandino's hold over people was not limited to military discipline but encompassed cultural and religious appeal as well, allowing his power to reach beyond his own troops. His followers (including his own brother Sócrates) believed in the rebel chieftain's mystical-magical powers. There are reports that peasant women and children followed Sandino to touch him or took things that he had touched to be relics (Bendaña 1994, 130); the peasants developed such reverence for Sandino that on at least one occasion they claimed to have seen a rainbow extend above his head (Belausteguigoitia 1985, 145). Although only a few dozen people outside his closest men had actually met him, he commanded impressive support in the hills. He enjoyed the advantage of a large network of informants and spies, many of whom were appointed by his "generals" with his authority; these people risked their lives to move weapons, supplies, and correspondence along secret trails throughout the region and promptly alerted the guerrillas about the movements of American troops in the area. Although sometimes outnumbered and always outgunned, Sandino commanded many advantages in the field, and his charismatic authority may have been his greatest asset.

**The Mission and the End**

Sandino emphatically denied that he had religious beliefs, for he (like Trincado) considered religions to be for people of backward minds. Asked about his religious convictions, he answered unequivocally: "Religions are a thing of the past. We are guided by reason" (Belausteguigoitia 1985, 172). From the EMECU, he learned to think of his own beliefs in terms of "science" and to scorn all religions as enemies of human evolution. Significantly, however, Sandino claimed to despise religion but not faith, and his notion of faith joined romanticism with spiritism: "Faith, I believe, is eternally childlike and creative; childlike, because it joins the real world with the world of the marvelous and although separating us from the doubt of skepticism and old age, transports us into the dream world of those early years in which, as the poet Wordsworth says, men still retain the memory of incarnation that has not yet been forgotten with the lapse of time and the loss of sensitivity" (Sandino 1981, 2:292).

More specifically, Sandino's cosmogony and cosmology—his understandings of the origin and the nature of the universe—were imbued with the scientistic speculations that he learned from the EMECU. He believed, for instance, that "ether was the first substance of the universe," which was preceded by "a great will, Love eternal and origin of all things"; this great will was God, who had one daughter, Divine Justice (who was the source of inspiration for his army) (Somoza 1936, 207). The earth, Sandino claimed, formed 123 million centuries ago, and humanity appeared 45 million centuries ago. In a circle of cosmic development and transmigration of spirits, the earth was a cosmic penal colony to which the spirits of the former inhabitants of Neptune were banished after the last judgment there; a tree was sent from Neptune, out of which men were born out of five-centimeter bags.[1] Later, Adam, Eve, and twenty-seven other "missionary spirits" were sent to regenerate the earth, and they are still here working for human redemption through continuous cycles of reincarnations. Sandino learned from Trincado (and apparently adopted as factual) a long list of reincarnations: Christ was in a former life Jacob, who was also Adam; the Virgin Mary was Eve; St. Paul was Moses. He professed that the twenty-nine missionary spirits were now members of his peasant army; though he still could not tell with certainty who each of his men was, he claimed to know that his wife Blanca was the Virgin Mary (200–10).

Moreover, although he never publicly speculated as to his own previous lives, Sandino clearly believed that he too was a reincarnated spirit—or perhaps something even more remarkable. On the one hand, if Blanca was

1. In Nordic mythology, the world-tree, Ygdrasil, survives the destruction of the world by fire and blood and bears a new man and a new woman (Weber 1999, 39).

the Virgin Mary, who once had been Eve, there was a good chance that Blanca's husband would be Adam or Jesus (a connection that would have rung true in the perception of the Segovian peasants). On the other hand, there is evidence that he considered himself an incarnation of Divinity or of Divine Justice. To be sure, Sandino is not known to have claimed explicitly that he was Divine Justice incarnate, but in the vast, complex array of images and symbols that he used, the implication often hovered just under the surface. For example, Sandino would present himself entering Jinotega in May 1927 at the head of twenty-nine riders, whom he later interpreted to be the twenty-nine spirits sent here to redeem this planet. Significantly, the rebel chieftain did not conceive of himself as one of the twenty-nine transmigratory spirits; rather, he was the commander of the twenty-nine, which amounts to a subtle self-identification as Divine Justice, the commander of the spirits. In another instance, Sandino described Divine Justice as "God's only daughter, born from His entrails" (Somoza 1936, 207; see also 175); he elsewhere used similar imagery when referring to himself, announcing to Pedrón in January 1930 that he was an incarnate, redeeming spirit born of a woman—and indeed calling himself "an instrument of Divine Justice"— and offering himself to him (along with a few bullets)(148). Whether one understands his imagery as referring to Christ or to Divine Justice, Sandino apparently intended to portray himself as the incarnation of God's only child. Finally, Sandino came to believe that Divine Justice was the animating principle of his EDSN: "the spirit that propels our army" (*la Justicia Divina quien impulsa a nuestro Ejército*) (224; see also 230). Conjoined with the passage from February 1931 (quoted above) in which Sandino wrote to Pedrón—again using the image of birth from a woman—to say that that he was the incarnation of the EDSN authority and that its animating spirit was in him (201), it becomes clear that Sandino perceived himself to be the incarnation of Divine Justice.

In addition to suggesting that he was divinity incarnate, Sandino on occasion appropriated biblical imagery and expressions from the Christian gospel. For instance, he closed some of his teachings by repeating Jesus' well-known phrase "He who has ears, let him hear" (Matt. 11:15; see e.g. Sandino 1981, 2:350). Such references have led some to affirm that he was a pious Christian (see e.g. Tayacán 1987), but Sandino did not believe in the divinity of Christ; indeed, one may easily be tempted to say that he thought of himself as Christ. The truth, however, was more complex. Sandino believed that Jesus had simply been the incarnation of one of the twenty-nine missionary spirits sent to renew the earth; moreover, Jesus was a revolutionary fighter who had introduced mankind to "the concept of liberty." Sandino claimed that "Jesus of Nazareth" had been a "communist and a revolutionary" who had "entered into open battle against Jerusalem's bankers one March 22, and having Prince Ur as military chief" (see Somoza 1936, 229). In essence, for Sandino, Jesus was an angel-like migrating spirit whose purpose was to assist the deity in the redemption of the world. Sandino himself, on the other hand, was God incarnate. Like the Bohemian Adamites, Sandino understood himself to be above Christ. He was no Christian; in fact, orthodox Christians might be inclined to qualify him a heretic.

Sandino shrewdly narrated events of his rebellion by evoking themes and imagery that are particular to the life of Christ. His story of the events at El Común Hill near Boaco (see Belausteguigoitia 1985, 91) offers a mixture of images from Jesus' transfiguration (see e.g. Mark 9:2–13) as well as the suffering at Gethsemane (see e.g. Mark 14:32–42): surrounded by a few men, tired and in tears, Sandino contemplated the betrayal of his country and transformed his involvement in the Constitutionalist War into the role of the staunch anti-American fighter, choosing to accept a likely martyrdom rather than to surrender his weapons. His forty-day descent to the inclement heat of the Atlantic coast to find weapons and Moncada's alleged offer to give Sandino money and power if he gave up his struggle (see Selser, 1:205) parallel elements of the story of Jesus' temptations by the devil in the desert wilderness (Luke 4:1–13). Fueled by his "sacred ire," Sandino spoke of throwing the Americans out of Nicaragua as Christ had done with the merchants at the temple (Sandino 1981, 1:362–63; see John 2:14–17). Finally, Sandino claimed to have been welcomed with palms and flowers as he rode his trademark mule at his arrival in the Segovian town of Jinotega with his twenty-nine men (Román 1979, 69), evocative of Jesus' triumphal entrance into Jerusalem on Palm Sunday (Matt. 21:4–9).

Along with his spiritual interpretation of the major figures of the contemporary history in which he was involved, Sandino revealed his eschatology and outlined the nature of the promised land that he envisioned. According to his 15 February 1931 manifesto entitled "Light and Truth," the earth's evolution would reach its final point—freedom and the "the kingdom of perfection"—in the year 2000 (Somoza 1936, 200). He anticipated that the chosen ones would be redeemed and would remain in an earthly paradise forever, while the others would be purged and banished to less evolved planets. In a letter to Abraham Rivera dated 14 October 1930, he explained the process: "The earth was a world of expiation where for millions of centuries Divine Justice held millions of refractory spirits to the divine law, but today the earth has accomplished its regeneration, and those refractory spirits will be cast upon other planets that are less advanced than the earth. In such a way, injustice will disappear from the earth and justice alone will triumph" (Somoza 1936, 176).

In searching for signs of the coming of the new era, the rebel leader believed in a close connection between natural occurrences and social, economic, and political events. Natural disasters, he thought, precede or announce social upheaval; thus, a series of catastrophes would inaugurate the final period. Some apocalyptic signals could already be seen, Sandino wrote to José Idiáquez, his main Honduran contact and supply master (see Somoza 1936, 224). In his letter to Idiáquez, Sandino was convinced that the ravaging earthquake that destroyed Managua in March 1931 was such a sign. He envisioned the Pacific and the Atlantic oceans meeting and covering everything except for the volcanic peaks over Nicaraguan territory (though he did not elaborate as to how the higher peaks in neighboring countries or elsewhere would be submerged under the circumstances) (Belausteguigoitia 1985, 178). The rage of waters, waves, and roaring seas are part of the traditional pool of apocalyptic imagery (see e.g. Luke 21:25), and to Idiáquez, Sandino stated his conviction that the earthquake held a deeper meaning as a portent of an impending "world conflagration" and that "the principal motive for the next world war [would be] in Nicaragua." Once again, Sandino suggested that Nicaragua was being punished for the sins of her evil sons; as he wrote to all his lieutenants, "Many of the catastrophes will happen in those places of the world where injustice reigns. We also know that two-thirds of humanity will be destroyed by the approaching world war" (Bendaña 1994, 188). The motifs of natural disasters and of warfare between nations as preludes to the end of the age appear in Matthew (24:6–8): "And you will hear of wars and rumors of wars; see that you are not alarmed; for this must take place but the end is not yet. For nation will rise against nation, and kingdom against kingdom, and there will be famines and earthquakes in various places." "This century," Sandino predicted with confidence, "will see extraordinary things" (Belausteguigoitia 1985, 197).

Evidence of the expected upheaval in human affairs was already visible in the prolonged and widespread economic crisis. Sandino had been out of Nicaragua in 1929 when the world economic crisis started, but it affected Nicaragua and his struggle significantly; by the time he returned in mid-1930, the country was experiencing much of its worst effects. Some economic indicators afford us part of the picture of the hardship. Nicaragua's economy was largely dependent (as it still is) on the export of agricultural and raw materials, the lion's share of which was coffee, a great deal coming from the northern regions where Sandino waged his war. (Half of all Nicaraguan exports went to the United States, and two-thirds of national imports came from that country.) Once the crisis set in, coffee production dropped to its lowest level ever (Tirado 1989, 40); coffee exports plunged 49 percent between 1931 and 1932, coupled with a 25 percent decline in market prices as compared to 1929 (Bethell 1991, 233). Overall, in 1928 Nicaragua exported products with a total value of $11.7 million, and it had a fiscal receipt of $5.6 million for the period from 1928 to 1929. In 1932, its exports dropped by over half, to $4.5 million, and from that year to the next the national fiscal receipt declined significantly, to $3.8 million. The gross domestic product declined slowly between 1929 to 1932 by as much as 32.9 percent (Bethell 1991, 233–34). Moreover, between 1926 and 1928, Nicaragua's debt ballooned from $6.96 million to $23.53 million; during the same period, the budget for the National Guard (*Guardia Nacional*, or GN) increased by 27 percent, which constituted 58 percent of national expenses (Dospital 1996, 109). The already ravaged economic picture worsened with the contribution of natural disasters such as the earthquake, drought, and the appearance of a disease affecting banana plantations (called the "mal de Panamá") in 1930.

In his 1931 manifesto "Light and Truth," the guerrilla rebel-turned-messianic prophet announced and defined the end of the present era. He predicted the "destruction of injustice on this earth" and the coming of "the reign of the Spirit of Light and Truth, that is, Love." As basis for those predictions, he reinterpreted the biblical Apocalypse of St. John, setting aside the notion of a transcendent paradise and dismissing the idea that "the world will explode and sink": "What will happen is the following. The oppressed people will break the chains of humiliation . . . The trumpets that will be heard will be the bugles of war, intoning the hymns of the freedom of the oppressed peoples against the injustice of the oppressors. The only thing that will sink forever is injustice" (Somoza 1936, 207–8).

His eschatological promise was imbued with a violent political design: the imminent war would be class warfare of global proportions, where the oppressor and oppressed would fight to the death and the oppressed proletariat would emerge victorious (Somoza 1936, 244, 253). "Only the workers and peasants will go to the end," he had cried one year earlier (Sandino 1981, 2:72). The existent sinful social and economic structure would be replaced, he announced. "Be certain, be very certain, be perfectly certain that soon we will have our triumph in Nicaragua," brought about by the lighting of the *"Explosión Proletaria* against the imperialists of the earth." The approaching catastrophe would happen in Nicaragua because it had been "chosen by Divine Justice to commence the judgment on the unjust of the earth" (Somoza 1936, 208). In Sandino's mind, it was clear that the beginning of both holocaust and paradise would take place in Nicaragua by divine ordination.

Sandino attributed three meanings to the term "revolution"*(revolución)*. Sometimes, the term was synonymous with mayhem or perhaps consternation; there was a "true revolution in my brain," he said after hearing accusations that he had sold out for 2,000 Mexican pesos (Bendaña 1994, 314). At other times, he used the term with its common meaning, as the preferred expression for coups and civil wars in which one Nicaraguan *caudillo* wrestled power from another. Sandino keenly understood such "revolutions" to be games of political musical chairs—bad for small countries such as his, he perceptively thought, for they fail to alter the structure of society and bring retrogression and disaster instead (Sandino 1981, 1:254). They are revolutions in name only. His third and final understanding of the term gives a more optimistic view: Sandino thought that true revolutions were a necessary process in the social evolution of mankind, believing that they had a purifying essence. Countries where there had been more revolutionary wars, such as Mexico, were more advanced, he believed (Sandino 1981, 2:59). In essence, we see here the second pillar upon which Sandino justified his own revolutionary actions. Earlier, he had come to the conclusion that enlightenment leads toward revolution; now, although hardly the discovery of an original argument, he had laid down that the goal of revolution is purification and progress.

It is difficult, if not impossible, to determine with any accuracy when Sandino began believing that he was endowed with his redemptive world mission. Such beliefs usually develop over long periods of time, but there is generally a pivotal moment in the lives of charismatic leaders that they interpret (almost always in hindsight) as the time when they received the revelation of their mission. Perhaps characteristically, Sandino described such moments to interviewers. To Román (1979, 50), he explained that in 1926 he had been pulled from Mexico to Nicaragua by a power outside of himself: "Without a fixed idea, without a determined purpose, dragged by a blind and irresistible magnetic force, I took the steam ship 'Méjico.'" To Belausteguigoitia, he mentioned that after his rejection of the Espino Negro

Accords he meditated and received his revelation at the top of El Común Hill on 4 May: "I came to understand that I was the one called to protest the treachery against my motherland and against the Nicaraguan ideals" (1985, 91). Millenarian leaders often fuse the private into the public (and vice versa); Sandino attributed great personal importance to the day upon which this revelation was received, 4 May, to the point that he thought that it should be declared a "national holiday because that was the day when it was proven that our national honor cannot be humiliated" (Selser 1960, 1:204). Sandino himself did not proclaim 4 May a national holiday, but he finally got his wish when the latter-day Sandinistas declared it to be the "Day of Dignity."

The goal of Sandino's self-proclaimed mission was far greater than that found in conventional accounts, namely the expulsion of the U.S. Marines from Nicaraguan soil. Although it is undeniable that Sandino was engaged in a war of national liberation against the Americans, it is at least equally true that his struggle became informed by his desire for the political and spiritual redemption of the oppressed of the world. Sandino's goal was much more than the practical political purpose of evicting the American invaders (as we will see in detail in the next chapter) but a wide-ranging eschatological one that would transform the world.

Sandino's spiritual impetus now illuminated his political actions. Trincado's doctrines provided Sandino with a framework that explained all levels of physical and spiritual, scientific and political reality. Trincado's beliefs filled his spiritual inclinations and fueled his political expectations in such a way that they became the firm ground on which to base new interpretations of himself and of his mission in even more radical millenarian aspirations.

## Modus Operandi

### The Man and His Organization

Sandino organized his men into eight columns, with a rigorous chain of command and "an absolute discipline" (Belausteguigoitia 1985, 131). All soldiers had a military rank; each column's leader was a member of Sandino's "Chiefs of Staff," with whom he sometimes consulted. At meetings, Sandino always spoke first and asked for suggestions later, but he tolerated no dissension. He alone decided on promotions of rank based on merit on the battlefield and loyalty to him (though there were no material advantages attached to promotions). Things were different in the battle-field, however, where Sandino granted his lieutenants a great deal of auton-omy, and each column was assigned a loosely defined territory.

Several personal aides kept careful records of proceedings, his corre-spondence, and his finances. It is remarkable that in spite of the terrible conditions of waging a guerrilla war in tropical forests and jungles and being in constant movement, Sandino always issued typed, properly stamped, and duly signed documents. He enjoyed formalities because they made him feel important, but it is thanks to that vanity and to his relent-less bureaucratic disposition that so much of his materials have been pre-served. From the archives of the U.S. Marines, for example, Macaulay quotes a description of Sandino taken from one of his fighters:

> Sandino is of medium height, very slender, weighs about 115 lbs.; educa-tion limited to primary grades; an extreme optimist and possesses unusual ability in convincing others of the feasibility of his most fantastic schemes; extremely energetic; explains his plans in great details to his low-est subordinates but often keeps his officers in doubt; is far from being cold-blooded and was never known to commit acts of cruelty himself; very religious and believes that for every wrong committed adequate punish-ment will be meted out to the offender, regardless of steps taken by agents of the law; he has little interest in acquiring money for personal use and rarely has a penny in his pocket; is very vain and sophisticated, fully be-lieving that his wisdom is infallible; he will not tolerate for long a subordi-nate of outstanding ability; feigns modesty at all times, but in fact is most vain and selfish. (Macaulay 1985, 57)

Sandino's vanity was coupled with a keen sense for flair and drama. Ibarra (1973, 169) reproduces a note that Sandino sent to his wife on 7 February 1933, only days after a peace agreement had marked the end of his revolt: as he was about to enter San Rafael, the guerrilla chieftain wrote ahead to de-mand that his wife arrange with the local priest for the tolling of the church's bells upon his entrance.

Sandino gave himself different titles at different stages of his life. He was originally named "General" by his men during the Constitutionalist War, a title that was often extended to almost any leader of a column in such circumstances. With his rebellious stance against Moncada, he styled himself the "Chief of the Mountaineers"; he then became "Supreme Com-mander of the [Liberal] Revolution," followed by "Defender of the National

Right," only to become a General again sometime later. He later elevated himself to the rank of "Generalissimo" and called himself the "Supreme Commander" of the EDSN. Following the peace accord in 1933, upon the formal dissolution of his ragged army and under the presumed threat of another American invasion some months later, he gave himself the new title of "Supreme Commander of the *Autonomista* Army, ruler of Central America." His most important and enduring title, however, was "César," signifying his self-image not only as a great military commander and ruler but also as an imperial god. Indeed, it was more than a title; used initially as his middle name and then as his first name, it erased his maternal name and thus concealed his illegitimacy, allowing him to become a new person in accord with his own definitions and dreams. Sandino never directly called himself a prophet or a messiah, but it is clear from his writings that he thought of himself as one or the other, and at times both. Thus, by taking the imperial title as his name, "César" Augusto joined his religious understanding to his military and secular ambitions of power and conquest.

Unwilling to meet the fate of Caesar, he surrounded himself with a personal guard, a tight unit composed of about thirty men who watched him day and night. He chose for the task boys as young as thirteen, in the hopes of shaping their minds and hearts: "They guard me, love me and obey me like a father. They form a fraternal organization among themselves" (Román 1979, 182).

However, Sandino's words masked a harsher reality. His army was made up primarily of hungry, barefoot, and ill-equipped *campesinos*, dressed in rags and with no military training. Previous Nicaraguan armies never wore fancy uniforms, but warlords at least paid their peasant soldiers some money and gave them food and clothing; by contrast, Sandino's men received no salary, turned themselves into virtual bushmen, and did not always have much in the way of clothes to wear or food to eat. Their general complained about their conditions, remarking in jest that they could not even wear the boots and uniforms of dead Marines because they were too large. A letter of extortion directed by the EDSN lieutenant Jesús Baldibia to a rancher in the Jinotega area shows, in spite of the abrupt and threatening tone, the pathetic needs of Sandino's men: Baldibia demands that he be sent 100 *córdobas* as payment in the service of Sandino's cause, or else, but pleads toward the end of the note that the sum be sent half in cash and half in khaki clothes and some underwear (Bendaña 1994, 183–84). Miguel Ángel Ortez, an important EDSN lieutenant, makes a similar plea for footwear and underwear in his "Operational Instructions" of 7 June 1930

(195–96). Under these circumstances and with no military power backing them, the guerrillas should not have been any match for the U.S. Marines or the GN (National Guard)—but they just kept coming.

The key to the EDSN's endurance lies primarily in the loyalty that Sandino's men showed to him over the years. Sandino seemed to care for his men with fatherly affection, and that affection was amply mirrored by his men, who referred to him fondly as "the old man" (*el viejo*). Most were illiterate and had never left the mountains; most had never seen the workings of electricity or an automobile, let alone an aircraft—until they suffered aerial attacks on their positions. Some of the lieutenants could barely read and write and so their chief taught them a little, perhaps understanding that literacy, like his religious beliefs, was a source of authority. Among the most loyal but also the most brutal of his men was Pedro Altamirano, known as Pedrón, who had been a fugitive and a smuggler in the sparsely populated frontier zone between Nicaragua and Honduras before joining Sandino. The "Latin American Legion" was the name symbolically given to the volunteers from elsewhere in Latin America who had joined the fight, some of whom worked very close to Sandino: Alfonso Alexander (Colombian), Gregorio Urbano Gilbert (Dominican), Esteban Pavletich (Peruvian), and Farabundo Martí (Salvadoran), to name a few.

The remarkable discipline demanded from Sandino's men mirrored their strong-willed commander, who did not smoke, drink, or gamble and who practiced vegetarianism. Traditionally, purity and asceticism have been symbolic ways to mark the separation of the eschatological community. In language known to (and used by) Sandino, St. Paul mixed war symbols, asceticism, and the coming of the apocalypse.

> For you yourselves know very well that the Day of the Lord will come like a thief in the night. When they say "there is peace and security," then sudden destruction will come upon them, as labor pains come to a pregnant woman, and there will be no escape! But you, beloved, are not in darkness for that day to surprise you like a thief; for you are children of light and children of the day; we are not of the night or of darkness. So then let us not fall asleep as others do, but keep awake and be sober; for those who sleep, sleep at night and those who are drunk are drunk at night. But since we belong to the day, let us be sober, and put on the breastplate of faith and love, and for a helmet the hope for salvation. (1 Thess. 5:2–8)

Sandino's men swore to protect the sovereignty of the motherland, and

their symbol was the red and black flag with a skull in the middle: red signified freedom and resurrection, black represented death and mourning,
and the skull signified that their fight was to the death (Belausteguigoitia
1985, 194; Román 1979, 63). Initially, the guerrilla chieftain ordered his
men "not to commit injustices in order to [continue to] enjoy God's protection" (Sandino 1981, 1:195). Thus, all black market activities and the traffic
of animals were prohibited, and no one was allowed to have more than two
horses (1:190). Soldiers who disobeyed the rules, abused peasants, stole, or
raped were summarily executed. However, as the war advanced the general
attitude toward rules loosened and much undesirable activity went on behind Sandino's back.

### Violence and the Administration of Justice

The year 1931 began with one bit of good news among a great deal of bad: on
13 February, the American secretary of state Henry L. Stimson announced
that the complete withdrawal of American troops would follow the upcoming 1932 election. Much enthusiasm filled the country; not coincidentally, perhaps, two days later Sandino issued his "Light and Truth"
manifesto, the most apocalyptic of his writings. However, the smiles
brought by the news of the future withdrawal dissipated in Managua with
the devastating destruction of the March 1931 earthquake. Publicly,
Sandino expressed his sorrow for the suffering that destiny had again imposed on Nicaragua (Sandino 1981, 1:167), but within his circle he interpreted the disaster as a divine sign of support for his cause: "[T]hings are
taking the color we require . . . Divine justice is flogging the enemy and we
need to finish the job" (Somoza 1936, 219). The last offensive was at hand,
Sandino kept announcing, and the increased level of violence that followed
his return from Mexico continued.

Through the success of his guerrilla tactics, Sandino became master of
a large territory (nearly one-third of the country's territorial extension). Personally or through his web of armed representatives, he named civil and
military authorities in the vast controlled areas, formally accrediting "official" papers to that effect (see e.g. Bendaña 1994, 199–200, 228, 240). In
early 1931, Sandino issued a communiqué with careful instructions as to
how his authority would be applied, detailing the hierarchical ranking and
the orders of command and of succession among the officials that he named
(244–45). Some areas were so firmly controlled by the rebels that citizen re-
quests to remove abusive governmental officials were made directly to the

guerrillas. Whether or not petitions of this type were heeded, they show a significant recognition of Sandino's de facto authority; petitioners might have appealed to the U.S. Marines or to the GN for the removal of the abusive official, if it was thought that either of these organizations were in charge (241–43). Through Sandino's network of his own officials and his armed bands, people were forced to pay arbitrary sums as contributions to his fight (e.g. 215–16, 183–84). Sandino ran a well-organized "government by extortion" (Crawley 1984, 62); his men even handed out receipts for monies and goods received—payable by the United States government, upon whose responsibility the rebels placed the precarious Nicaraguan situation (see Bendaña 1994, 202, 207). One of these receipts or a statement declaring that the bearer was friendly to the rebels were desirable documents, offering a guarantee of safe passage and personal security to the bearer, his workers, and his property. Fulgencio Hernández wrote to one of his chosen victims: "If you do not pay the [aforementioned] contribution, I warn you not to continue picking coffee in your plantation because you have no guarantees for your hacienda nor your peons" (215). To be found in Sandino-controlled territory without a rebel guarantee bore drastic consequences, including possible accusation of spying or treason and a brutal execution. Thus, a guarantee became an item of exchange for money in extortion threats. The guarantee documents were not without problems, of course: possessing them could be interpreted as collaboration with the guerrillas if the bearer ran into the Marines or the GN.

Stern measures were applied to those without guarantees, to those who disobeyed the dictates and pronouncements of Sandino or of his officers, and to those who refused to pay. EDSN collectors were instructed to make examples of offenders by taking or killing their cattle, burning their houses and crop fields, and taking family members as hostages. Typically, Sandino wanted to win or to keep the support of the rural poor, and he gave precise instructions only to take from the rich; these instructions were followed, for the most part, even when he was away in Mexico (Bendaña 1994, 197). However, the notion of wealth was relative for the destitute peasant soldiers who executed the orders, and personal scores were often settled under the guises of patriotic collections, giving rise to abuses. If such abuses touched Sandino's supporters and he found out, he usually intervened with a strong punishing hand against the offending party (236–37). He otherwise justified his army's looting and other abuses by arguing that it was "unjust that the men [who] struggled for the liberation of Nicaragua [had to] wear rags" (Sandino 1981, 2:200).

Less fortunate were those executed. The gruesome executions performed by Sandino's men are as famous for their lethal skill as they are for their supposed originality. As Sandino's official seal shows, the tool of rebel (and therefore, in his view at least, divine) justice was the machete. Decapitations were the order of the day, but it was not considered enough to behead a condemned man; rather, guerrilla soldiers administered what they called *cortes* (cuts) that ranged from laceration to abominable mutilating combinations, causing death after extended suffering. (Perhaps not coincidentally, *corte* also means legislature or court of law.)

> The most famous was the *corte de chaleco,* the "vest cut": the offender's head was lopped off with a machete, after which his arms were severed at the shoulders and a design was etched on his chest with machete slashes. Pedrón invented the "vest cut" and applied it often until he tired of it in 1930 and ordered that all "traitors" receive the *corte de cumbo* instead . . . the "gourd cut." An expert machete man sliced off [the top] portion of the victim's skull, exposing his brain and causing him to lose his equilibrium [and to suffer through] hours of agony and convulsions before death. Less sophisticated was the *corte de bloomers,* by which the victim's legs were chopped off at the [back of the] knees, eventually producing death through bleeding. These three *cortes* were the most popular among the guerrillas, but there were . . . others that were . . . applied to the bodies of dead enemies: the "tie cut" [*corte de corbata*], by which the subject's throat was cut and his tongue pulled through the slit, and the "cigar cut" [*corte de puro*], by which the victim's penis was amputated and placed in his mouth. (Macaulay 1985, 212–13)

Another *corte* consisted in slashing open the abdomen of a decapitated man and then placing his own severed head in the abdominal cavity.[2] A regiment of child guerrillas (who also guarded Sandino) had the task of swarming the battlefields with machetes in order to finish off wounded Marines and to collect their weapons, equipment, and personal possessions (Texeira 1978, 266). The marauders were given a name that concealed their macabre activity: the choir of angels (*el coro de angeles*).

2. See also Maraboto 1929, 16. For more examples of Sandino's brand of violence, see Sandino 1981, 1:129, 173, 226, 235, 252, 320; 2:61, 122, 148–49, 173, 181, 185, 187, 200–205, 216–18, 237, 244, 247, 255, 262, 311, 329; Belausteguigoitia 1985, 188–90; Gilbert 1979, 55; Román 1979, 162; Bendaña 1994, 187–88.

The violent aspect of Sandino's rebellion is a thorny subject. Some commentators downplay it and some overemphasize it, but it remains little (it if at all) understood by either side. The atrocities seem initially to have been directed at the U.S. Marines and may have begun as early as 1927. At the end of the conflict, in 1933, Sandino claimed that the Marines had begun beheading Nicaraguans first, so in retaliation he had ordered their heads to be placed on sticks by the side of mountain trails as an act of vengeance (Román 1979, 162). (Indeed, Macaulay [1985, 228–29] documents some Marine atrocities.) However, Schroeder (1996) has shown that Sandino's particular brand of violence did not originate with him but rather was a legacy of the crudely violent political culture of the Segovias and a carryover from the Constitutionalist War. A contemporary of Sandino, a peasant gangster leader named Anastasio Hernández, resorted to the same savage executions and terrorist tactics in the service of powerful Conservative families of the region, whose aim was to terrorize political rivals and to deter others from supporting them. Hernández's activities expanded from May to mid-November of 1927, at which time he was defeated by a murderous rival Liberal gang led by José León Díaz, who later joined Sandino. Thus, in Schroeder's view, Sandino's appropriated the existing "basic tools of political struggle" used by Segovian élites. What was indubitably original about Sandino was his justification for the use of violence.

Two stages are discernable in Sandino's approach to violence: before and after his membership in the EMECU. In the first stage, Sandino and his fighters sacrificed themselves and their victims at the altar of the limited objective of national liberation, crystallized in the struggle to evict the foreign occupying force and to rid the country of treasonous collaborators. Thus, violence was framed primarily in an appeal to honor, nationality, race, party, and class membership. During this stage, Sandino appealed to God for help in a manner no different than the way we have seen Nicaraguans (and Segovians in particular) pray and make petitions, as belief in God and in predestination gave the rebels strength and protected them; for example, announcing the arrival of the "bloodiest battle that Central America ha[d] ever seen", Sandino cited as motivation "the honor of [his] motherland and its race . . . strengthened by [his] belief in the supreme being" (Sandino 1981, 1:207). In November 1927, in one of his many exaggerated battle reports, Sandino wrote: "Destiny has marked traitors and invaders [of the motherland] as terrible delinquents, punishing them with slow agony to make better felt the expiation of their dark fault" (Selser

1960, 1:271). Although the imagery of purification by violence suggests some level of spiritual development, the permeating sentiment of this passage is still racial nationalism. By contrast, after his personal embrace of the eschatologically oriented ideas of the EMECU, the limited goals of Sandino's struggle were transfigured into more explicitly religious and cosmic terms. Thus, in the second stage of his approach to violence, Sandino and his fighters sacrificed themselves and their victims for the benefit of a radical, universal transformation of the cosmos. Although there is no single moment at which one can identify a dramatic transformation, the trajectory is clear. After his return from Mexico in 1930, Sandino was writing about the divine inspiration of his forces (Sandino 1981, 2:150), and EDSN violence was justified by a heavy reliance upon apocalyptic discourse. By early 1931, he was committed to a cosmic battle between good and evil that would bring about the end of the world; although he continued to evoke nationalistic, racial, and class symbols (the concern for party virtually vanishing), their use shifted to the context of an impending millennial holocaust, as shown in the Light and Truth manifesto and in correspondence of February and March 1931.[3] Although Sandino's crude violence may well be grounded in Segovian barbarism, his justifications for the violence paralleled the unfolding of his own understanding of himself and his army; in essence, what took place was not purely a shift at the level of phenomena but a qualitative spiritual leap (which previous commentators have all too easily missed). In the early days of his rebellion, Sandino believed that he and the EDSN were on the side of the angels; from 1930 onward, Sandino believed that they themselves were the angels.

Moreover, the shift had practical as well as philosophical implications, such as in Sandino's understanding and treatment of traitors. All along, the gruesome violence was directed to more than just the occupying forces: Nicaraguans who were considered traitors were also executed. In November 1927, Sandino issued a decree identifying the "traitors to the motherland" as anyone giving or receiving help or protection from the occupiers

3. It is worth noting that Ramírez's collection includes only three pieces from February and one from March 1931 (Sandino 1981, 1:159–66), thus avoiding the most visibly apocalyptic period in Sandino's life. For a more accurate picture, one needs to consult Somoza (1936), which includes in its totality the spiritist and cosmological discussion in the letter to Abraham Rivera (208–10) that Ramírez selectively slashes. Ramírez's work also conveniently excludes the 3 February 1931 letter addressed to Pedrón (199–201).

and anyone that dealt with them or represented them (Sandino 1981, 1:174). Anyone against Sandino was for the enemy, and anyone for the enemy was against him. As hardline as this position was, however, he had yet to turn against those claiming neutrality, and Sandino publicly urged his men to be fair in extorting money and goods from landowners, to employ minimum force, and to remove and burn doors and windows from the homes of the uncooperative so as "to make the punishment humorously visible" (2:201). He denied for some time that his men committed crimes, later arguing that impostors using the name of his cause were at fault. (Indeed, Sandino was partially correct about this: some assassinations that Somoza later attributed to Sandino had in fact been committed earlier by Anastasio Hernández, in the free-for-all of murdering gangs roaming the Segovias after the Constitutionalist War of 1926 and 1927 [Schroeder 1996, 405].) Privately, however, the rebel leader encouraged the executions (see Somoza 1936, 166–68; Bendaña 1994, 234), and his only known objection to the decapitations was procedural. In a congratulatory letter to sergeant Marcial Rivera, he wrote: "The traitors to whom you have administered vest cuts in your last tour are justly executed and this [supreme] command has no comment to that effect, except to say next time you are prohibited from going about putting little pieces of paper on the corpses announcing that you have executed them. In future, you will not write those papers giving account of anything" (Somoza 1936, 307). Sandino encouraged and condoned the executions, but he did not want to admit it in public or to take responsibility.

Perhaps allowed by such anonymity as well as by his own spiritual transformation, the definition of treason—already quite loose—became looser toward the end of 1930, as Sandino's apocalyptic fantasies grew and as he became more and more intolerant of those who did not abide by his decrees. He gave orders to execute for treason any merchant refusing "to share" his salt or medicine with the peasants, as well as any peasant refusing to take a share of the stolen goods (Somoza 1936, 177–78). Neutrality became a dangerous luxury after his declaration that it was "a crime to cross one's arms before the liberating struggle" of his army (307). Sandino was not bothered by the carnage and at times made intriguing arguments that it was all for the protection of his people: "If we do not decapitate them [the enemy], they will continue to assassinate the oppressed people" (Bendaña 1994, 234). (This may suggest that the beheaded would not reincarnate.) Convinced that he was punishing evildoers, Sandino was unrepentant. In the same May 1931 letter that urged the decapitations to continue, Sandino proselytized two of his lieutenants, giving them his teachings on evil and intention and inviting them to read it to the troops:

> Do not ever do anything that may bring you to hell.
>
> Hell is the remorse of our conscience when we have committed unjust acts.
>
> Try to be angels, not devils.
>
> Angels are those people that in the opportune moment present themselves before human beings bringing relief.
>
> Devils are those ungrateful people who do evil deeds to families or to people who live honestly.
>
> Often we do evil deeds involuntarily, and that is purgatory.
>
> Purgatory is in the remorse that we feel in our conscience when we commit evil deeds involuntarily, but we feel satisfied when we try to cleanse our responsibility with good deeds. (157)[4]

The eclectic nature of Sandino's understanding—mixing an orthodox Catholic teaching such as purgatory with his selective notions of absolution and virtue—is palpable. Evil is only evil if one hurts good people, and good actions can cleanse involuntary misdeeds. It is remarkable but consistent that this spiritist lesson accompanies an order "to extend the terror and to chop heads off." Significantly, this kind of directive is not found before 1930, the year in which Sandino declared himself to be divine incarnation. Sandino did not worry about his station on these matters: "My conscience is clear," he boasted, "I enjoy the satisfaction of a job well done [and] I sleep like a healthy baby" (Alemán 1951, 115). In one instance, he even claimed to have derived enjoyment from seeing a scene of bodies shredded by machetes: "It was a beautiful picture," he exclaimed, "worthy of showing to the whole world as an example" (Somoza 1936, 245).

After 1930, as reflected both in his propaganda and in his operations, the scope of Sandino's cause widened to include the goals of the EMECU. Sandino instilled in his men the belief that they themselves were an in-

---

4. I have chosen to translate this passage from Grossman's presentation of the document rather than the version appearing on pages 233–35 of the same publication, because the former is more fluid and elegant. Sandino directed this letter to Inéz Hernández, a brother of the infamous Segovian bandit Anastasio Hernández, who terrorized the northern departments of Nicaragua on behalf of the local and national Conservative bosses between May and November of 1927 (see Schroeder 1996).

strument of divine punishment: "We have been sent to serve as whip and punishment for their [the Americans' and the traitors'] unrestrained crimes," he declared (Sandino 1981, 2:58). In the killings, he linked his political campaign for national sovereignty against the United States with his religious plan for world redemption. He believed that the executions were carried out "with the maximum love of liberty," claiming only to eliminate "those who commit[ted] offences against liberty and [those who] sought to impose slavery upon us" (2:187). (Dospital [1996, 26] calls Sandino's approach "selective terrorism.") He admitted that these actions were "drastic [but necessary] measures for the benefit and health of the nation" (Somoza 1936, 281). Such was "the price of liberty," he said, almost hinting at regret (Belausteguigoitia 1985, 188).

*The Eradication of Darkness*

Whatever or whoever became identified as an obstacle to progress acquired the character of an evil to be removed at all costs. Sandino's explanation that "divine justice is rigorously cold, and when it is detained by evil, it becomes agitated and transforms itself into electric energy that melts evil and opens the way" (Somoza 1936, 224) seemed broad enough to justify anything. All of it, according to Sandino, was a predestined cosmic battle for control of the universe, a war between good and evil: "Spirits battle incarnated or not incarnated," he often repeated, in the understanding that the battle for Nicaragua was part of that universal war (Belausteguigoitia 1985, 177). The objectives of warfare (whether conventional, guerrilla, or even nuclear) are limited, earthly goals: territory, resources, power, or the annihilation of the enemy. In Sandino's mind, both sides used similar tactics, but to different moral ends: "The practices of our army and those used by the enemy in the White House are about the same but the difference is that the spirits of light protect our army [whereas] the spirits of darkness are those that favor the so-called White House" (Somoza 1936, 202).

"Life is never over because the spirit always survives," Sandino thought, and hence his remorselessness (Belausteguigoitia 1985, 172). He thought that human lives and individual goodness or evil were predetermined; since it was in the fate of a man to be wicked, his execution might have been the deliverance of his wicked condition, a liberating chance allowing him to reenter the cycle of reincarnation at a higher plane. This understanding was extrapolated to the social context when he wrote that "revolution is synonymous with purification" (Sandino 1981, 1:163; see also 166). Above and beyond the tactical political imperatives for the use of terror, therefore, Sandino also attributed a deep spiritual purpose to it.

A survey of the justifications for EDSN violence reveals three principal motivators. The first was one of the most typical forms of human self-gratification: vengeance. Sandino's peasant soldiers often used violence in a tit-for-tat manner, as a response to some of the (real or perceived) killings and abuses of the U.S. Marines; in other instances, violence served as a means of settling personal scores or an expression of vanity and power.

Second, EDSN violence was employed with a tactical, functional utility in mind, which in turn had two different manifestations. One function of violence was to instil terror in the outside community. Schroeder sees this phenomenon as a component of the political culture of the Segovias, where "every attack had its surviving eyewitness [as] a clear sign that gang leaders assigned to them a role of audience, or chroniclers, charged with re-membering and telling their kin, neighbours, friends, and fellow commu-nity members what they had seen and experienced" (1996, 441). Machiavelli believed that it is better to be feared than to be respected, and Sandino understood the notion well: "We try to *impose* respect [for us] among people who for fear [of the enemy] might hurt the cause of Nicaragua's freedom" (Bendaña 1994, 218; emphasis added). In fact, respect cannot be imposed, for it must be freely given; if it is coerced, it ceases to be respect and becomes fear. Sandino's purpose was therefore to instil a fear greater than any fear the enemy could instil in the population, and the guer-rillas succeeded in spreading fear and terror into the Segovian inhabitants and beyond. The other functional objective of extreme violence was simply as a means of conserving scarce bullets (Román 1979, 80). A similar effi-ciency is recognizable in Nazi concentration camps, where administrators resorted to the use of gas to kill prisoners en masse as the most efficient means of accomplishing their objective of extermination while conserving bullets for the battlefield.

The third central motivator for the use of extreme violence was a com-bination of duty and necessity. Sandino believed that it was the duty of himself and of his men to purify Nicaragua and the world of undesirable, corrupting elements; gruesome violence and its implementation were sim-ply a necessity in the accomplishment of their duty (Bendaña 1994, 233–35). To be sure, these concepts of duty and necessity were ideologically motivated, and their purpose changed with the development of Sandino's disposition and ideas. Originally it was a purely political cause that appro-priated religious language such as purity and redemption. According to

Sandino, Nicaraguan traitors "had no right to live" (1981, 1:166);[5] they were hindrances to the liberation of the motherland, and he emphasized that "the purity of the cause [needed] to be maintained at any price" (Román 1979, 79). One of his army's perceived duties was therefore to maintain the purity of all of the things that Sandino understood initially to be amalgamated in his cause: party, race, social class, and nation. Moreover, it was necessary to clean up those who resisted the message, who chose to remain ignorant, and thus Sandino expanded the scope of his attacks to include neutral parties; those who rejected the life of the spirit represented an obstruction in the path of universal redemption. The rebel leader believed that ignorance gave rise to envy, which in turn gave rise to injustice; the coming of the Kingdom, the final triumph of justice over injustice, would occur "when the majority of mankind [came] to know that they live[d] by the spirit" (Somoza 1936, 207). Ignorance, therefore, was but a transient stage in human development and one that the enlightened were duty-bound to combat in order to become the majority and thus to help along the arrival of the Kingdom. This might be achieved by active proselytizing, as indeed Sandino undertook; another way was the direct elimination of unbelievers. Relishing in the thought of ruling Nicaragua and in expectation of the cleansing that would follow, Sandino told Abraham Rivera that "we will sweep with brooms made of bayonets everything that obstructs human progress" (Somoza 1936, 209; see also Bendaña 1994, 217).

With increasing intensity after his return from Mexico in 1930, Sandino's struggle ceased to be merely a political struggle with sprinkles of religious symbols, becoming instead enveloped in his beliefs about the approaching end of the world and the final struggle between his forces of light and those of darkness. Significantly, this change was in part a response to Sandino's failure to deliver a final defeat upon the U.S. Marines at his return; thus, the infusion of a radical eschatological direction into the renewed violence of 1930 and 1931 marked the failure of prophecy and the eschatologizing of his struggle (see chapter 6 for a further historical and theoretical discussion of the phenomenon of prophetic failure). It is no coincidence that Sandino's return from Mexico produced radically millenarian pronouncements, a dramatic swelling of his ranks, and an intense wave of violence to cleanse the region and to rush the apocalypse that would precede the end.

5. See also "Interview with Two [Former] *Sandinista* Youths: Captains Manuel María Avila and Moisés Alberto Escobar," *La Prensa*, 19 Feb. 1933, 1.

As noted above, Sandino used biblical and Christian symbolism to describe himself and other key players in modern history. The bankers of Wall Street (who in Sandino's eyes controlled American politics) were the descendants of the Golden Calf, and the 30 pieces of silver for which Judas had sold Christ had miraculously appeared in the vaults of Wall Street as a sort of curse (Sandino 1981, 1:331). The American Marines were the representatives of the Golden Calf, defenders of an evil materialistic empire; the same indictment was made against the clergy (Somoza 1936, 230). Thus, bankers, Marines, and clergy all were seen as obstacles in the march of the new Levites toward the Promised Land (Sandino 1981, 1:326). The image implicitly compares Sandino to Moses at the head of the Levites in the desert wilderness, a common move among those who have preached violence in the name of God. At his descent from Mount Sinai, Moses said: "Whoever is for the Lord, come to me." He then echoed God's command: "Each man strap a sword to his side. Go back and forth through the camp from one end to the other, each killing his brother and friend and neighbor. You have been set apart to the Lord today, for you were against your sons and brothers and he has blessed you this day" (Exod. 32:26–29).

# 5

# Peace and Death

> I am a fatalist and an optimist. No one dies the day before one is meant to. Suppose they kill me! So what? . . . It is not easy to be alive and to be a hero forever. Only dead can one become a hero and also become a symbol. That is to say, in death one also contributes, and perhaps even more.
>
> —Augusto C. Sandino, in an interview by José Román

## The Way to Peace, a Tactical Retreat

### War and Conquest

IN MARCH 1931, a civil war began brewing in Honduras. Sandino, concerned about an attack against him should the Conservatives take control in that country, elaborated possible countermeasures: if attacked by Honduras, he would retaliate by "proclaiming the Union of Central America, under the name of *Comuneros de Centroamerica*" (Somoza 1936, 216). Historically, the *Comuneros* were Spaniards who had petitioned Charles V for more open forms of governing and for local control of taxes, until their rebellion was crushed in 1521. Sandino anticipated that all workers and peasants would join him and that with their help he would expand his struggle against the United States and its allies throughout Central America. He later claimed to have sent delegations the following month to contact labor movements in Central America in an attempt to secure their support for the new project. The new state would be founded for the proletarian class; according to Sandino, the re-creation of the defunct Central American Federation would exclude the "bourgeois element." "Only we, the workers and peasants of Central America, will be able to restore our federation," he proclaimed (224). Nothing seems to have come out of the meetings, however, and it is not clear that they ever took place.

*117*

Beginning in February, the military successes of his troops led Sandino to believe that he would soon have "military, civil, and religious control of the republic" (Somoza 1936, 208). Indeed, guerrilla operations expanded over several departments, and Sandino's followers gained virtual control of the northern countryside at the same time as they made much progress into the department of Zelaya, on the Atlantic coast. However, they largely failed to sway the Indians to their cause or to receive endorsement from a significant portion of the population; they also failed to seize and occupy any cities (Brooks 1998). Sandino grew impatient.

Sandino also grew increasingly nervous and suspicious. He suspected Zepeda of treasonous motivations when the latter suggested that Sandino grant interviews to some American journalists. Sandino refused the suggestion and later advised his men of his new attitude toward Zepeda: "We will not break with Zepeda because it is not convenient to our cause. We need him to continue his propaganda work abroad, but we will not trust him much" (Somoza 1936, 243). It would seem that Sandino had learned some practical discretion from his ruptures with Turcios, Martí, and the Mexican communists. His newfound prudence became more apparent a month later when he also became angry at Gustavo Alemán Bolaños, his Nicaraguan propagandist in Guatemala, for proposing to support Conservative Evaristo Carazo's bid for the Nicaraguan presidency. Sandino replied politely this time, rejecting the idea and informing Alemán Bolaños that he had no room for political maneuvers at the moment; rather, "our army will wait for the coming world conflagration in order to begin developing its announced humanitarian plan in favor of the world proletariat" (253). Later, Sandino revealed his contemptuous feelings toward Alemán Bolaños to José Idiáquez: the "poor devil," Sandino said (almost echoing his words against Turcios), had "idiotic pretensions" in thinking that he could tell the guerrilla leader what to do and what to say. Though Sandino promised never to write to Alemán Bolaños, he may have been posturing for Idiáquez' sake (254–56).[1]

Overcome by the possibility of more betrayals, Sandino became more isolationist and advised self-reliance. "We must convince ourselves that we

---

1. For their part, Idiáquez and Alemán Bolaños were at odds with one another over Sandino's savage methods. In a note sent through Idiáquez dated December 1930, Alemán Bolaños had advised Sandino to "cut off the ears" of a few enemies and to "take some departmental capitals and hang their local leaders in public squares as an example." At the bottom of the same note, Idiáquez had intervened, urging the guerrilla chieftain to disregard Alemán Bolaños's advice and to cease the cruel executions (Alemán and Idiáquez, 1930).

are alone and we have no other alternative than to triumph or die," he told his men (Somoza 1936, 243). This was not a simple paranoid attitude but a conclusion that he had reached about the present state of affairs. Zeal stemming from his new beliefs and his disappointments with politicians in Mexico had made Sandino ill-disposed toward political maneuvers. The final victory still was not in sight; he grew so frustrated that he threatened to start burning entire towns if he could not take them, but he never followed through on this threat (256).

Moreover, his army's successes in the field brought their own troubles. Initially, it had been encouraging that the more territory the rebels controlled, the more their ranks swelled. However, the fact that the eight EDSN columns had been designed to be self-sufficient made it difficult for Sandino to communicate with his lieutenants and to keep a steady flow of supplies moving to reach the troops; these problems only increased with the addition of more men. As a result, attacks against civilians, killings, kidnappings, and extortions in the countryside intensified. Sandino issued orders to merchants and landowners in the northern region to make contributions or pay the price (Somoza 1936, 287–88; see also 280–82).

Sandino's desire for advances in urban areas continued, but he realized the difficulty of capturing cities unless the inhabitants joined in the effort. Thus, on Independence Day (15 September) 1931 he called upon the people of León, the second largest city in the country, to join him. León was a Liberal Party stronghold where Sandino enjoyed some labor and student support. In a confusing attempt at a flattering pun, he argued that León had inherited the spirit and leadership of the whole country after its independence from "the Spanish Lion" (*León español*). Now that traitors threatened the country, he proclaimed, the same spirit had moved to "the virgin jungles of the Segovias," and so he called on the patriotic *leoneses* to try to recover that spirit of leadership by rising and joining the "good sons of Nicaragua" (Somoza 1936, 263–64). No such uprising took place.

*Political Maneuvers and the New Conditions*

It did not take very long for Sandino to revoke his unwillingness to make political deals or to look for political alternatives that would advance his position. Toward the beginning of December 1931, Sandino modified his tactics and pursued a course of action that led to the creation of the Committee for the Liberation of Nicaragua (*Comité Pro Liberación de Nicaragua*) in El Salvador (Somoza 1936, 293). His expectation of "world conflagration" and of taking "control of Nicaragua" remained unchanged, but there was now a puppet political organization to carry the agenda off the battlefield. Sandino would entrust retired Nicaraguan general Horacio Portocarrero to be the new president; in return, Portocarrero would choose a cabinet whose absolute obedience to Sandino's army was required (294–96). Sandino had made it clear that he wished to control all the civil, military, and religious institutions of the republic. Should his plan succeed, the new arrangement would ensure him prompt dominion over the first two institutions.

Sandino hinted at what would follow: "Our army prepares to take the reins of our national power. We will then proceed to the organization of great Nicaraguan workers and peasants' cooperatives, which will exploit our own natural resources for the benefit of the Nicaraguan family in general" (Somoza 1936, 354). He called for a wide election boycott and ordered his troops to sabotage telegraph lines and to attack and burn polling stations, arguing that voters, if allowed, would confirm the enslavement of Nicaragua (357, 356). The electoral battle was almost a repetition of the Constitutionalist War, with Juan Bautista Sacasa as the Liberal candidate and Adolfo Díaz as the Conservative. Betraying more frustration and desperation over his inability to make urban advances and to interrupt the election, Sandino argued that casting a ballot was "high treason" and an evil display of darkness in "moments of so much light" (Sandino 1980, 62).

As November 1932 approached, so did the date of the American withdrawal, filling the population with much anxiety. Both Liberals and Conservatives had reservations as to whether the infant GN (National Guard) was competent to deal with the Sandino menace by itself. The election took place as scheduled on 6 November, and Sacasa was elected president in generally fair proceedings. Sandino's influence may have been felt, however; a large but undetermined number of voters did not register, feeling threatened by the guerrillas. Moreover, 31 percent of registered voters did not vote, up 20 percent from the last election but similar to the 1920 and 1924 elections; it is thus impossible to tell whether the participation ratio was a drop to regular levels or a result of Sandino's campaign of terror. However, of the registered individuals that did not vote, 58 percent were located in the areas controlled by Sandino, which indicates some, if limited, influence (see Vargas 1989a, 111–40 for a more detailed analysis of the election).

The election results were not known for a few days, and during the delay Sandino considered his options. He notified Pedrón on 9 November that he planned to ask Sacasa (should he have won) to appoint EDSN mem-

bers to the key ministries of war, finance, and foreign relations and to secure control of the military garrisons in Managua and Granada (Somoza
1936, 373). The objective, Sandino said in another letter addressed to two of
his lieutenants, was "to obtain enough war *matériel* to enable us to sustain
a conventional (*campal*) war" (377). A coup was brewing. However, the actual demands that Sandino later presented to the president-elect were different and concealed the objectives that he had outlined privately: his
proposal to Sacasa demanded the withdrawal of American troops (already
under way), the formal institutionalization of the EDSN as the national
army of Nicaragua, the government's acceptance of (and backing for)
Sandino's long-planned Latin American conference in Argentina, and finally the right of the people to oust the president (Sandino 1981, 2:252).

The right to insurrection for which Sandino asked seems at first impression close to John Locke's views on the dissolution of government. In
light of Sandino's understanding of popular sovereignty, however, the parallel fails to hold. Locke, in the *Second Treatise on Government,* had argued
that when conflict arises between one group and the ruler, and the existing
laws are silent or inadequate to meet the need, the governed citizenry has
the last word (1988, 427). Sandino, by contrast, approached it from the opposite direction: he claimed that he and his peasant army knew best from
the start, and that they would correct the evils of the élites as well as the
ignorant mistakes of the electorate.

Sacasa ignored the rebel's demands but not his negotiating gesture. In
the meantime, Sandino cleverly continued to explore other options to improve his chances. He wrote to the foreign minister of El Salvador, asking
him not extend formal recognition to the newly elected Sacasa government
but instead to recognize his own "provisional government" in the territories that he controlled (Sandino 1981, 2:260). Such a development would
have boosted Sandino's negotiating position with Sacasa. The rebel also
looked for ways to improve his bargaining position in the field, and as soon
as he learned that the American Marines had withdrawn their airplanes in
mid-November, he alerted his men to move forward and to seize urban
areas (Somoza 1936, 376–78). There is no record that the Salvadoran minister responded, however, and the shrewd attempt to outmaneuver Sacasa
failed; moreover, Sandino's troops were unable to take any urban center.

Sandino conceded that Sacasa wanted peace and took some encouraging steps by naming delegates to represent him at a likely table of negotia-
tions. Furthermore, Sofonías Salvatierra and his Patriotic Group (*Grupo
Patriótico*) (made up of secondary political figures independent of the tradi-

tional parties) approached Sandino after the election, urging him to take advantage of the favorable conditions for peace that existed with Sacasa's advent to the presidency. Sandino justified his peaceful mood to his would-be delegates on Christmas Eve 1932, convincing himself that the people now wanted Sacasa to negotiate with him: "Today we have been informed that the Nicaraguan people in general have awakened in patriotic response to the exploding sound of our liberating weapons and are unanimously concerned that Dr. Sacasa should reach an agreement with our army" (Salvatierra 1980, 108). It was an unconventional interpretation of the recent election results, an interpretation that he could not have offered in 1928 for the simple reason that then it was his enemy Moncada who was the victor.

### Romantic and Tragic

Sacasa was sworn in as president of Nicaragua, and his nephew Major Anastasio Somoza García was appointed director in chief (*jefe director*) of the GN, on 1 January 1933. The very next day, the Marines were gone.

Sandino was in a critical military position. The civil war in Honduras had intensified toward the end of 1932, posing a serious threat to his designs. As he feared, the Conservatives seized power in Honduras and began to patrol the border regularly in order to stop a return flow of insurgents who had fled to Nicaragua. As a consequence, Sandino's supply line from Honduras was reduced to a trickle and his rearguard was now closed for the first time since his guerrilla activities had begun. Eventually, the Honduras military struck a border patrol agreement with their Nicaraguan counterpart that further tightened border security, to Sandino's detriment. Ample room to run and hide is the key to a successful guerrilla warfare strategy, and Sandino's theater of operations was being reduced. He feared that he could now be easily trapped.

Still, Sandino would not admit to anxiety about the changing conditions in the field. He maintained his stance that President Sacasa needed to deal with him in order to legitimize the new government, essentially repeating the argument that he had made to Moncada in 1926: the guerrilla leader was the see of untainted national authority and the new president should seek anointment from him in order to validate the will of the electorate. After all, Sandino claimed, Sacasa had abandoned him in the patriotic struggle, and so the rebel *caudillo* had moral authority over the elected president (Salvatierra 1980, 106).

Sandino demanded that Sacasa detail his plans for his four-year term in office and promise that no secret arrangements had been made with the United States. He abandoned his demand for control of the key ministries and of the armed forces, calling instead for the abrogation of the Bryan-Chamorro Treaty and for support for his Latin American conference. He also resurrected and modified his earlier plan to found his own village, asking for what amounted to the creation of an autonomous department for him and his followers. The new department, on the disputed border between Honduras and Nicaragua, was to be called "Light and Truth" (*Luz y Verdad*) after Trincado's system of ideas (Salvatierra 1980, 135–36). However, when he pushed for the assembly to acknowledge formally his patriotic greatness in rejecting the Espino Negro Accords, his friend Salvatierra dissuaded him (139).

For his part, Sacasa did not want to miss the opportunity to bargain with Sandino and to bring peace to the country. Plagued with internal problems in the GN, he saw an urgent need to reach a settlement. He appointed Sofonías Salvatierra as his minister of agriculture and as head of the government negotiating team, which quickly traveled to meet the rebel leader. Thus, there was much activity at San Rafael during the last two weeks of January 1933, as the presidential commission waited for Sandino to agree to meet with them in order to prepare the way for a future meeting with Sacasa. Sandino could not make up his mind; in spite of all the gestures of good will and all the promises on the part of the government, it still took the insistent intercession of Sandino's pregnant wife to get the guerrilla finally to agree to meet with the commission. She appealed to her husband's fatherly instinct and to his sense of predestination in convincing him to accept the president's good will:

I beg of you in the name of little Augusto that we do our best for all three of us to be happy. . . . You know, my love, that I will be the first victim if we do not accomplish anything. . . . I have confidence in your tenderness that you will not let me perish. . . . Our little boy kisses you. If only you could see how he jumps now. Come and see your little child. Do not think of abandoning him because he will be your happiness. At this moment there appeared a rainbow in the West, a good sign. Come little daddy. Don't make me cry so much. (Somoza 1936, 427)

Eventually, Sandino accepted Sacasa's peace proposal as a good omen and he finally allowed the government commission to come meet him.

On the morning of 1 February, after a long sleepless night, Sandino—

who a month earlier had warned that they "could arrive at peace in Nicaragua as though by incantation" (Sandino 1981, 2:255)—announced to the presidential envoy: "I woke up feeling romantic and tragic. I think we have to make peace in the next five days or I will kill myself [*o me mato*] and the only way is for me to go deal directly with President Sacasa" (Salvatierra 1980, 173).[2] The following night was special to Sandino, who placed tremendous importance on dates and anniversaries: on the previous 1 February, his once close comrade Farabundo Martí had been executed; five years earlier, 2 February was the date upon which Sandino had returned to the hills after his trip to the coast, where he had initially collided with Moncada. Moncada was out of office and, from Sandino's perspective, the circle was completed. Ironically, 1 February was also Major Somoza García's birthday.

Salvatierra seized the opportunity; he wasted no time in arranging for safe conduct and air transport for Sandino to travel to Managua that same day. At noon, Sandino made an emotional landing in the capital, where he was met and driven by Somoza García to the Presidential Palace. With the same awkward tension between indecisiveness and rashness with which Sandino had rebelled and rode into the mountains in 1927, he had now come to make peace. At day's end, only a few minutes before midnight on 2 February 1933, a peace agreement was signed.

## "A Society of Mutual Help and Universal Fraternity"

### *Saving Face*

The peace agreement acknowledged the noble and patriotic crusade of General Sandino, who formally accepted the authority of the Sacasa government and pledged a gradual surrender of his weapons. The second clause in the agreement called upon the signatories "to use all adequate rational and judicial means to strive for the complete political and economic sovereignty of Nicaragua," a clause that later proved to be fatal given Sandino's radical, conspiratorial nationalism and his esoteric understanding of rationality. Sandino's men were granted amnesty for all acts committed since

---

2. Macaulay's translation of this passage reads "to make peace in the next five days or I'm dead" (1985, 245; see also Salvatierra 1980, 179–80). However, the presence of the reflexive pronoun *me* reveals Sandino's dramatic allegation that he would kill himself, just as he had earlier promised if his cousin María Mercedes rejected him.

May 1927, and they were allowed to settle in the Coco River basin, where they would establish an "agricultural cooperative." Sandino was allowed to keep a force of one hundred "auxiliaries," in principle under presidential command but headed by Sandino's trusted follower and friend, EDSN general Francisco Estrada; this auxiliary force would be independent of the GN and its status would be reviewed in one year. The rest of the peasant force would give up its arms by 23 February of that year under the supervision of Salvatierra, who had been designated presidential delegate to the northern departments to make Sandino feel more at ease (Sandino 1981, 2:278–80).

The guerrilla commander pressed for many additional demands. One was an Orwellian request that all national records referring to the guerrilla *caudillo* as a "bandit" be purged or destroyed; not unsurprisingly, this request was denied. Overall, however, in order to obtain the peace, the Nicaraguan authorities had carefully avoided injuring Sandino's pride and had accepted an agreement that allowed the rebel to save face and to appear glorious. Sandino turned in his old, run-down weaponry at the indicated time and place, and he was allowed to keep for his auxiliary guard the few good weapons that he presented. Although almost everyone suspected that Sandino had hidden the rest of his weapons in the mountains, the compromise was pushed through. Such compromise, however, was meaningful primarily to the politicians; warriors are lovers of victory. This particular peace was not the preferred solution of the director of the GN, and as time would reveal, neither was it Sandino's.

Sandino's apparently sudden mood to be peaceful and politically accommodating drew different reactions from different quarters at home and abroad. Some immediately interpreted it as a sign of heroic greatness (Vasconcelos 1990); at the other extreme, the Mexican Communist Party renewed their accusations of treason.

Back in the mountains, although the accords insisted that the area would remain under the official jurisdiction of the Jinotega department, subsequent decrees virtually granted Sandino his own dominion in a substantial portion of territory—36,000 square kilometers, or one-quarter of the country. In his new domain, Sandino moved to uphold his end of the treaty by setting up an agricultural and industrial cooperative for his men in the prescribed territory. The organization and initial work for the cooperative began as a camp in the remote area of Güigüilí, near the source of the Coco River.

Popular mythology and the ideology of some latter-day Sandinistas have romanticized the period following the peace accords, during which

Sandino retreated to the hills after supposedly deposing his weapons. According to this view, once the U.S. Marines left Nicaragua, Sandino excluded himself from political activity as he withdrew from the battlefield; Sandino is thus interpreted like a Roman dictator who, after having done his patriotic duty to resolve the national crisis of foreign occupation, withdraws to pursue a bucolic project with his men but is then betrayed and murdered. However, the story is much more complex; as one historian has recently pointed out, "the political interpretation of the last year [of Sandino's life] is an open problem" (Wünderich 1995, 332). Indeed, the evidence suggests a different story: instead of retiring, Sandino pursued similar goals by different means.

*The Threefold Redemption*

The new cooperative was established to pursue three distinct but related neocolonial objectives: economic, political, and spiritual. At the economic level, the cooperative was organized on two fronts, one agricultural and one industrial. In turn, the agricultural front had two aims: self-sufficiency in the production of corn, beans, vegetables, and common staples for local consumption, and the cultivation of cash crops such as bananas and tobacco destined for commercial export. The industrial front sought the exploitation and transformation of gold and timber. The work began in earnest; Sandino was full of enthusiasm and initially spent much of his time drafting feasibility reports for the government and establishing trade contacts with merchants downriver on the Atlantic coast, through whom he expected to distribute a large share of the production. He wrote to J. A. Fagot, a trader in Cabo Gracias a Dios, asking him if he had any ideas for business ventures and proposing in turn to sell him for cash on delivery gold, rubber, and cotton (Dospital 1996, 170). The cooperative became the central preoccupation of his life: "After the expulsion of the Marines, this cooperative is the most important thing there is" (Román 1979, 102).

His designs for the region were grandiose. Sandino expected to open the Coco River to commercial navigation for several hundred kilometers, from Güigüilí to the Caribbean, and to transform Güigüilí into a vital and modern inland port that would rescue the region from its primitive condition. He expected the government to finance all of his projects and to provide capital for industrial and agricultural equipment, or at least to serve as his guarantor in obtaining loans from local bankers. However, neither the financing nor the loan guarantees materialized, for Sandino failed to show that he had secure markets for the agricultural products, timber, and gold that he wished to export.

Sandino's immediate practical concern was to provide employment for his men and to secure a steady flow of funds from the state in a variety of ways. The one hundred auxiliaries would receive army salaries; a congressional order voted 120,000 *córdobas* (one *córdoba* was then equivalent to one American dollar) for the execution of the peace accords and for a series of public works destined to provide employment in the region; in fulfillment of Sacasa's campaign promises to provide "peace, work, and bread," 25,000 *córdobas* were allocated by Presidential Decree 296 for the production of wheat and flour for the north; and finally, legislation granted de facto municipal status to the cooperative, giving it a five-member local council, whose salaries were paid by the national treasurer. Sandino had ensured that his people were well looked after.

To the credit of Sandino and his men, the cooperative project advanced and became somewhat prosperous. By January 1934, the Güigüilí camp had gained the appearance of a little town, with streets lined by houses; there were plans for a clinic, a school, a landing strip, and five additional camps in the surrounding area. On 12 January, Güigüilí was granted formal municipal status.

The desired economic development was tied to a second set of objectives that were political in nature. Sandino wished to rid Nicaragua of American businesses as well as the American Marines, and he worked to push U.S. companies out of the area and to assert Indo-American sovereignty. Sandino planned to invite a Mexican company to set up shop in the region to displace the United Fruit Company and "also to push out the Yankee companies from the mines" (Arrieta 1971, 22). This approach was consistent with Sandino's search for "absolute political and economic sovereignty." In Sandino's mind, having sovereignty meant freedom from American influence, but given his views on race, he saw no contradiction in diminishing Nicaraguan sovereignty in favor of a Latin American state. Indeed, he believed that the cooperative project was imperative because he had persuaded himself that the United States "was making preparations to colonize Central America" (Sandino 1981, 2:179).

Sandino wanted more than economic renewal and political strength, however; he also dreamed that the region would become a vibrant "center of cultural life" (Dospital 1992). In its pursuit of this third set of objectives, the project was closely connected with the implementation of the utopian ideals of the EMECU. In July 1933, Sandino declared himself "dedicated to the foundation of a society of mutual help and universal fraternity" (Sandino 1980, 67). He adopted the EMECU's motto Ever Further Beyond as the cooperative's own motto, finally replacing his earlier Free Motherland or Death (*Patria Libre o Morir*).[3] Alongside the red and black banner of the EDSN, the town flew the flag of Trincado's Hispano-American Oceanic Union (the UHAO); the Nicaraguan flag was not present. Thus, the so-called Coco Project was an attempt to create a prototype commune according to many of the EMECU principles that Sandino had learned from Trincado's followers and that he hoped he would later extend to the whole world: "If I succeed in making even this first unit run, the future will take care of the rest," Sandino wrote to his master (Román 1979, 103). Perhaps in return, Sandino was named vice president of the UHAO (Hodges 1992, 5).

Even before the peace accords had been signed, Sandino had requested that a senior member of the EMECU be sent from Mexico to assist him. He should be, Sandino wrote, "a brother resigned to self-sacrifice and well versed in the works of spiritism in order to facilitate our spiritist communications" (Somoza 1936, 240). Again, in October 1932, he requested help from Jaime Schlittler of the EMECU in Mexico City. His insistence on this point demonstrates the seriousness that he attached to it. Sandino's personal choice was his friend Francisco Vera from the Yucatán *Cátedra*, but Vera politely turned down the offer, citing personal reasons (see Vera 1932; Schlittler 1932).

The delivery of material progress to the region required leveling forests in order to construct new cities, but these new cities would be unlike any existing ones. Sandino described the idyllic project to visiting sympathizers.

> We will all be brothers. . . . We are going to build cities and schools. We will bring carpenters, mechanics, leather artisans and tailors from the Pacific region so that we have everything. One thing though, there will be no vagrant drunkards, exploiters or selfish people. Everything will be arranged in cooperatives. There is abundance of gold, and we will buy abroad all we

3. Bendaña points out that the formula Ever Further Beyond also belonged to Bakunin (though he gives no reference), suggesting that there was a connection between Sandino and the Russian anarchist (1994, 133). If one follows Hodges's arguments, one might agree that Sandino was intellectually indebted to European anarchists—but the connection was through Trincado, who adopted the expression as his school's motto. There is no evidence that Sandino read Bakunin.

need with it. It is ridiculous that in Nicaragua we have copper and nickel coins. They ought to be made of gold because we have it in such great quantities. Now, the peasants have nothing, but they will have everything. (Arrieta 1971, 21)

It was Sandino's wish to create a perfect social arrangement in which everyone would be happy and would lack nothing material. There would be abundant employment and riches for everyone. He boasted to city-dwellers: "I hear talk of people unemployed here [in Managua] and I just laugh when over there [in the hills] there are so many riches at one's reach; one ought to go to those mountains and get it" (Salvatierra 1980, 238).

Individual property was at the root of fratricidal wars, Sandino declared to *La Prensa* on 7 July 1933. The cooperative was therefore a model for the ideal form of land tenure, and he favored "state owned land" (Belausteguigoitia 1985, 185). This statement may sound like bolshevism to someone unfamiliar with the context, but in Sandino's understanding it was not; in order to make the distinction, he proclaimed himself a "rationalist communist." The expression was an adaptation from the precepts of Trincado, who despised Soviet communists because their radical materialism denied man's spiritual dimension. For Sandino, "rational" meant holy and enlightened, implying that there was a spiritual connection between his political ideas and supreme reason. Even so, the idea of state ownership constituted a deviation from Trincado, who thought that ownership in any form was evil because everything belonged to everyone.

In order to achieve his objectives, Sandino understood the need to deal with the situation of the aboriginal inhabitants of the region. Claiming that the Indians had been "abandoned and exploited" first by the feudo-colonial system and then by the capitalists, he said that he felt responsible for their fate: "If I do not assume their incorporation into national life, who will?" (Román 1979, 100). Sandino acknowledged that the Indians were intelligent and was fascinated by the fact that many spoke English. At the same time, he also pitied "the poor Indians" for the way that they chose to live, and he concluded that they needed his enlightenment and his guiding hand to be successfully integrated into civilized society: "This is where I want to come in with civilization to lift them up and to make true men out of them" (Belausteguigoitia 1985, 193; see also Román 1979, 98). Abraham Rivera, who knew the Indian ways well and spoke several of their dialects, advised him against this approach, but Sandino would not pay heed.

Essentially, Sandino wanted to undertake the colonization and integration of the natives of the Coco basin, an assimilationist attitude that seems inconsistent with the pro-Indian rhetoric of the 10 July 1927 manifesto. Whereas Sandino had earlier claimed authority from his mystical link with the Indian race, he now adopted the patronizing attitude of a colonialist who saw them as inferior and as less than true men. He seemed driven to bring the European way to them whether they liked it or not. Thus, there was little difference between Sandino's position toward the natives and that of the European religious proselytizers who had arrived 400 years earlier. The liberation and enlightenment of the Indians became an added but central aspect of his new crusade, related in all of its facets to his broader economic, political, and spiritual plans; the rebel leader saw the civilizing of the Indians as connected to the overall picture of Nicaragua's development, stating that "only with the civilization [of the region] could Nicaragua become a country of dignity and respect." He referred to his development project as "the plan for the redemption of this zone" (Román 1979, 99). "What the Indians need is education and culture to know themselves, to respect and love one another," Sandino declared (Belausteguigoitia 1985, 172), the notion of "knowledge of self" evoking Trincado's trinity of body, soul, and spirit. If the Indians attained knowledge of self, as Trincado preached it, they could then be delivered and redeemed.

Sandino's expressed desire for "religious control" of his country was animated by a theocratic vision of a universal commune, which he wished to begin establishing through the Coco Project in Nicaragua. Since mid-1931, he had been rereading Trincado's Los cinco amores with the intention of "forming [the] first government of the Universal Commune." Sandino expressed his regret at not knowing of Trincado's plan for the UHAO before elaborating his own "Plan for the Realization of Bolívar's Supreme Dream," for the two visions were connected in his mind (Somoza 1936, 239). Although he had elaborated his own plan in the middle of the rebellion, just prior to travelling to Mexico, the plan was still alive; he had a new approach but had not abandoned his grand ideals. "The great dream of Bolívar's is still in sight," he said, "the great ideals, all ideas, have their phases from conception through perfection until their realization" (Belausteguigoitia 1985, 197). With the Coco Project, in his view, Bolívar's dream had reached the realization phase.

The Coco cooperative was therefore the foundation of the universal commune, which included plans to feed the peasants, bring economic development to the region, expel the foreign companies, and redeem the Indians out of their presumed subhuman culture. Future cooperatives would lead to continental federation and then expand to encompass the world: "We do not think that the whole solution is in political nationalism. Above the nation, [there] is the federation, continental first and then broader until the totality is attained," Sandino had declared, outlining the steps that the greater plan needed to undergo before completion (Belausteguigoitia 1985, 199). This vision has consistently eluded the attention of the many who claim that Sandino's struggle was purely nationalist. In fact, Sandino hoped that his project would lead to world government. *La Nueva Prensa* cited Sandino on 26 February 1933: "Borders will have to disappear and the Americas will bring to reality the dream of the great liberator. But my ideal does not end there. How great and sublime it would be that once this is realized, Europe and the other continents would form a great confederation, the great human fraternity." In essence, Sandino was attempting to embody the five circles of *Los cinco amores:* family, friends, region, nation, and universe. The EDSN, the primordial core and see of spiritual renewal, constituted the inner circle of the family. The cooperative, which grouped the biological families of EDSN fighters, constituted the second circle of communal friendship; this in turn would extend first to the region of the Segovias (the third circle) and then to the nation as a whole (the fourth circle). From the nation (which for Sandino was multifaceted, itself consisted of three levels: Nicaragua, Central America, and the Indo-Hispanic race), it would expand outward until it reached the final worldwide or universal circle.

The cooperative was also to become a haven for revolutionaries from all corners of the world, emulating the policy adopted by Mexico following its own revolution. Sandino was clear on this point: the "proletariat from all of Central America and from anywhere in the world should arrive to this region" (Sandino 1981, 2:326). The invitation even transcended racial distinctions, for it was extended to foreigners, (which for Sandino meant non-Indo-Hispanic [Román 1979, 129]), so long as they did not come to exploit the locals. Once again, implied in Sandino's view is the understanding that race determined economic disposition, class belonging, and political allegiance. The cooperative was thus very much a part of the political eschatology of redemption for the chosen ones, the oppressed.

Sandino's commitment to the cooperative was therefore irrevocably tied to his religious and political outlook. He was so convinced of the righteousness of his new crusade that he believed that he would be killed because of it. He had become more and more fatalistic, a disposition that became more acute as the northern project advanced and seemed to gain success. Just after the peace accords, Sandino confessed to José Román how he felt: "I will not come out of here. I know that they will kill me because of these ideas, not the Marines but the Nicaraguans. I know it and it does not matter to me because that is my destiny, the same destiny that brought me here. But at least I will have planted the seed that will one day give fruit" (Román 1979, 59).

## Collision Course

### Conspiratorial Scenarios

Sandino was aware of the conditions that had led him to make peace. He admitted to Alemán Bolaños that he had been "forced by circumstances" to take a new course of action and that once the Marines had gone "the enthusiasm of people cooled off even though the country was still subject to intervention by less visible political and economic means." He also admitted that he and his troops were physically spent and economically exhausted and that they lacked the necessary equipment to continue the fight. They could not run to Honduras nor obtain help from El Salvador (Alemán 1951, 160–61). It was an unusually detached and realistic assessment of his own position, but it was not destined for public consumption.

In addition to his objective strategic analysis, the guerrilla leader concurrently announced to Lidia Barahona just a few weeks after surrendering his weapons that the Marines' withdrawal only represented an American tactical retreat under the pressures of the international community and of his army. Sandino's own strategy of retreat thus emulated the alleged American one. He concocted a scenario to show that the Marines were coming back within months; "The peace was signed [by us] in order to prevent the return of armed intervention," but that return was already at work behind the scenes (Somoza 1936, 481). In a separate letter to Barahona's husband Humberto two months later, Sandino alleged that the U.S. State Department had approached him through companies in the Atlantic region of Nicaragua before the 1932 election to offer him money and war *matériel* so that he might continue his war against whatever government took office in Managua after the Marine evacuation. At the same time, he claimed that the United States was willing to grant a loan of $2 million to Nicaragua's government to fight against him. Sandino concluded from these alleged offers that the United States coveted the continuation of the war as an opportunity to return within a year under the pretext of pacifying the nation (486). The guerrilla commander confided to Lidia Barahona: "That is the secret for which I do not leave the northern region, so that I can be ready also for the chance to restore our political and economic independence." He had convinced himself that the Marines had imminent plans to return and it was thus imperative that he stopped the enemy's new designs in order to prevent another fratricidal war (481). In essence, Sandino had an interest in showing to the Nicaraguan left that he still was struggling, albeit quietly, to maintain the motherland's liberty. It was this version of events that he came to believe.

Because Sandino believed that the Americans had shifted their plan of conquest of Nicaragua and Latin America to a political arena, behind the scenes, he planned to meet their challenge on that level while also remaining vigilant on the battlefield. He was clear that the best means to achieve that goal would be to take over the Nicaraguan government, and he therefore sought to establish a new force in the country's political arena. At the same time, he was somewhat careful not to make things too difficult for Sacasa's presidency. In May 1933, Sandino traveled to Managua for a meeting that he described to the press as "a response to the aspirations of several groups wishing to organize themselves in a new political party called *Autonomista.*" The meeting was an attempt at establishing an umbrella organization for all of the left-wing groups in Nicaragua. When the meeting was banned by presidential order, Sandino accused the traditional parties of fearing the development of his project, but he was careful to declare his support for the Sacasa regime at the same time (Somoza 1936, 496–97).

Nonetheless, the *Autonomista* project continued, and bits of its platform soon were revealed. It was familiar rhetoric: the United States was trying to dominate the country through political and economic strings attached to the local bourgeoisie; the new party's goal, as its name suggested, was to secure and uphold national autonomy. The first step in their program was the establishment of a new constitution, Sandino arguing that the current one was tainted because it had been crafted under foreign intervention. For the same reason, the party also proposed to "eliminate the Liberal and Conservative parties" (Arrieta 1971, 21). In Sandino's assessment, both of the traditional parties lacked the moral and political purity to elaborate a new constitution because of their collaboration with the occupying American forces; moreover, the country would remain under foreign influence "for as long as the government belonged to a particular [traditional] party" (Sandino 1981, 2:320). "Only the nascent *Partido Autonomista,*"

Sandino claimed, "will be able to give Nicaraguans a clean constitution" (Somoza 1936, 506). The new party, Sandino hoped, would be the political means to "build a new Nicaragua, and get rid of all the putrefaction," with the help of the workers and peasants (Arrieta 1971, 14, 18).

Whereas Sandino previously argued that the EDSN was the savior of the country, the new *Autonomista* party now occupied that role. In reality, he had traded one institution for another for the sake of public consumption, but his disposition remained unchanged. The new party was a collective endeavor and also was linked to the comprehensive work of the cooperative. Francisco Estrada, chief of the auxiliary forces and Sandino's right-hand man, was under the impression that "the organization of the new party . . . [would] end all past sectarian attitudes and fuse into itself all the entities that exist[ed] in the country." According to Estrada, Sandino wanted to create a one-party state and to control the totality of the new Nicaragua (Somoza 1936, 498).

The new party project continued until Sandino decided to drop it at the beginning of October 1933. Never one to commit himself to a single approach, he had concurrently backed another political venture called the National Unification of Nicaragua (*Unificación Nacional de Nicaragua*). In October, he offered two hundred *córdobas* to radical labor chieftain Norberto Salinas Aguilar to rent a house in Managua for the movement's headquarters, hoping to attract and recruit workers and students. The project, however, never got off the ground; Sandino and the Nicaraguan left were far too unstable to coalesce.

Sandino had an admirable military instinct, but he possessed few political skills. He was almost incapable of politics; as Wünderich (1995, 273) observed, "As soon as he would enter into politics, he would not do much more than to formulate general principles." The leadership and decision-making abilities that he displayed on the battlefield were absent in the civic arena, and when removed from the midst of the peasants, he became unimpressive, changeable, frivolous, irresolute, and uncharismatic. One Peruvian journalist who interviewed him in Mexico in 1930 had this to say:

> His face is dry, hard. . . . His eyes say nothing; one might say that they had never seen anything. He does not know how to smile although he laughs frequently . . . [O]ne might say that his laugh does not laugh . . . it is very uncomfortable . . . he is just insipid. Although he doesn't know how to talk, he is expressive, vehement; he says everything he feels, sometimes

that which he does not feel. . . . He is the Creole [*mestizo*] type, one hundred percent, a talker—in general, a bit swaggering. (Macaulay 1985, 159)

Aware of his deficient political skills, Sandino chose to rely for counsel on aspiring labor leaders, some of whom were more radical than Sandino himself. One such adviser was Norberto Salinas Aguilar, who pushed him incessantly to return to armed conflict; Ibarra (1973) identifies Zepeda, Salinas Aguilar, and Escolástico Lara as the people that pushed Sandino to war with the National Guard. In a 3 June 1933 letter to Sandino, Escolástico Lara (who was named interim leader of the EDSN when Sandino was absent) reported to the guerrilla chief about a secret meeting with Vicente Lombardo Toledano, Mexico's minister of education and a caustic, radical, Marxist-Leninist labor leader. During the meeting, Lara writes, they discussed Lombardo's willingness to contribute a shipload of weapons for Sandino to overthrow the government (Somoza 1936, 502). Sandino prudently avoided that option, however, because in his estimation it would have played right into the American trap. Sandino still wished to overthrow the newly elected government and to place his own man at the helm of the country—such ambitions rarely dissipate overnight—but he had adopted a calculating, piecemeal approach to achieve his goals.

Still, the rebel was not entirely at ease with this new approach and seemed a little defensive about his new tactics. As he wrote to Alemán, "there was no right to demand [from me] the [complete] independence of Nicaragua overnight" (Sandino 1981, 2:331). Similarly, he felt the need to assert to Humberto Barahona: "The program is not dead; it is still standing" (Somoza 1936, 486). The willingness to play a waiting game showed once again Sandino's ability to adapt to new circumstances while holding fast to his ultimate goals: "We need to inspire confidence in order to be in the position to proclaim the presidential candidate of our choice," he wrote to his closest men (490). He still dreamed of becoming, as he wrote to Lara and Salinas Aguilar, "the decisive factor in the nation's destiny at the first opportunity that present[ed] itself" (536).

During this period, Sandino claimed to have uncovered another, more bizarre American conspiracy. In the early days of his rebellion, Sandino had argued for the existence of an American conspiracy to keep the Central American republics from uniting so that they could be easier prey to foreign exploitation. Now, however, he flipped the argument around: in fact, the United States was fostering the union of all of the Central American countries in order to make its colonization project more expedient. The operation was orchestrated by Wall Street and had been started by the pro-American dictatorships in Guatemala, El Salvador, and Honduras; geography dictated that Nicaragua was next. Fortunately, according to Sandino, there already was opposition to the deceiving American designs in the form of a "unionist tendency" driven by the people (Sandino 1981, 2:326). Harnessed by his leadership, that popular tendency would be successful in resisting the latest American penetration attempt. In addition to helping foster an increased sense of unity within Nicaragua, the claim was also likely an attempt to smear the administrations in those countries that had turned their backs on Sandino.

The rebel leader believed that the United States maintained control of Nicaragua through the National Guard; in his view, the GN was in the military field what the traditional parties were in the political, the imperial proconsul. He identified the GN as his principal enemy: "The elements of our country's military, who operated in alliance with the invaders, continue to be our enemies" (Somoza 1936, 481). Indeed, insofar as Sandino's immediate objective was to capture power in Nicaragua, the GN was his principal and most formidable opponent: in the words of Ramírez, "According to the conjunctural conditions of his struggle, Sandino stops his armed resistance but his project to seize power is still in vigor . . . having as permanent objective the elimination of historical parallels and the elimination of the National Guard" (Sandino 1981, 2:439). The third-party agenda became futile as it became clear that the greatest and most threatening force opposing him came not from the traditional parties but rather from Somoza García and the GN.

Overall, then, ample evidence exists to contradict the conventional, romantic understanding that after the elections Sandino withdrew to the hills and retired from military activity and from political life in order to pursue a bucolic project with his men. In fact, the cooperative project was both a front and a means to an end. It was a front in that it allowed Sandino to secure some legitimacy and some funds while he plotted to betray his new benefactor, President Sacasa. Mixing Marxist-Leninist jargon into Sandino's goals, the latter-day Sandinista Sergio Ramírez acknowledges his hero's cunning strategy to seize power: "We cannot interpret his way of focusing his agrarian demands as isolated from the context of the struggle because in the ultimate instance, what persists in Sandino is the fundamental project of seizing power" (Sandino 1981, 2:439). At the same time, the cooperative project was a means to an end in that Sandino intended his cooperative to be a prototype to be emulated by the world—indeed, a harbinger of that world's millennial end. Similarly, Dospital (1996, 68) has observed that Sandino's apparent retreat to the hills was really a strategic move designed to "buy time" and "to gather the strength that will allow him to launch his fight at another time." Sandino's scheme to wait for the propitious conditions to launch his takeover is what Paige has called "Sandino's secret" (1997, 177).

*Crisis and Irresolution*

Conspiracies aside, Sandino had legitimate reasons to dislike and to mistrust the National Guard. Since the peace accord, the GN had attacked and killed Sandino's men whenever possible; between April and October 1933, 104 confrontations apparently occurred between the two forces (Vargas 1989b). A GN report analyzed the Sandino situation as follows: "We have not stopped thinking that the common enemy of the Republic and of the National Guard is General Sandino, whether this is in the military, the political or the economic order" (Dospital 1996, 177). Sandino protested to President Sacasa and complained about the attacks to anyone who would listen, but nothing was resolved. Sandino also accused the GN of being an unconstitutional body. Francisco Estrada, who shared this opinion, alerted the auxiliary troops in September 1933 that they might have to return to the struggle (Somoza 1936, 537–38).

Moreover, Sandino was setting himself up on a collision course with the ambitious GN director, Major Somoza García—who, to complicate matters, also had his eyes on the presidency. Sandino looked upon Somoza García with his usual bravado: "General [sic] Somoza is thinking of destroying me. And what is General Somoza worth? He is worth the job that he has. Otherwise no one would give him a second look. I am a real *caudillo*. I might be disarmed but with one signal I would have people by me right away because they do believe in me. But I do not want [more] war" (Salvatierra 1980, 234). It was becoming apparent that there were two armed groups in Nicaragua, the leaders of which were competing for the presidential chair, with President Sacasa (who feared Somoza García more than he did Sandino) caught in the middle. Aware of the president's dilemma, Sandino continued to profess his loyalty to him while in fact remaining independent.

At the beginning of June, Sandino was dealt a fateful personal blow: his wife Blanca died while giving birth to a healthy baby daughter, Blanca Segovia. At the death of his wife, Sandino took his wife's young cousin Angelita to be his consort. However, Sandino's own health was weakening as well, as a result of the recurring bouts of malaria that he had contracted during his years in the mountains.

Another unexpected event occurred on 1 August 1933 when an enormous fire consumed the army weapons depot in Managua, not far from Somoza García's offices. Panic ensued; Sacasa declared a state of emergency, raised a militia of seven hundred men, and immediately informed Sandino. Convinced that the incident was a GN conspiracy to take over the presidency, the rebel chieftain mobilized six hundred armed men, immediately placing them at Sacasa's disposal (Somoza 1936, 520–21). Of course, the peace agreement had allotted weapons for only one hundred auxiliaries, and so Sandino was forced to explain how the additional five hundred had come to be armed as well; despite his claim that the extra guns came from revolutionaries in Honduras, Sandino's trick of hidden weaponry was exposed. The secret was out. Somoza García had long been suspicious of the president's treatment of Sandino, and he was now certain that the rebel had made a fool of the GN by not surrendering all his weapons.

Ibarra (1973, 200–205) claims that the fire was a plot by Sacasa to tame Somoza, but there is no corroborating evidence for this view. Although the full story of the blaze may never be told, it was undeniably—like the Reichstag fire—a catalyst in an already volatile political situation. If we believe Ibarra, mistrust reigned among the main three players. Sandino reacted to the crisis outlandishly, proclaiming on 16 August the Union of Central America and the founding of a new Autonomist Army of Central America (*Ejército Autonomista de Centroamerica*) two days later. His early fantasies of triumphing as if "by incantation" had resurfaced. He traveled to Managua to talk to GN director Somoza García in an attempt to reduce tensions. They gave each other mutual assurances of respect.

The proclamation of Central American union called on all the region's governments to adhere to the Autonomist Army and to become states in the new federation. Sandino allocated ministerial portfolios to each country and outlined electoral rules to choose a president in the future. He claimed that the United States was increasingly infiltrating the domestic and external politics of the five small countries and that the time had come to stop this unwanted influence.[4] His spiritist system of ideas was his cen-

---

4. To Sandino's mind, Central America consisted of the five republics that had been federated in the nineteenth century: Guatemala, El Salvador, Honduras, Nicaragua, and Costa Rica. Neither Panama nor Belize figured in his scheme.

tral explanatory device: "The spiritual vibration of the Indo-Hispanic race is turning toward the Central American Autonomist Army" to save its racial dignity, he wrote in his "Supreme Proclamation of Central American Union by the Autonomist Army of Central America" (Sandino 1981, 2:349). The newly formed army's guidelines acknowledged Sandino as the "Supreme Commander" and "Supreme Moral Authority of Central America," and Sandino refused to recognize the authority of any Central American government that did not submit to him (Somoza 1936, 527–30).

The situation heated up a few degrees at the approach of 17 February 1934, the reviewing date for the status of Sandino's auxiliaries. Salinas Aguilar pressed Sandino not to give up his arms and incited him to resume the armed struggle as the only available alternative. He even proposed a coup d'état: with 30,000 *córdobas,* he said, they could bribe an officer at the weapons arsenal in León, which would enable them to take the city to launch a full-scale attack from there (Somoza 1936, 552–56).

Sandino was ambivalent at a time when firmness and decisiveness were greatly required of him; he wished neither to fight nor to give up his weapons, but he continued to listen to his bellicose advisors. He again wrote to Sacasa questioning the legitimacy of the National Guard and hinting that he would not give up his weapons when the time came. Angered at the intimation, Sacasa summoned him to Managua, where Sandino arrived on 16 February 1934. In an interview published in *La Prensa* on 17 February, Sandino reiterated his intention not to surrender his weapons; he asserted that according to the letter of the peace agreement he was only bound to do so before a properly "constituted authority," which in his view the GN was not (for more on this view see also Somoza 1936, 495–96). The same day, Somoza García declared to *La Nueva Prensa* that he and his officers were finding it impossible to continue in a situation where there existed a state within a state. Personal ambition aside, Somoza García had accurately assessed Sandino's role within the present situation.

The dramatic clash of the two military chieftains continued to unfold in the pages of the national press, which itself was interested in infusing as much sensation into the situation as it could. On the next day, Sandino made his intentions apparent and indulged his self-importance by digging in his heels when a journalist brought up Somoza García's objections. Asked if he did not think that the GN's duty was to ensure that there would not exist two states within one, he answered: "The fact is that there are not two, but three states. [There is] the power of the president of the Republic, that of the National Guard and my own. The Guard does not obey the president, we do not obey the Guard because it is not within the law" (*La Prensa*, 18 February 1934). Missing or ignoring the implicit warning in the journalist's question, Sandino chose instead to enflame the situation; with his statement, Sandino placed himself at serious risk in Managua, facing an increasingly impatient but now openly challenged Somoza García. To be sure, Sandino tried to soften the tone of his remarks by pointing out that if he and the president did not reach an agreement, he would leave the country rather than start another fratricidal conflict. The cautious remarks may have come too late, however, as they were not afforded the same weight in the press reports that followed.

Sandino remained in Managua to continue talks with the president, and he and Sacasa exchanged letters in the subsequent days. Sandino wrote to the president asking for guarantees for his men in the cooperative and for "correction to the structure and procedures of the National Guard" (Salvatierra 1980, 241). From Sacasa's response, dated two days later (20 February), we learn that the president was open and conciliatory; he was willing to form a partnership with Sandino in the opening of a gold mine in the Segovias, and he also also agreed "to improve the operations of the National Guard," thus making bona fide concessions to the rebel that were clearly detrimental to Somoza García and his aspirations. President Sacasa would seek to introduce a reform bill that would drastically reduce the GN's size within the next six months. Such a reduction of the GN required the parallel disarmament of Sandino's men; however, the language of the peace agreements guaranteed that Sandino could keep his auxiliaries, who had been officially placed under "presidential authority" and thus were considered to be under and not outside government control. In a small concession to the GN, the president vowed to send to the northern region a "Presidential Delegate . . . with the special charge of collecting all weapons found outside the control of the government, as well as attending to the protection of the men" that had fought under Sandino's command (Salvatierra 1980, 243). However, given the vague language of the proposal and Sandino's proven ability and willingness to hide his weapons, this concession was virtually meaningless. (Both letters were published in the local newspapers on 21 February 1934.) It was later learned that the president intended to appoint retired general Horacio Portocarrero, an EDSN man and a coconspirator with Sandino against the Moncada administration, as the presidential delegate to the northern departments. At the end of the day, Somoza García's GN would have diminished powers in the country and less control in the north as a result of the changes.

On the evening of 21 February, Sandino met with Sacasa in a friendly atmosphere at the presidential residence where they celebrated the newly achieved agreement, hailing it as another advancement toward peace in the country. As Sandino and his entourage made their way out of the presidential grounds, Somoza's men picked them up. Sandino was led away and executed alongside Pablo Umanzor and Francisco Estrada that same night. The GN also surrounded and attacked Salvatierra's residence, where some of Sandino's men, including his brother Sócrates, were lodged; all the EDSN men were killed, except for one that escaped. Similarly, the next day, the GN descended upon Güigüilí, razing the cooperative and killing most of its members. The Sandino question was brought to an end, with the exception of a few fighters in the hills; Pedrón himself was finally captured and killed in 1936, the same year that Anastasio Somoza García became the ruler of Nicaragua. Tears flowed in some quarters, while in others there was jubilant celebration. The first *sandinista* rebellion in Nicaragua, with the all-too-familiar contest for power of one armed group against another, was over.

# 6

# Sandino's Millenarianism

> Here is the core of the religious problem: Help! help! No prophet
> can claim to bring a final message unless he says things that will
> have a sound of reality in the ears of the victims. . . . But deliver-
> ance must come in as strong a form as the complaint, if it is to
> take effect; and that seems a reason why the coarser religions,
> revivalistic, orgiastic, with blood and miracles and supernatural
> operations, may possibly never be displaced. Some constitutions
> need them too much.
>
> —William James, *The Varieties of Religious Experience*

## Patterns of Millenarianism

**PORTIONS OF THE SANDINO MYTH** coincide with the man's
own self-perception: Sandino was a warring prophet-messiah. Thus, we
may further our understanding of his life and actions by comparing him
with other warring prophets-messiahs and with other revolutionary religious leaders who have emerged across ages and cultures in similar conditions. This requires situating Sandino in the field of millenarian beliefs.
Millenarian religions are no ordinary religions; they operate at the convergence of religion and politics. They are driven by a dream of deliverance
from suffering and oppression by divine powers. To study them is to study
why men and women seek salvation and perfection in this world (Lee
1988, 5).

The term *millenarian* is derived from the word *millennium*, itself
formed from the Latin words *mille* (a thousand) and *annus* (year)—literally,
a period of a thousand years. *Millenarianism* refers to a tradition that
emerged from Jewish apocalyptic writings and made its way to Christianity
through the Apocalypse of St. John. As John envisions in Revelation 20,
Christ will return to defeat and imprison the devil and to establish the

Kingdom of God over which He will rule for one thousand years; Christian martyrs will be raised from the dead and made royal priests, and at the end of the millennium the devil will be freed only to be finally destroyed at the hands of the Messiah. This victory will lead to the resurrection of the dead, the Last Judgment, and the redemption of God's people.

Although the term *millenarian* traditionally has been used to designate specifically religious movements, millenarian ideas have implications broader than those conventionally associated with religions, and secular ideologies of revolutionary movements may also be termed millenarian (Barkun 1986). Indeed, millenarian characteristics are found in many contemporary social and political movements; as the concept of the millennium has come to denote an expected age of perfection and happiness on earth, movements of any sort that pursue this type of salvation may be classified as millenarian.

As an initial example of the political expression of millenarianism—highlighting the issue of violence that is so prominent in understanding Sandino—let us briefly consider some of the many revolutionary, communist, egalitarian, or anarchist groups of the late Middle Ages in Europe: the Taborites and the Adamites of Bohemia, Tomas Müntzer, and John of Leyden. Like Sandino himself, there have been numerous cases of self-divinization in millenarian figures: Tanchelm believed himself to be possessed by the holy spirit, Müntzer understood himself as the "living God," and the Adamites were convinced that they were "superior to Christ" (Cohn 1970, 49, 236–38, 219). As a suggestive parallel to the political movement around Sandino, consider the Taborites and the Adamites. Between 1420 and 1421, commanded by different leaders and having undergone several mutating phases, these groups pursued the establishment of a classless society, where all would live as brothers. Believing themselves to be the "Elect," the Taborites began a class war against the "great" (whom they considered driven by avarice) and set out to conquer the neighboring lands at the cost of much blood, with the intent of moving outward into larger territories and eventually the world. They held property in common and issued proclamations changing the feudal power arrangements of bonds, dues, and services and setting up new regimes in every territory that they controlled; a system of dues or taxes by extortion was established. The Taborites also became involved in a national war to defend Bohemia against invading foreign forces. After a short period of transition, they dwindled, only to give rise to a new group under new leadership, with a more radical set of beliefs: the Adamites, who thought that they were better than Christ and who held the doctrine of the Free Spirit, believing that God dwelled in them as the Saints of the Last Days. By the time that the Adamites came under the leadership of Adam-Moses, they wanted to set up a world government; some believed that the Virgin Mary was among them, and some regarded themselves as the avenging angels, whose mission it was to go about the world wielding their swords until all the evil ones had been cut down. In October 1421 they were finally exterminated, but their influence was felt in central Europe for at least another generation (Cohn 1970, 214–22). Because the millennial vision of salvation is one of radical transformation, the idea that all that exists must be destroyed is not uncommon; the twentieth century has yielded monstrous examples of this sort of radical behavior. Many times, revolutionary millenarian movements encounter their own deaths at the hand of the authority that they challenge.

From its Judeo-Christian and European roots, the millenarian impulse often has flourished in the boundaries between different cultures and societies, sometimes emerging where foreign cultures collide. For example, in *The Religions of the Oppressed*, Vittorio Lanternari (1963) proposes that the European millenarian tradition has continued in colonized continents, where the encounter between indigenous peoples and the technologically more advanced Europeans has often undermined the foundations of native religious and cultural beliefs. This encounter provokes sufficient doubt in the natives to erode their realm of meaning and to cause them great alienation, and so they seek to escape the alienating condition by replacing their defeated gods with Judeo-Christian symbols as a means of manifesting their aspirations for salvation and for freedom from domination. Thus, the desire to escape domination leads to the creation of a religion that promises millenarian salvation, in which the hope for the spiritual salvation promised in the gospel is translated into social and political salvation.

From the documented cases of millenarian movements from around the world, the Americas during the nineteenth and early twentieth centuries afford numerous examples. In the United States, the Ghost Dance among the Plains Indians promised that God would restore Native greatness by rewarding them with plenty and by ejecting the white man from their land (Lanternari 1963, 151–57). In Canada, David Wilson and the Children of Peace rebuilt "Solomon's Temple" to await the coming of the Jewish messiah who would abolish British rule (Schrauwers 1993), and Louis Riel promised deliverance to the Métis, whose way of life and existence appeared to be threatened by the flow of white immigrants westward (Flanagan 1996). The Rastafarians in Jamaica believed that Emperor Heile Selassie of Ethiopia was their messiah and that he would transport them back to Africa, away from oppression (Lanternari 1963, 159–65). In Brazil, at the turn of the century, peasants in the Contestado Rebellion resisted the advance of capitalist development and republican nation building in favor of a God-chosen monarchy (Diacon 1991). Later in Brazilian history (and contemporary with Augusto Sandino), the Joazeiro movement led by Father Cicero (Romao Batista) also rebelled against the republican government and proclaimed the rule of the Holy City and the restoration of the Golden Age (Lanternari 1963, 192). In the later twentieth century, speculations about the state of the environment, race, and religion in the United States have sparked millenarian movements among such diverse groups as environmentalists (Lee 1995), Black Muslims (Lee 1988), and white supremacists (Barkun 1997), as well as among various religious and other groups (see e.g. Anthony and Robbins 1995; Barkun 1994, 1995; Kaplan 1997).

Thus, Sandino's millenarianism takes its place in a long (and continuing) line of New World religious and political movements. Moreover, Sandino's war of resistance against the American occupation can be seen as resembling those of typical nativistic resistance movements. He promoted a religion promising final political and spiritual deliverance to a people whose freedom was threatened by a foreign force of occupation and by the advancement of white landowners over the agricultural frontier. His religion, although fundamentally different from the mainstream Catholicism practiced by most Nicaraguans, used familiar Christian symbols to convey his message of redemption to his followers. It also provided a greater justification both for political action and for violence.

Working toward a more general theoretical understanding of these phenomena, Yonina Talmon defines millenarian movements as those that expect "imminent, total, ultimate, this-worldly and collective" salvation (1968, 349). Norman Cohn, in *The Pursuit of the Millennium*—his seminal study of millenarian eruptions from the early Christians to the sixteenth century—adds "miraculous" to his own list of characteristic elements (1970, 15). For Talmon and for Cohn, viewing salvation as *imminent* means that the end of the present order of things is at hand. The time left may vary; it may be days, months, or even years, but it is to occur soon and suddenly. Not surprisingly, millenarian leaders call on the faithful to begin immediate preparations. The expected salvation is *total* in that it will involve a complete transformation of the world—not simply improvement or reform, but perfection itself. War and hatred, poverty and calamity, illness and poverty—all earthly afflictions will disappear, giving way to a world of peace and love. Millennial salvation is considered *ultimate* in that its arrival is expected at the end of a process believed to be presently unfolding in time; nothing is usually expected to follow once the period of bliss has been attained. In other words, time is viewed as a predetermined flow of events leading toward a final stage of future perfection, the end of time. *This-worldly* salvation means that the rewards of perfection will be obtained here on earth, not in a distant heavenly paradise. More precisely, millenarian movements often interpret paradise as having a dual nature, both immanent (terrestrial) and transcendent (otherworldly), the two aspects fused in the apocalyptic hope of the Heavenly City descending upon the earth. Millenarian expectations for salvation are *collective* in that the awaited redemption is to be granted only to a defined group, the elect; millenarian believers expect to obtain redemption on account of their membership in a group and not because of their individual virtues. Finally (for Cohn), the attainment of perfection is *miraculous* because believers expect that the awaited transformation will be accomplished with the help of divine or supernatural forces.

How do Sandino's life and thought relate to these six characteristics? Sandino was convinced that the final redemption of mankind on earth was imminent—indeed, it had begun in this century and would culminate in A.D. 2000 with the Last Judgment of mankind. The present era, therefore, marks the end of the development of this planet. In 1931, he emphasized the urgency and the need for preparation by announcing that the "hecatomb"—the conflagration that would usher in the end of the world—would "be played out in the last sixty-nine years that remain[ed]" (Somoza 1936, 106).

According to Sandino, millenarian redemption was total, involving the complete transformation of the planet and of the essence of mankind. The announced "proletarian explosion" would consist not of simple social modifications but rather of a radical transformation of reality, bringing about a world of love, justice, and perfection on earth; in his understanding of his own role in this transformation, Sandino expected to command all aspects of people's lives—military, political, and religious. He endeavored to reach the all-encompassing fifth circle of Trincado's love, both through armed struggle and through the establishment of peaceful cooperatives in the northern region of Nicaragua.

Moreover, with certain qualifications, Sandino saw salvation as ultimate: he envisioned the flow of time as a movement toward a final stage of universal "spiritual development," which, once reached, would become permanent and unchangeable. Therefore, what had begun in Nicaragua in 1912 (the year of origin enshrined in his new calendar) was in fact the ultimate stage of development in the history of the earth. However, Sandino qualified this sense of ultimacy by placing the earth in a broader cosmic context. The process of development that was taking place on earth, as he understood it, was part of the greater development of the whole universe; just as he thought that every political or social revolution contributed toward the ultimate liberation of humanity, he also believed that the attainment of perfection on this planet would be a contribution to the accomplishment of the universal paradise. Once the final stage was fulfilled on this planet, nothing would replace or reverse it—but the larger cosmic process of universal evolution would continue elsewhere, on whichever planet the impure spirits would be banished, there beginning another cycle of expiation and redemption.

Consequently, the salvation that Sandino promised was also this-worldly. Perfection itself, it is clear in Sandino's writings, was to be reached here on earth and not in any celestial place. The love, the justice, the joy, and the boundless riches were an earthly promise, rewards for an already determined spiritual evolution and for the victory of the forces of light over those of darkness.

Moreover, as one aspect if its this-worldliness, Sandino's doctrine had a collective aspect, for he believed that the rewards of perfection would be granted to the elect group as a whole—in particular, to the oppressed. At the same time, it is important to discern the several layers within this collectivism. At the inner core one finds the EDSN, among whom (according to Sandino) were found the twenty-nine missionary spirits sent to redeem this world; the EDSN was therefore the moral beacon of the world, whose first task was to awaken the people of the Segovias. The Segovianos, in turn, would awaken the people of Nicaragua; his country, Sandino thought, had been chosen to be sacrificed for the freedom and independence of a new race, "the Latin American Nationality." From among the oppressed peoples of the world, that new race had been chosen to defeat and to conquer the northern Anglo-Saxon oppressor. Thus, Sandino and his men were called upon to carry out the ultimate work of God: the liberation of the oppressed and the final elimination of the oppressors of the world.

Finally, Sandino expected that some of the events of the final days would occur miraculously. Extraordinary natural disasters, supernatural forces, and divine guidance would assist in the transformation of the world. Overall, then, Sandino's hopes and his unique blend of religious beliefs do indeed correspond to the six characteristics identifying millenarianism.

## Conditions and Goals

Generally, the circumstances under which millenarian movements appear (and disappear) exhibit a discernable pattern. Norman Cohn, calling millenarianism "the messianism of the poor" (1970, 61), remarks that millenarian movements typically attract the poor, the oppressed, and marginal segments of society such as landless peasants and the unemployed, all of whom would understandably be responsive to promises of deliverance from suffering. In understanding the experience of such groups, we may introduce the notion of *multiple deprivation*—"the combined effect of poverty, low status, and powerlessness." Sheer physical deprivation may lead to an obsession with material security or with bodily healing, but poverty alone does not necessarily lead to millenarianism. Rather, it is often a combination of afflictions—poverty, social rejection, and the inability to influence political change—that produces a fertile soil for millenarian ideas. These conditions, when combined, can spark the kind of desperation that seeks relief in fantasies such as the "myth of the elect" and "role reversal" (Talmon 1968, 354).

However, poverty, low status, and powerlessness are often relative, and so Barkun proposes the concept of *relative deprivation* to refer to the perception of differences between social groups (1986, 34–35). Deprivation is relative because it is evaluated according to subjective perception rather than some absolute criterion; the larger the perceived disproportion of wealth and power between groups, the higher may be the chances of discontent. This view helps explain why not only the poor erupt into millenarianism; as Talmon notes, millenarianism has also been observed among members of a middle class or a "frustrated secondary elite" (1968, 356) who experience relative deprivation.

In connection with cultural and physical peril, situations of disaster have been identified as a catalyst in the emergence of millenarian movements. Barkun (1986, 51) defines *disaster* as "a severe, relatively sudden, and frequently unexpected disruption of normal structure arrangements within a social system . . . resulting from a force, 'natural' or 'social,' 'internal' to a system or 'external' to it, over which the system has no firm control." Disaster does not affect everyone equally, however, for "disaster is to some extent in the eye of the beholder"; in particular, rural societies are more susceptible to the "disintegrative effects" of disaster because of their social compactness and vulnerability (60, 69). In a study of Asian and African millenarian movements, Adas also finds this susceptibility "among peasant groups" (1987, 113). Overall, Cohn asserts that eruptions of "revolutionary millenarianism [take] place against a background of disaster" (1970, 282).

In response to shared social conditions such as these, millenarian movements can be understood as sharing certain goals as well. They are often *revivalistic*—that is, they are not only reactions to misery and material hardship but also agents of positive and desirable social change.[1] Emphasizing the "subjectivity" of millenarian responses, Wallace interprets millenarian activity as a means of "revitalization" for a threatened culture (1956, 256). Talmon writes that millenarianism can be understood as a "search for a tolerably coherent system of values, a new cultural identity and a regained sense of dignity and self-respect" (1968, 355). Adas finds that these movements provide "a sense of vision and purpose for the future that otherwise appeared perilous and uncertain"; millenarian ideas help the oppressed to "recover their lost status" and to "restore legitimate rule" (1987, 112–13). They are said to give people the kind of confidence that "transforms inferiority into superiority" (Talmon 1968, 369).

Millenarian eruptions also perform what Worsley calls an *integratory function*. In his study of Melanesian cargo cults, Worsely found that millenarian movements offered to groups that lacked unity, social organization, and political institutions the opportunity to integrate and to overcome their traditional divisions in order to face a common threat—namely, the cultural crisis resulting from the arrival of Western colonialists. The shock of crisis jolts such groups out of their prepolitical existence, and they eventually foster the development of tighter social units and secular political organizations (Worsely 1968, 227–31). Lanternari agrees that reforms become instituted as millenarian ideas secularize, and that raising "popular awareness of the need for change . . . pave[s] the way for reform in the cultural, political and social structure of secular society" (1963, 322).

In evaluating the conditions and goals of Sandino's millenarianism, we must start with the man himself. Sandino experienced his own life as a se-

---

1. This sense of "revivalism" is somewhat different than the term's common usage, which refers to "an approach to religion designed to stimulate interest by appealing principally to emotions" (Vollmar 1967, 448).

ries of personal injustices and frustrations. Considered a social outcast from birth, he experienced deprivation and social stigma. He also endured hardship because of his mother's habits and because of her abandonment of him. He rejected his mother and rebelled against God (the God of the Catholic Church, that is), faulting Providence for dealing him a bad hand. As a young adult, Sandino found it difficult to accept his improved fortunes, letting his violent temper get him in trouble; as a fugitive, he drifted in search of fortune and adventure. Thus, his religious preferences can be partly understood—on a personal level, at least—in light of his refusal to face the reality of hardship and of his obsessive search for something better, always more just and comfortable. (The misery and suffering of his youthful years may also have helped to produce in him the unchecked ambition of his adulthood, when he thought very highly of himself and was happy to shower himself with honors and titles.)

For Sandino, a better and more comfortable life meant a life of fame and honor, and so when the opportunity presented itself he turned his quest toward public life. Indeed, perhaps to a greater extent than for most people, Nicaragua's social and political condition intersected with Sandino's personal experiences and beliefs. Thus, Sandino transferred his personal preferences and desires for recognition to a search for glory in the social realm. In particular, the social dimension of his beliefs became rooted in his perception that the imperialistic advances of the United States were to blame for Nicaragua's (and his own) situation.

Significantly, Sandino came to adulthood in the Segovias, where the northern way of life was changing rapidly under the pressure of regional, national, and international circumstances. The most affected were peasants and Indians. Agricultural development and legal reforms displaced indigenous populations as coffee became the major export crop in the latter part of the nineteenth and the early twentieth centuries. The advance of the agricultural frontier threatened the peasants' livelihood, their traditional economy was challenged, and many ended in dispossession; an early rebellion, sparked by rumors of oppression, had resulted in a bloodbath. Most peasants thus faced two options: to become day laborers under oppressive conditions, or to withdraw or move further beyond the frontier. Even when peasants adapted to the oppressive life of laborers, their security was often threatened by civil wars, in which they were forced to serve whatever party their employer embraced.

Moreover, the northern region's situation was a microcosm of the disorder afflicting the whole country. Because American officials ran

Nicaragua's finances, many Nicaraguans believed that the political inability and servility of their ruling élite threatened their national sovereignty and by extension their very existence. Traditional political institutions—including the Conservative and Liberal parties—were unable to offer solutions to their age-old feuds (Stimson 1991, 23–24). In fact, they were a reflection of the chaos; the domestic political élites and their uncompromising attitudes had sunk Sandino's country into crisis and despair.

Thus, in the 1920s and 1930s, the peasantry of northern Nicaragua were caught in an unstable period of transition, the region's former order shattered and a new one not yet established. These conditions made the Segovias a fertile soil for a message of hope and deliverance to be preached and to be received. Hinterland societies such as these experience a sense of decay and powerlessness in the presence of outsiders and of a changing world; in Wallace's terms, they react to a "threat of damage" to their social order (1956, 265) by becoming more receptive to promises of deliverance and of regeneration.[2] Generally, situations of effective or perceived cultural disintegration form the background for the emergence of nativistic movements; the movements themselves are often triggered by catalysts such as plagues, droughts, famines, wars, and natural disasters.

The same pattern applied to Sandino's rebellion. Nicaragua was (and sadly continues to be) a country with an unstable political and natural environment; Sandino's war of liberation was preceded by the Constitutionalist War and by a grasshopper plague. Whatever agricultural activity had remained undisturbed by the Constitutionalist War came to an end with the grasshoppers; corn, the staple of the Nicaraguan diet, had to be imported, and scarcity and high prices could not be averted. The situation was later aggravated by the 1929 world financial crash, when exports fell because of the depressed economic conditions of the country's most important buyer and benefactor, the United States. In 1930, Nicaragua was struck by drought and by a disease affecting banana plants. Moreover, Sandino's war itself, waged in the heart of coffee country, also contributed to the desperation because much of the coffee production (which then accounted for

2. In other colonized lands, the same general circumstances have given rise to millenarian movements, often sparked by the threat of destruction of a native way of life by the arrival (or increased activity) of white settlers. In 1847, for example, the Mayas of the Yucatán saw their existence threatened by the arrival of new settlers and their plantations; they rebelled, eventually fighting for nearly fifty years while expecting deliverance from the "Talking Cross" (Reed 1964).

over half of the nation's exports) dropped, prices fell, and there was labor unrest fueled by Moncada's inability to deal with Sandino and to bring the American occupation to an end. Nature made a further contribution with the March 1931 earthquake that destroyed most of Managua.

Disaster must threaten a people's physical existence, not just their culture, in order to trigger millenarian reactions. Indeed, the better conditions of life in the cities may explain why Sandino's message did not spread to the whole country. By contrast, in the isolation of the northern countryside and mines, peasants and Indians labored in dire conditions and were paid in company bonds redeemable only at the company's stores. Thus, Sandino's arrival in 1926 to a chaotic and uncertain setting was coincidental, but his leadership and message came to fill a cultural, political, and religious need for Indians, miners, and peasants alike. He created a cohesive brotherhood, a tighter social unit, and a new identity that promoted change and offered deliverance.

However, history cannot be explained or analyzed purely through reference to social circumstances. Human lives are not determined wholly by social events; although the social environment does present parameters within which human development is accomplished, single individuals can make decisions that shape their own and others' lives. True, there could have been no *Sandinismo* without Sandino, but neither would *Sandinismo* have existed were it not for the deliberate decisions of men and women to listen to him, to follow him, to accept his prophecies, and to use his iconic image in pursuit of their own ends and visions.

## Leadership

Leaders are an important element in the millenarian mix. Although the presence of leaders is not a precondition for the birth of millenarian movements, they usually do precede the movement or emerge from within it. An atmosphere of disaster may test the abilities of conventional leadership, leaving the way "open to emergent leaders" (Barkun 1986, 87). According to Cohn, even in the case of a rebellion with limited goals, there sometimes appears "somewhere on the radical fringe, a *propheta* with his following of paupers intent on turning this one particular upheaval into the apocalyptic battle, the final purification of the world" (1970, 284)—a scenario remarkably parallel to Sandino's appearance at the end of the Constitutionalist War.

There is a fortuitous element at play in the appearance of millenarian leaders, the contingent convergence of social needs with the personal traits of an individual at a particular time. These personal traits are more likely to appear where a tradition of charismatic leadership already exists (Barkun 1986, 86–88). According to Max Weber, *charisma* is "a certain quality of an individual personality by virtue of which he is set apart from ordinary men and treated as endowed with supernatural, superhuman, or at least specifically exceptional power or qualities. These are not accessible to the ordinary person, but are regarded as of divine origin or as exemplary, and on the basis of them the individual concerned is treated as a leader" (Weber 1947, 358–59; cited in Worsley 1968, xii). For Weber, a leader's charisma is associated with the notion that a prophetic or divinely ordained mission has been given to an individual, from which (rather than from merely personal attributes) the leader derives his or her authority.

Millenarian leaders are typically classified as either *prophets* or *messiahs*. Biblical prophets are leaders who claim their authority as spokespersons for God; indeed, the Greek word *prophetes* simply means "spokesman," and the prophet's mission is to proclaim God's message (see McCarthy 1967, 866–67; Redmond 1967, 861–66). A prophet is distinct from a priest; where priests act within institutions and carry out duties as guardians of an established tradition, a prophet works outside institutions with unmediated authority, which rests upon the prophet's particular divine charisma, visions, revelations, and at times miraculous works. In the Weberian sense of the word, then, the prophet is charismatic (Flanagan 1996, 84–85).

Prophets understand their mission through revelation; a prophet may be called to his mission through voices and visions from God or from the angels. Often the message is interpreted in hindsight after leaders have committed themselves to a cause; some call this an "awakening," defined as a "critical period when the leader's new spiritual identity is formed" (Wallis 1982, 39, 14). However experienced, revelation—derived from the Latin *revelare*, to disclose or to unveil—is an unexpected receipt of profoundly significant knowledge, giving the recipient a new outlook on the world and on himself. It is presumed to be a supernatural communication, beyond the natural capacities of an individual. In biblical prophecy, revelation also has a public dimension, usually addressed not only to an individual but also to an entire people (Dulles 1967, 441–44). Convert to a truth that must be shared with others, the prophet desires to see his or her own conversion replicated in others; to the indifferent and to scornful unbelievers, however, the prophet offers not hope but punishment. A prophet articulates and explains the ills that affect the community and announces redemption as well as punishment.

A messiah is generally described by many of the characteristics that describe the prophet, but with a crucial difference: the messiah is not merely a messenger but a divine savior—the one expected to bring the awaited Kingdom of God to its fulfillment.

One common characteristic both of prophets and of messiahs is the use of magical power in many forms. Adas (1987, 119) found that there were trusted healers and possessors of magical or extrasensory powers among the leaders that he studied. Powers similar to magic can also be manifested in divination or in premonitions; astrologers, for instance, believe that the movements of celestial bodies have a close correspondence with natural events and with human actions, and that these correspondences can be studied in order to make predictions about history and the world. On a more popular level, natural phenomena such as storms and earthquakes are often seen as determining or revealing events in the social realm. By contrast, magic proper involves the actual transformation of things, the casting of spells to make things change and become other than what they were. Significantly, the exercise of power does not necessarily involve magical potions, ritual sacrifice of animals, or other overt physical acts; sometimes just speaking is enough. As Northrop Frye points out, in primitive societies there is almost no room for abstraction, and the concepts of subject and object are hardly separate; the result is a belief in the magical power of words, in the capacity of words themselves to change things or to bring a new reality into being upon utterance (Frye 1990, 5–6).

In the conceptual dichotomy of millenarian leaders as prophets or as messiahs, Sandino was a mixture of both; more precisely, he began as a prophet and developed into a messiah. Initially, his central concern was with preaching his beliefs, and he was successful in converting many of his men. At the same time, it is important to keep in mind that he had no intention of dedicating all his time to proselytizing activity; although he wished to institutionalize his beliefs, he (like Trincado) despised traditional priests and did not understand himself as either priest or missionary. Rather, Sandino was a revolutionary prophet who intended to liberate his people from foreign and domestic oppression. He wanted to bring to them the message of the new age of freedom, justice, and right; he wanted to awaken the people of Nicaragua to their mission for Latin America and for the world; he wanted to announce the coming of the millennium at the end of the century and to warn his people about the imminent apocalyptic calamities that would precede it. He was a prophet in military garb.

Over the course of his public career, however, Sandino transformed himself into a messianic figure as well. As the incarnation of Divine Justice in Trincado's system, he was the equivalent of the Son of Man, the divine force that had broken through history to usher in the end times. As messiah, Sandino wanted to redeem his region (the Segovias), his country, his fellow workers and proletarians, and his race. The imagery is close to that of the early Christians, where Christ is expected to return from the dead in order to stand in judgment of all; as Paul writes, "[H]e has fixed a day on which He will have the world judged in righteousness by a man whom He has appointed, and of this He has given assurance to all by raising him from the dead" (Acts 17:31). However, the more appropriate model is drawn not from the Christian tradition but from the Jewish one, not Christ but David—a military champion who would defeat Israel's enemies, reestablish the Jewish nation to its political glory, and install himself as king. In this sense, Sandino became a messiah both in his own eyes and in the eyes of his followers.

As a prophet-messiah, Sandino drew on several different sources to justify his authority. The content of his message was one of these sources. It is clear that the initial message that he brought to northern Nicaragua was the political ideology that he had absorbed during his first trip to Mexico, his first political awakening. His contact with those ideas changed his worldview and his orientation significantly; he ceased to be a drifter, defined what he wanted, and learned where and how to get it. As with other prophets, Sandino's experience of personal illumination in his contact with revolutionary ideas while in Mexico was followed by a need to give those ideas public expression in his own country. The feeling of having attained the truth propelled him to propagate his discovery in order to reach out and to help others. Therein arises the prophet's sense of mission, as Sandino's private search for the perfect place was transformed into a public endeavor.

However, his dream of a perfect place soon ceased to be a search and became the pursuit of a cause, for in Sandino's case perfection was not to be found but to be built. The pursuit of the cause brought together the personal goals of the early Sandino with the revelation that the Mexican revolutionaries offered to him—that his dreams needed to be constructed and shared with others. His private pursuits and desires, therefore, moved the pursuit of his cause. It was accommodated to satisfy his personal wants and aspirations, his passions and dreams, but was not the result of inner transformation.

In its public dimension, his message became an indictment of the present world and of the human condition—imprisoned by an evil economic system, thirsting for money and power, and lacking in concern for justice and for the brotherhood of men. Sandino formulated a vision of shameful occupations, humiliations, and violations of Nicaragua and of other nations of the hemisphere; he wanted to show that the future of the so-called Indo-Hispanic nations would be no less than cultural and political collapse at the hands of a predatory empire. This situation was not hopeless and unchanging, however, because all the suffering and humiliation would come to fruition in the final defeat of the Americans. That was the message that Sandino promoted in order to awaken the masses and to "gain control" over them (Román 1979, 49). In effect, this message offered a reinterpretation of reality, what Wallis calls "reality construction" (1982, 55).

Later, Sandino's desire for honor and glory grew amidst a series of disappointments, and his role was transformed once again. Only months into his rebellion, he began presenting himself as a Christlike figure, even if only by analogy: "My love for my motherland and my people is enormous and that is why I am willing to forgive everyone. . . . I knew that the people are ungrateful, but I still forgive them. . . . He who wishes to be a redeemer must die by crucifixion, must imitate Jesus Christ in resignation and say: 'Forgive them Father, for they know not what they do' " (Sandino 1981, 1:199–200). Toward the end of his second trip to Mexico, Sandino considered himself the incarnation of Divine Justice, suggesting to the mind of the Segovian inhabitants that he was Jesus returned. This self-portrayal as Christ—even if, for him, Christ was just another revolutionary prophet— had a significant effect on his followers; like Christ, Sandino would die and return at the coming of the millennium, and thus he came to project an aura of divine infallibility. Sandino's own self-image, however, was slightly different: a Davidic messiah at the head of twenty-nine warring spirits.

Thus, we witness the prophetic role turned messianic: Sandino believed that he was called not only to bring the divine message but also to inaugurate the final phase of human development on earth, first through violence and then through his agricultural communes (which did not preclude the use of violence). His new revelations no longer came directly from social and political ideologies but rather in the form of visions during dreams and meditation sessions and from a voice that talked to him on a mountaintop in the Segovias. The new message was compatible with (but not the same as) the old one: he still sought liberation for the working class, but he understood this liberation not merely in terms of material comfort and historic recognition but rather as the establishment of the Kingdom of God on earth and as the promise of spiritual life eternal. Moreover, in his attempt to apply the message that he had received from the EMECU, his understanding of power shifted; he now wished to install a theocracy where he would control the totality of national life, ban all religion, abolish the traditional political parties, and partition the land in cooperatives for the workers. Like Caesar, he would become god and emperor.

In his pursuit of power, Sandino's influence on the peasantry can be partially explained by his magic-like beliefs and practices. He met with no incredulity when he spoke of telepathic communication with his followers (especially in times of battle when the senses were believed to be more acute) or when he encouraged them to trust their instincts in their movements as though those instincts were revelations and guidance from the divine or directly from him. His regular use of horoscopes to make predictions was also impressive to peasants and to Indians; his visions, premonitions, and predictions—along with his beliefs in the transmigration of souls and in electromagnetic and psychic communications among living beings—were a source of awe to the simple peasants, most of whom did not even know what electricity was.

Sandino also cultivated charismatic authority through the power of his proclamations and announcements. He spoke with overwhelming certainty and was convinced that his pronouncements acted like magic spells that would radically alter the nature and outcome of events. This was evident in his reaction to the arrival of the Conservatives to power in Honduras; later, after the explosion of the weapons depot in Managua, he rushed to proclaim the Union of Central America, the formation of the Autonomist Army, and his rule over the region as countermeasures. Even more closely linked to magic was his belief that the continuous repetition of certain phrases would lead him to victory.

Overall, to the extent that the people of the Segovias believed in the view of the world that Sandino presented and accepted that he had extrasensory and supernatural powers, his authority was unchallenged. It was thanks to Sandino's ability to convey his beliefs to his followers that he managed to organize and to channel the anarchic nature of peasants into a disciplined and well-oiled fighting machine, capable of standing up to a superior enemy that possessed much better weapons and huge technological advantages such as radios and airplanes. In turn, the fact that so superior an enemy did not defeat them made Sandino and his followers believe even more firmly that they had been destined for great things; he interpreted his nondefeat as a victory.

As a psychological counterpoint to his sense of authority, Sandino suspected and mistrusted anyone who was not deeply committed to him. His break with Turcios, his fight with Martí, and his constant mistrust of "intellectuals" and of schooled people such as Alemán Bolaños or Zepeda emanated primarily from his lack of complete authority over these individuals. In Mexico, he was disappointed in the way that he was treated both by the government, who had not bowed before him, and by the communists, whose respect for him did not go beyond their calculations about how much use they could get out of him to embarrass the government. His lack of political wisdom—evident in his handling of political affairs in Managua after the peace treaty—showed how uncharismatic and awkward he was outside of his circle of admiring supporters and friends.

As another strategy for retaining power in relationship both with the ignorant and with the educated, Sandino was always careful not to reveal his underlying thinking. He had been taught early about the esoteric value of knowledge; inspired by a tradition in which knowledge is to be administered piecemeal to the initiated, he learned to keep his overarching strategy to himself, unless he felt that his interlocutor would be receptive beyond doubt. When that was the case, he pontificated upon his views overtly and was usually convincing. However, despite his caution, he did not have much influence outside of the peasants' circle; he remained inadequate, suspicious, and insecure among the urbane or the socially sophisticated, hardly knowing how to relate to them. The more he tried to impress them, the more bizarre he appeared; the more elaborate and the fancier the vocabulary he used, the more his listeners became aware of the gibberish that he spoke. Sandino once said that his biggest fault was that he talked a lot (Román 1979, 29), and he seems to have mostly talked about himself. Among the peasants that seemed to have worked well; among people of independent critical capacity, however, fewer individuals were likely to trust him. As Nietzsche remarked, the more one talks about oneself, the more one has to hide (1966, aph. 169).

To be sure, although Sandino was not successful in influencing most of the literate foreigners who joined him, one must avoid the inference that the peasants followed him only because they were uneducated and foolish. They followed him because his message was appealing to them; most important, they followed him because he articulated their dreams for a more just society. At the same time, he was able touch a chord among people such as Román, Beals, and Belausteguigoitia, who—in spite of their education and against their professional objectivity—were earnestly receptive to his message.

In the Middle Ages, millenarian prophets usually were former members of the clergy, mystic travelers, or drifters; in the modern world, nativistic leaders are often found among fugitives or former soldiers who have been exposed to white society's notions of progress and technology, or among disaffected members of a middle class. In either era, leaders typically have lived a richer life than have their suffering people and have seen benefits and riches in the outside world. For his part, Sandino's wider experience and travels gave him the confidence (a confidence that he otherwise may not have possessed) to lead the unenlightened peasants without fear of being challenged; moreover, his worldliness also made him a bit of an outsider, which attracted attention and admiration and which impressed the locals. At the same time, his familiarity with the people's history and his command of the local symbols and idiom endeared him to them; Sandino had after all grown up in a small village himself, initially raised by an Indian mother and surrounded by the Indians of the southeastern plateau. Thus, Sandino's profile fits that of other millenarian rebels.

## Ideas and Beliefs

As we have seen, apocalyptic leaders do not appear in a vacuum. They are preceded by a pool of ideas and symbols conveying a yearning for radical deliverance from suffering. To be sure, conditions of disaster, coupled with the presence of leadership, are bound to produce some sort of rebellious reaction; such rebellion is most likely to be effective and lasting, however, only in the presence of ideas that provide a cohesive framework for a movement.

Millenarian beliefs include various elements: an explanation of reality (Barkun 1986, 56), an indictment of the present world, a retrieving of a glorious past, and a rejection of an imperfect future. Through these beliefs, prophetic leaders explain the circumstances of mounting evil and decay and present answers to these problems in unequivocal terms: quick and sweeping changes. In this sense, the prophetic leader and the prophetic message are sometimes inseparable. A prophet is the interpreter of good and evil, proposing solutions to a world of chaos that the common people can understand (Adas 1987, 119). As a variant on the prophetic role, some modern millenarian leaders have been trained in esoteric traditions as members of secret societies or religious sects. From this perspective, the prophetic message is attainable only by those who have received illumination; those who have been chosen to receive this illumination must themselves act upon it (Billington 1980).

Eric Hobsbawm, in *Primitive Rebels,* explores the conditions and development of rebellion both in the absence and in the presence of "the right kind of ideas" (1965, 106). Hobsbawm distinguishes the millenarian figure from the revolutionary, who has the tool of ideology and the organizational skills to mobilize and to establish a movement (59). The revolutionary claims to have knowledge of the world and to possess the necessary solutions to fix it; to the revolutionary's technological mindset, no problem is unsolvable. However, Hobsbawm's framework has been critiqued effectively by Barkun, who—although he agrees that apocalyptic "movements require some ideology as a necessary condition"—believes that the "distinction between revolution and millenarianism is . . . largely artificial" (1986, 181, 123). Hobsbawm's conceptual distinction does not address the in-between, where most apocalyptic movements seem to be found.

Ideology provides a framework for the interpretation of a reality that goes beyond the local setting; it corresponds to local experience at the same time as it places that experience in a more ample context, thereby validating it in some way. This may account for the syncretic nature of millenarian ideals: images and symbols are often adopted as they become available, without regard for their philosophical or other compatibility—all that matters is their usefulness in expressing chiliastic hope.

Certain religions and dispositions have been identified as conveyers of millenarian ideas. Generally, religions with a linear view of history and a preordained eschatology—elements that have the "power to bridge future and past" (Talmon 1968, 359)—may promote millenarian symbols. Notions of an earthly paradise and the idea of the divine working within history must be available in either religious or secularized versions; communist doctrine, for instance, relies on variants of these beliefs to express its future hopes for mankind. By contrast, religions with notions of a purely spiritual salvation or with a repetitive and cyclical understanding of existence are, apparently, rarely conducive to millenarian dreams (Talmon 1968, 353). However, themes and ideas within cyclical systems such as theosophy have occasionally been adapted in the construction of elaborate millenarian expectations; such was the case with Louis Riel (Flanagan 1996)—and, as I have argued here, with Augusto Sandino.

At the heart of the belief system that motivated Sandino's millenarianism was anti-imperialism. Convinced that the United States wanted to control the world and that there would be a sort of domino effect at play in Latin America, he considered it vital to stop the U.S. aggression in Nicaragua—to arrest an expanding world empire and also to fight for freedom and justice for the oppressed classes. In Sandino's eyes, the Anglo-Saxon United States was the common economic and cultural enemy of the chosen Indo-Hispanic race, warring against their language and tradition. Therefore, the ejection of U.S. troops from Nicaragua, Sandino thought, was the most immediate task for the liberation of Indo-America. His interpretation of anti-imperialism was not static, however: as he matured in his spiritist thinking, the national and racial clash also became a cosmic battle for control of the universe. Sandino came to believe that the United States represented the forces of evil and his own troops represented the soldiers of light; Americans stood in the way of human purification and attainment of the realm of perfection (for a restatement of this by one of his latter-day followers, see Borge 1988, 88). Class, nationality, and race therefore became symbols of spiritual renewal for Sandino as much as they did for his contemporaries in Italy and Germany. It was on behalf of his people, Sandino had predicted, that the spirit would speak. His cry for the redemption of the oppressed was intricately linked with the promotion and preservation of the new redemptive race-nation. (At the same time, his principles sometimes proved flexible when that suited his purposes; in his quest for power, he was willing to hand over power to the Americans rather than to be outmaneuvered by his rival Moncada, and later he demonstrated the same willingness to relinquish Nicaragua's "absolute sovereignty" over its territory in exchange for Latin American protection against the United States.)

Sandino, like many in his country still today, was liberal in name only. For example, his anticlericalism was not true liberalism: although he manifested animosity toward institutional religion and likely absorbed this disposition from traditional Liberals in Nicaragua (as well as from radicals in Mexico), Sandino sought to install his own government in Nicaragua based on the religious precepts of the EMECU. He attacked the churches, but he did not separate his own religious beliefs from his political plan; Sandino wanted an official state religion, a theocracy, thus violating the classic liberal separation of church and state as well as the pluralist principle. Indeed, Sandino was not a pluralist but a dualist; he interpreted the world (in the typical Zoroastrian tradition) as a battle between the forces of light and the forces of darkness and thought that those not with him were against him. Similarly, Sandino was not the democrat that some have taken him to be.

He did appeal to the democratic principle of the will of the majority when that will favored his own, but if it did not, he quickly dismissed it as being either ignorant or co-opted by force. His dismissal of the will of the Nicaraguan electorate during two consecutive fair elections is a case in point.

Thus, much of Sandino's thought appears as typically millenarian. Various other aspects are more complex, yet still suggestive. A common concern among millenarian prophets is the construction of genealogies that connect them to the Jews, who offer an archetypical model of prophetic leadership and of a people chosen by God. Sandino did not have an elaborate genealogy of his own, but his belief in the transmigration of souls fulfilled something of the same function, by allowing him to believe that among his followers were gathered the spirits of the greatest people in history: Abraham, Moses, Peter, Mary, and so on. He often spoke of his enemies as worshippers of the Golden Calf, picturing himself and his men as the carriers of the tradition and mission of the Levites, who would again see the chosen people through to the Promised Land.

Similar to many millenarians, Sandino predicted that there would be a transitional apocalyptic period of blood, suffering, death, and calamity before the millennium arrived. His message was that the transition period had already started and was marked by the calendar that he had created. Millenarians place importance on the past and glorify the future; little emphasis is usually placed on the present, except as a strategic springboard. Sandino sometimes idealized a period of freedom before the arrival of the white race in America, and he originally considered the Spaniards (not the Americans) to be his people's oppressors; after he embraced the EMECU's ideas, however, he stopped blaming the nationality of Master Trincado and even spoke of Spain as a "predestined nation" (Belausteguigoitia 1985, 199). Indeed, because he equated culture with European traditions and language, he needed the Spanish influence upon Indian practices in order to hold the Indo-Hispanic race above the Anglo-Saxon enemy. Paradoxically, however, he rejected the Catholicism of many of his followers as a European religion at the same time as he heartily embraced material progress, scientism, and the language of rights—all products of the Anglo-Saxon culture that he so much loathed.

That was the extent to which Sandino looked to the past. He knew little or nothing about the pre-Columbian way of life, and he was somewhat confused about the present status of the Indians, accusing the white race of simultaneously exploiting them and abandoning them like animals in the jungle (Belausteguigoitia 1985, 193). The most important feature that he drew from the natives was their resistance to the European invaders, but he also believed that the Spaniards had improved the Indians, resulting in the birth of the new chosen *mestizo* race (Belausteguigoitia 1985, 200). Rather than concerning himself to any great degree with the past, Sandino looked to the future and had no delusions about re-creating the pre-Columbian past that he understood so little. Salvation was placed in the future economic development of the region, in the creation of a homeland for the chosen race, in the prospective canal and the riches that it would create, and in the mission that God had conferred upon the new race. Overall—as with many millenarians—Sandino's orientation to the past and to the future was primarily an attempt to address the threat of destruction that he believed faced his world, his race, his class, and his people in the present.

Sandino was frustrated by the impotence of Latin Americans in the face of the increased presence of the United States in the region and by the decadence of Hispanic order and culture. His own people's backwardness and conformity frustrated him; in discourse evocative of the core ideals and doctrines of the Enlightenment, he thought that ignorance was the great enemy and that scientific education would lead his people out of ignorance (Belausteguigoitia 1985, 200). In his federation, he hoped to create the means with which to resist this cultural erosion, to create a new order in the world, and to build an empire that would finally crush the Anglo-Saxon one.

The development of Sandino's political ideas and his concern for liberation ran parallel to his quest for personal honor and recognition and to his self-image as revolutionary savior. Sandino's millenarian vision was a vision of misplaced hope for himself and for those who followed him.

## Reaction to Failure

Sandino's millennial movement also illustrates what scholars refer to as the failure of prophecy—the behavior of groups in the aftermath of failed predictions. What happens, for example, when a group predicts the end of the world for a certain date and it does not materialize? To be sure, Sandino's grandest prediction—that the world would end in the year 2000—was only proven incorrect long after his own death, far too late to have any impact on his movement. Rather, during his lifetime, the most important instance of the failure of prophecy involved his predictions of a final defeat of the forces of occupation: while in Mexico during his second trip, Sandino promised that he would deal the final blow to the U.S. Marines upon his return to Nicaragua.

When predicted events do not occur, some members respond by simply leaving the group. The most intense followers, however, often find it difficult to leave or to admit that they were wrong in the face of the ridiculing comments of those who never accepted the movement. These adherents then have two options: resuming proselytizing with greater intensity than before, or reinterpreting or de-eschatologizing the doctrines of the movement. Ernest Benz, in *Evolution and Christian Hope,* introduced the concept of "de-eschatologization" to describe "the removal of the original basic attitude toward the end of time in the Gospel message" (1968, 23–26). This process began as a slow "shift of emphasis" that culminated in Augustine's reinterpretation of scripture, lifting the anxiety of the expectation of the Kingdom of God and Christ's Second Coming. Whereas the early church fathers had believed in the imminent coming of the Kingdom, Augustine transformed that expectation by positing that the Kingdom of God on earth had already found its fulfillment in the Universal Church; thus, Augustine successfully emptied the terrestrial church of its millenarian orientation, allowing it to direct its energies toward a more institutional and even political existence. However, the apocalyptic texts that had fostered the experience and had inspired the millenarian beliefs of the early church were left untouched by Augustine's de-eschatologizing, and they would continue to make available a rich pool of symbols for future generations to express their millenarian longings.

The seminal work on this topic, *When Prophecy Fails* by Leon Festinger, Henry Riecken, and Stanley Schacter (1966), is a careful study of the development of a millenarian group calling themselves the Seekers. The group's leader, a woman who claimed to receive revelations from extraterrestrial beings, announced that the world would be destroyed on a specific date and that believers would be whisked from the earth in a spaceship to avert the catastrophe. The date arrived— and nothing happened. Festinger and his colleagues examined the ways in which individual Seekers reacted after the "disconfirmation" of the prophetic message. When predictions are not matched by reality, the believer experiences "cognitive dissonance": "Two opinions, or beliefs, or items of knowledge are dissonant with each other if they do not fit together . . . if they are not consistent or . . . if one does not follow from the other." Furthermore, "dissonance produces discomfort and, correspondingly, there will arise pressures to reduce or to eliminate the dissonance" (25, 26). Given the engaging nature of millenarian beliefs, one cannot easily turn away from the discomfort of dissonance by ignoring or rationalizing it. The discomfort can be reduced, however, by the sheer addition of more believers: "[I]f more and more people can be persuaded that the system of beliefs is correct, then clearly it must, after all, be correct" (28). Thus, some believers resort to proselytizing, trying to win more people over to the "faith."

In essence, rather than questioning the basis of their belief, followers attempt to reduce the inner conflict by altering the outside features; rather than undergoing personal transformation, they attempt to change what causes or reminds them of the conflict. Five conditions are required for this process to take place: beliefs must be held with conviction; there must be a strong commitment to act on that belief; the possibility of disconfirming a belief must exist; the disconfirmation must take place; and the believer must have social support following disconfirmation (Festinger, Riecken, and Schacter 1966, 4). When these conditions are present, believers begin a campaign of conversion around them so that they can readapt the environmental conditions to their beliefs and reduce the discomfort of dissonance. The possibility of the reinterpretation of doctrine following the failure of prophecy may involve issues such as changes in the date of expectation, blaming failure on a misreading of the divine revelation, and so on; it may also cause the believers to reinterpret their reading of history.

Sandino's situation upon his return from Mexico fits these five conditions. Sandino held his beliefs in earnest and was convinced that the expected Mexican aid would enable him to eject the Americans from Nicaragua, giving him victory. He committed himself and many of his men to the Mexican trip because he believed in the payoff: he willingly endured exile and accusations of treason, hunger, and poverty, and even more costly still, he sacrificed his pride in the attempt to achieve his desired end. Even when he became a part-time spiritist in Mexico, he always remained a committed revolutionary. Similarly, those who stayed and fought on during his absence also believed in the promise of victory; their actions too reflected their commitment to their beliefs. Sandino repeatedly announced that the coming victory would take place at his return, opening the possibility for disconfirmation, and when he returned humiliated and empty-handed, the disconfirmation was verified. Finally, Sandino was not abandoned, for he enjoyed the support and encouragement of his followers.

Sandino's promise was contingent upon the expected massive monetary aid and weapons, and as he became aware that he might not get his wish, he began to experience the discomfort and pain of dissonance. Thus, even before his return, rather than admitting the prospect of failure both of his trip and of his predictions, and rather than facing the thought that he might have been unworthy of all the honors that he believed he deserved, he reinterpreted his role as that of a suffering messiah. In the face of what he understood to be betrayal at the hands both of the Mexican government and of his former communist friends, Sandino reinterpreted his trip by announcing a prophetic mission: that he had been destined to fail so that he would become exposed to the evil and corruption of the world (Somoza 1936, 208–10). He proceeded to alter his surroundings by preaching and converting his men to the new faith. Significantly, however, rather than de-eschatologizing his mission, Sandino preached an intense eschatologically oriented message, prophesying the fulfillment of his new message by the end of the century in the form of the final victory of good over evil at the end of time. He resumed his war and his violent means with greater intensity than ever, and he preached with vigor in letters and manifestos that were read aloud to the peasant soldiers. His soldiers became daring zealots, an army of God.[3] Thus, Sandino's response to the failure of his prophecy conforms to the reactions observed by Festinger and his colleagues, with a significant variation: Sandino's prediction involved an event in time, and failure prompted (in addition to strong proselytizing and the setting of a new date) an eschatologizing of what until then had been a political struggle.

**Millennial Certainty and Revolutionary Politics**

Whether or not they have faced the failure of prophecy, millenarian movements have often attracted adherents who have experienced failure, defeat, or oppression of other sorts. According to Cohn, these groups have not only dreamed of role reversal but also have believed that they were collectively superior to all other people; uncertainty and despair were filled by promises of eternal glory, the group became "obsessed by the apocalyptic fantasy, and filled with the conviction of its own infallibility set itself infinitely above the rest of humanity and recognized no claims save that of its own supposed mission" (1970, 16, 283, 285). These are the same traits that Cohn

3. The Basque chronicler Belausteguigoitia remarked the religious dimension of Sandino's crusade, observing that Sandino (like Oliver Cromwell) had instilled great zeal in his peasant troops, "made a religious sect out of his army," and ignited in them "the fire of a new revelation" (1985, 130–31).

also noted in modern revolutionary and totalitarian movements—indeed, a potential that exists in all movements of this kind.

The certainty and zeal with which millenarian movements embrace fantasies to relieve their existential anxiety is what Eric Voegelin terms *gnosticism*. Voegelin identifies the first influential manifestation of this gnosis in the speculations of the thirteenth-century monk Joachim de Fiore, a medieval monk who devised a system of thought dividing history into three ages conforming to the three persons of the Holy Trinity: the age of the Father, the age of the Son, and the coming age of the Holy Spirit. According to Voegelin, Joachim's vision of the tripartite meaning of history set aside Augustine and the uncertainty of human existence by bringing back into profane history the notion of a transcendent eschatological direction. Many millenarian fantasies have since incorporated the central components of Joachitic speculation; his partition of history and related symbolism, for instance, reemerged in the secularized thinking of G. F. W. Hegel and Auguste Comte (through which it shaped Gámez's tripartite Nicaraguan history), to be developed by Karl Marx into a political system. Each these thinkers believed that they had discovered the meaning of history—a false belief, according to Voegelin: "The problem of an *eidos* in history . . . arises only when Christian transcendental fulfillment becomes immanentized. [It] is a theoretical fallacy. History has no *eidos*, because the course of history extends into the unknown future. The meaning of history is an illusion" (1952, 120). In his early writings, Voegelin (1986) showed that what he called "political religions" are gnostic movements that in their search for earthly spiritual fulfillment, final salvation, and meaning in their lives, replace the world-transcendent symbols of the Christian faith with profane symbols such as race, class, and nation. Indeed, Voegelin refers to such movements—hypostases of the human longing for eschatological, transcendent salvation—as spiritual disorders.

Norman Cohn too, in his early groundbreaking work, regards millennial movements as spiritual disorders. Later, however, in his *Cosmos, Chaos and the World to Come* (1993)—which traces the millenarian disposition to an element present in Zoroastrianism, late Judaism, and early Christianity—Cohn is more inclined to see millenarian outbursts as a product of religious and spiritual development than as a pathological expression. Expanding on this view, Flanagan locates millenarianism "as part of the repertoire of political behavior," a specific response to political life, not simply as the province of fringe, radical groups in colonized or backward societies or as "an exotic response to catastrophic shock" (1995b, 165). Because politics involves managing conflict and situations of conflict generate anxiety, millenarianism constitutes a possible response to that anxiety with its vision of a "conflict-free millennium."

Flanagan (1995b) sketches three types of political dispositions: monism, dualism, and pluralism. Monism, the "philosophy of oneness," is present in the belief that a social group is a homogenous whole, undivided and unfettered by conflict or cleavages. Monism may take forms such as populism and totalitarianism. Dualism interprets the world in terms of the presence of two clashing forces: the warring of two nations to the death, perhaps, or an internal dichotomy based on class, gender, or race. Pluralism is the notion of accepting and promoting the presence of a variety of ideas and points of view, which takes form in liberal democracies and constitutional régimes. Millenarian movements can be monistic and dualistic, but in the end most are dualistic, for as Flanagan points out, the monistic are typically single-minded in relation or opposition to a pluralistic model. In the context of complex plural (political) societies, millenarian movements are bound to be ignored as utopian or will violently clash with the mainstream values of the group. The Salvation Army and the Natural Law Party figure among the former; the radical racist right and radical antiabortion groups in North America are among the latter. The wider implications of Flanagan's argument in the political realm are similar to the conclusion that James reached about radical religious millenarians: they are here to stay.

What are we to make of the imposing record of violence on the part of medieval and modern millenarian movements? Millenarian ideals, it has been argued, supported the rise of Hitler's Nazi revolution, for Hitler too argued that Germany lacked purpose and integration and suffered under the unjust burden of the peace of Versailles, and he successfully articulated a strengthened German identity through racial symbolism (Rhodes 1980). There is a certain fallacy in the assumption that change and relief from suffering are necessarily goods in themselves. The study of movements headed by the likes of Hitler, Pol Pot, Stalin, and others may lead us to question the notion of a "religion of the oppressed," for in many instances millenarian movements have also become the religion of the oppressor. Under the weight of suffering and uncertainty about the world, religions, ideologies, and myths emerge; paradoxically, it is one's disposition toward this ultimate uncertainty that greatly determines what kind of religion (or politics) one will embrace. James is correct in doubting that radical millenarian movements can disappear, for it does seem that some constitutions need them too much.

In his views on and uses of violence, Sandino was closer to the pattern of a modern revolutionary millenarian than to that of a nativistic cult. The ideas that guided and misguided his actions are ancient, but his impatient disposition is radically modern, indebted to the tradition that has embraced progress and that is unwilling to wait for the world to change or to rely on Providence. Given that Sandino believed that semidivine spirits populated his troops, he (much like the medieval Adamites) had no reason to wait for God to transform the world; that was in fact the mission of the twenty-nine spirits. In that sense Sandino, a mechanic by training, represents *homo faber*, the maker of worlds who will help the millennium arrive regardless of the cost. Like Dostoevsky's Raskolnikov, he believed that history was "an ocean of blood" (Sandino 1981, 1:330), but he was bolder—perhaps more like Koestler's Ivanov, unconcerned with the sacrifice of as many lives as it takes in order to see his understanding of history fulfilled (Koestler 1980, 131). Sandino was the typical twentieth-century millenarian revolutionary who, like his European contemporaries, was prepared to destroy the world in order to save it. Convinced of the divine necessity of his cause and supported by his beliefs in transmigratory spirits, Sandino was able to justify greater and more intense violence. His justification came from God Himself, incarnate in him. As a messiah, Sandino believed that he was helping to realize the grand design of God. It is easier, after all, to justify the kind of violence that Sandino practiced when one has the certainty that the extermination of evil will hasten the arrival of the millennium.

It is worth remarking, if only in passing, that the military and political movement that later claimed to follow in the footsteps of Sandino in Nicaragua, the FSLN, presented an equivalent message of hope and redemption for its followers and exhibited the same pattern of action and reaction as its martyred hero. The latter-day Sandinistas both appropriated the image of Sandino and emulated many of his actions. However, a full discussion of the relationship between Sandino and the later Sandinistas cannot be pursued here and awaits a careful study of its own.

Millenarian religions can be understood either as representing a constructive experience and a developing mechanism for their societies or as expressing a pneumopathological flight from reality. Of course, no millenarian movement can be described fully by either of these extremes; millenarian figures and movements are highly dynamic and complex, and they develop in a multitude of ways that defy any single mode of classification. We may agree with Voegelin that a gnostic element may be discerned in all of these movements, but we must keep in mind that not all gnostic millenarian movements develop into totalitarian systems. There exists an array of circumstances and factors bearing on each individual movement— including particular religious beliefs, political experiences, the movement's position in the balance of forces, and its ability to produce change through political means—that determines the movement's ultimate orientation.

That being granted, we must still agree with Cohn that the potential for radical totalitarianism is always present in radical millenarian movements. My examination of Sandino's development and record do not allow for a classification of his millenarianism as a constructive one. To be sure, the peasant movement headed by Augusto Sandino was crushed at a moment of temporary and strategic retreat, and there is no way of telling precisely what it would have become. We do know what it was in its time, however, and the historical evidence seems clear. Belausteguigoitia once lamented that is was a "pity that Nicaragua [is] such a small country" because he thought a man of Sandino's stature deserved "a greater country . . . maybe the whole of Latin America" (1985, 137). Judging by Sandino's boundless ambition, his self-absorption, his theocratic disposition, his zealous plans to control the totality of Nicaraguan life, his racism, and his record of violence, it is safe to speculate that a larger movement, controlling a larger territory, might have meant only greater atrocities and bloodshed.

### Sandino Vive

This book has drawn attention to the religious dimension of Augusto Sandino's life and experiences and has mapped the development of his millenarianism. Such an approach allows us to see that Sandino acted in accordance with a pattern that is characteristic of many other millenarian prophets and messiahs in Third World countries—and is similar to the modern gnostic element that fueled totalitarian régimes over the past century.

In thus fusing Sandino's politics and his religiousness, we avoid the mistake (characteristic of so many of his latter-day critics and followers alike) of seeing the sacred and the profane as clearly delineated and mutually exclusive polarities. Wunderich, for example—like a good Marxian— sees the apparent gap between the religious and the mundane aspirations in Sandino as a contradiction that must be resolved, if it is to make sense. Sandino, he writes, "secularized *all* religious ideas, and referred them to the practical goal of national liberation. . . . His message uses apocalyptic language. . . . but it is not a religious message. *It contradicts the transcendental orientation.* . . . He separates history from cosmology. . . . His nationalism and his communitarian ideal did not mystify the political, but rather politicized his cosmic vision" (1995, 152–53; emphasis added). Seeing religion in general not as an activity grounded in human experiences of the divine but as flights of fancy that are divorced from reality (141), Wünderich is insensitive to the validity of religious attitudes, including those of millenarian political religions in particular. Indeed, Wünderich's position on Sandino's religious "digression" (130) puts into question the moral and spiritual commitment of Sandino's beliefs. Wünderich's conclusion that Sandino's religious ideas constituted a means to the secular end of his struggle is close to Hodges's (1986) arguments that Sandino was a populist demagogue and a skilled manipulator; in Wünderich's view, Sandino—with his "singular *pretension* to believe himself justice incarnate" (*la singular pretension de creerse encarnación de la justicia*)—was a faker (Wünderich 1995, 318; emphasis added). I pay Sandino the greater compliment of actually taking seriously his own ideas and his profession of faith. What Wünderich sees as a contradiction that needs resolving is in fact the manifestation of a typical tension of human existence, a tension only exaggerated (not created) by the peculiar disposition of millenarian figures.

Sandino's life is an example of what human beings are capable of when—engulfed by pride, lost in despair, and crushed by the anxiety of their existence—they search for relief and final salvation in absolute worldly certainty. Many would blame religion or religiousness in general. To think that religious hope is to blame for these results, however, is to draw the wrong conclusion. "It is in hope that we are saved," Augustine noted, "[b]ut hope that is seen is not hope" (1958, 19.4) True hope is "the faith of things not seen" (Heb. 11:1), which requires spiritual fortitude: "For how can a man hope for what he sees?" Augustine asked, "but if we hope for what we do not see, we wait with patience." Patience is a quality strange to revolutionists; its absence suggests that we look into their nature to understand their excesses.

If Salman Rushdie's insight about Nicaraguans is correct—that in order to understand their living one must first come to an understanding of their dead—then the study of an influential Nicaraguan figure like Augusto Sandino can only contribute to our comprehension of present-day Nicaragua. With Sandino's story in mind, it may be easier to understand why a man like Marco Antonio Bonilla, claiming to be the son of God at the

Oriental Market in Managua during Easter 1992, was able to draw large crowds of people in search of a favor, a miraculous cure, or a simple blessing. It may be easier to understand that witches are unionized in Nicaragua. It may be easier to understand the Sandinista difficulty in accepting the 1990 and 1996 election results and how their threat of violence seeks justification in the defense of what they call the gains of their revolution.

Rushdie's remark is insightful not only because it identifies that many Nicaraguans easily connect Sandino and Christ but also because it shows that millenarian expectations in that country may still be floating on the surface. It should not come as a surprise, therefore, that a great number of Nicaraguans still identify with and revere the figure of Sandino.

IN the compact truth of the Maya-Quiché myth of genesis, the world was engendered by Tepeu, the Lord, with the assistance of Gucumatz, a mythical half-celestial and half-earthly creature represented by the plumed serpent. They met, and from their meditations, words, and counsels the earth was born; from the immobility and silence of darkness, the world came into existence. In the experience of the Maya-Quiché, the power and wisdom of the Creator were mediated and complemented by the serene fellowship of the mystical serpent.

In a sense, Sandino—mystical and practical, humiliated and proud— combined both lord and plumed serpent of the Maya-Quiché creation myth, as he attempted to bring the world out of darkness, to recreate it in the light of the revelations of the new age. Instead of serene words and meditations, however, he brought blood and revolution.

# Works Cited

Note: A fuller bibliography of materials by and about Sandino, including reproductions of some of the primary sources cited here, may be found at the Sandino website, http://www.sandino.org.

Adas, Michael. 1987. *Prophets of Rebellion: Millenarian Protest Movements Against the European Colonial Order.* New York: Cambridge Univ. Press.

Alemán Bolaños, Gustavo. 1951. *Sandino el libertador: Biografía del héroe americano.* Mexico City: Ediciones Caribe.

Alemán Bolaños, Gustavo, and José Idiáquez. 1930. Letter to Augusto C. Sandino, 30 Dec. Photocopy in possession of the author.

Anthony, Dick, and Thomas Robbins. 1995. "Religious Totalism, Violence and Exemplary Dualism: Beyond the Extrinsic Model." *Terrorism and Political Violence* 7, no. 3: 10–50.

Arias Gómez, Jorge. 1972. *Farabundo Martí: Esbozo biográfico.* San José, Costa Rica: Editorial Universitaria Centroamericana.

Aristotle. 1990. *Nichomachean Ethics.* Trans. David Ross. Oxford: Oxford Univ. Press.

Arrieta, Nicolás. 1971. *Habla Sandino.* Masaya, Nicaragua: Privately printed.

Augustine. 1958. *The City of God.* Trans. Gerald G. Walsh, Demetrius B. Zema, Grace Monahan, and Daniel Honan. New York: Image.

Barbusse, Henri. 1928. "Carta al General Sandino." *Amauta* (Lima), no. 19: 92–93.

Barkun, Michael. 1986. *Disaster and the Millennium.* New Haven, Conn.: Yale Univ. Press.

———. 1994. "Millenarian Groups and Law Enforcement Agencies: The Lessons of Waco." *Terrorism and Political Violence* 6, no. 1: 75–95.

———. 1995. "Understanding Millennialism." *Terrorism and Political Violence* 7, no. 3: 1–9.

———. 1997. *Religion and the Racist Right: The Origins of the Christian Identity Movement.* Rev. ed. Chapel Hill: Univ. of North Carolina Press.

Beals, Carleton. 1932. *Banana Gold.* Philadelphia: Lippincot.

Belausteguigoitia, Ramón de. 1985. *Con Sandino en Nicaragua: La hora de paz.* 2nd Nicaraguan ed. Managua: Editorial Nueva Nicaragua.

Bendaña, Alejandro. 1994. *La mística de Sandino.* Managua: Centro de Estudios Internacionales.

———. 1995. Speech given at the Olof Palme Conference Centre, Managua, in commemoration of the 61st anniversary of Sandino's execution, 21 Feb. Complete text available at http://www.tigerden.com/~berios/sandinosoc.txt.

Benz, Ernest. 1968. *Evolution and Christian Hope: Man's Concept of the Future, from the Early Fathers to Teilhard de Chardin.* Trans. Heinz G. Frank. New York: Anchor.

Bethell, Leslie, ed. 1991. *Central America since Independence.* New York: Cambridge Univ. Press.

Billington, James H. 1980. *Fire in the Minds of Men: Origins of the Revolutionary Faith.* New York: Basic Books.

Blavatsky, H. P. 1972. *Isis Unveiled* (1877), in *Collected Writings,* vol. 1. Wheaton, Ill.: Theosophical Publishing House.

———. 1992. *The Key to Theosophy: An Abridgement.* 3rd printing. [Wheaton, Ill.]: Theosophical Publishing House.

Bolaños, Pio. 1984. *Génesis de la intervención norteamericana en Nicaragua.* Managua: Editorial Nueva Nicaragua.

Bolívar, Simón. 1976. *Simón Bolívar: Doctrina del Libertador.* Ed. M. Pérez Vila. Caracas: Biblioteca Ayacucho.

Booth, John A. 1985. *The End and the Beginning: The Nicaraguan Revolution.* 2nd rev. ed. Boulder, Colo.: Westview.

Borge, Tomás. 1988. "Intervención en la Plaza de la Revolución 'Carlos Fonseca' en el primer encuentro de la policía y los niños." In *Los primeros pasos: Revolución popular sandinista.* Mexico City: Ediciones Siglo Veintiuno.

———. 1989. *La paciente impaciencia.* Havana: Ediciones Casa de las Américas.

Brockett, Charles D. 1990. *Land, Power and Poverty: Agrarian Transformation and Political Conflict in Central America.* Boston: Unwin Hyman.

Brooks, David. 1989. "U.S. Marines, Miskitos, and the Hunt for Sandino: The Rio Coco Patrol in 1928." *Journal of Latin American Studies* 21: 311–42.

———. 1998. "Rebellion from Without: Culture and Politics Along Nicaragua's Atlantic Coast in the Time of the Sandino Revolt, 1926–1934." Ph.D. diss., Univ. of Connecticut.

Campos Ponce, Xavier. 1979. *Sandino: Biografía de un héroe.* 3rd ed. Mexico City: Edamex.

Cohn, Norman. 1970. *The Pursuit of the Millennium: Revolutionary Millenarians and Mystical Anarchists of the Middle Ages.* Rev. ed. New York: Oxford Univ. Press. (First edition published in 1957.)

———. 1993. *Cosmos, Chaos and the World to Come: The Ancient Roots of Apocalyptic Faith.* New Haven, Conn.: Yale Univ. Press.

Crawley, Eduardo. 1984. *Nicaragua in Perspective.* New York: St. Martin's.

Cuadra, Pablo Antonio. 1978. *El nicaragüense.* 8th ed. Managua: Editorial Universitaria Centroamericana.

Darío, Rubén. 1973. *Antología Poética.* Buenos Aires: Editorial Kapelusz.

———. 1988. *Selected Poems of Rubén Darío.* Trans. Lysander Kemp. Austin: Univ. of Texas Press.

Diacon, Todd A. 1991. *Millenarian Vision, Capitalist Reality: Brazil's Contestado Rebellion, 1912–1916.* Durham, N.C.: Duke Univ. Press.

Dospital, Michelle. 1991. "Sandino y la Escuela Magnetico-Espiritual de la Comuna Universal." *Cátedra: Revista de Ciencia, Cultura y Educación* (Managua) 1, no. 1: 48–54.

———. 1992. "La construcción del Estado Nacional en Nicaragua: El proyecto sandinista, 1933–1934." Paper presented at the First Central American Congress of History, Tegucigalpa, Honduras, 13–16 July.

———. 1996. *Siempre más allá . . . : El movimiento sandinista en Nicaragua, 1927–1934.* Managua: Instituto de Historia de Nicaragua.

Dulles, A. 1967. "Revelation (Theology of)." In *Catholic Encyclopedia,* vol. 12. New York: McGraw-Hill.

Eliade, Mircea. 1959. *The Sacred and The Profane: The Nature of Religion.* Trans. Willard R. Trask. New York: Harcourt.

———. 1991a. *The Myth of the Eternal Return.* Trans. Willard R. Trask. Princeton, N.J.: Princeton Univ. Press.

———. 1991b. *Yoga: Immortalidad y libertad.* Trans. Diana Luz Sánchez. Mexico City: Fondo de Cultura Económica.

Festinger, Leon, Henry Riecken, and Stanley Schacter. 1966. *When Prophecy Fails: A Social and Psychological Study of a Modern Group that Predicted the Destruction of the World.* New York: Harper Torchbooks.

Flanagan, Thomas. 1995a. "On the Trail of the Massinahican: Louis Riel's Encounter with Theosophy." *Journal of the Canadian Church Historical Society* 37, no. 2: 89–98.

———. 1995b. "The Politics of the Millennium." *Terrorism and Political Violence* 7, no. 3: 165–75.

———. 1996. *Louis "David" Riel: Prophet of the New World.* Rev. ed. Toronto: Univ. of Toronto Press.

Fonseca Amador, Carlos. 1980a. *Ideario político de Augusto César Sandino.* Managua: Secretaría de Propaganda y Educación Política del FSLN.

———. 1980b. *Sandino: Guerrillero proletario.* Managua: Editorial Nueva Nicaragua.

Frye, Northrop. 1990. *The Great Code: The Bible and Literature.* Toronto: Penguin.

FSLN (Frente Sandinista de Liberación Nacional). 1977. *Plataforma general politico-militar del F.S.L.N.* N.p.: Dirección Nacional del Frente Sandinista de Liberación Nacional.

Fuentes, Carlos. 1985. *Latin America at War with the Past*. Montreal: CBC Enterprises.

Gámez, José Dolores. 1889. *Historia de Nicaragua*. Managua: Imprenta El País.

Garraty, John. 1979. *The American Nation: History of the United States*. 4th ed. New York: Harper and Row.

Gilbert, Gregorio Urbano. 1979. *Junto a Sandino*. Santo Domingo: Editora Alfa y Omega.

Girardi, Giulio. 1987. *Sandinismo, marxismo, cristianismo: La confluencia*. Managua: Centro Ecuménico Antonio Valdivieso.

Glick, Thomas F. 1991. "Science and Independence in Latin America (with Special Reference to New Granada)." *Hispanic American Historical Review* 71, no. 2: 307–34.

Gould, Jeffrey L. 1993. " '¡Vana ilusión!' The Highlands Indians and the Myth of Nicaragua Mestiza, 1880–1925." *Hispanic American Historical Review* 73, no. 3: 393–429.

———. 1998. *To Die in This Way: Nicaraguan Indians and the Myth of Mestizaje, 1890–1965*. Durham, N.C.: Duke Univ. Press.

Gould, Robert Freke. N.d. *History of Freemasonry: Its Antiquities, Symbols, Constitutions, Customs, etc*. London: Caxton.

Haya de la Torre, Victor Raúl. 1927. *Por la enmancipación de América Latina*. Buenos Aires: Gleizer.

———. 1928. Letter to Froylán Turcios. *Ariel* (Tegucigalpa) 4, no. 60: 1185.

———. 1936. *El antiimperialismo y el APRA*. Santiago de Chile: Ediciones Arcilla.

Hobsbawm, E. J. 1965. *Primitive Rebels: Studies in Archaic Forms of Social Movements in the Nineteenth and Twentieth Centuries*. New York: Norton. (Originally published in 1959.)

Hodges, Donald C. 1986. *Intellectual Foundations of the Nicaraguan Revolution*. Austin: Univ. of Texas Press.

———. 1992. *Sandino's Communism: Spiritual Politics for the Twenty-First Century*. Austin: Univ. of Texas Press.

Huntington, Samuel P. 1997. *The Clash of Civilizations and the Remaking of World Order*. New York: Touchstone.

Ibarra Grijalva, Domingo. 1973. *The Last Night of General Augusto C. Sandino*. Trans. Gloria Bonitz. New York: Vintage.

IES (Instituto de Estudios del Sandinismo). 1986. *General Augusto C. Sandino: Padre de la revolución popular antimperialista, 1895–1934*. Managua: Editorial Nueva Nicaragua.

Invernizzi, Gabriele, Francis Pisani, and Jesús Ceberio. 1986. *Sandinistas: Entrevistas a Humberto Ortega Saavedra, Jaime Wheelock Román y Bayardo Arce Castaño*. Managua: Editorial Vanguardia.

James, William. 1958. *The Varieties of Religious Experience: A Study in Human Nature*. New York: Mentor. (Originally published in 1902.)

Kaplan, Jeffrey. 1997. *Radical Religion in America: Millenarian Movements from the Far Right to the Children of Noah.* Syracuse, N.Y.: Syracuse Univ. Press.

Kardec, Allan. 1979. *Le livre des esprits.* Montréal: Presses Sélect.

Knight, Alan. 1986. *The Mexican Revolution.* Vol. 2, *Counterrevolution and Reconstruction.* Cambridge: Cambridge Univ. Press.

Koestler, Arthur. 1980. *Darkness at Noon.* New York: Penguin.

Lanternari, Vittorio. 1963. *The Religions of the Oppressed: A Study of Modern Cults.* Trans. Lisa Sergio. New York: Knopf.

Lee, Martha F. 1988. *The Nation of Islam: An American Millenarian Movement.* New York: Edwin Mellen.

———. 1995. *Earth First! Environmental Apocalypse.* Syracuse, N.Y.: Syracuse Univ. Press.

Locke, John. 1989. *The Second Treatise of Government.* Ed. Thomas P. Peaedon. New York: Macmillan.

Macaulay, Neil. 1985. *The Sandino Affair.* Durham, N.C.: Duke Univ. Press. (Originally published in 1967.)

Machiavelli, Niccolò. 1984. *The Prince.* Trans. P. Bondanella and M. Musa. New York: Oxford Univ. Press.

Maraboto, Emigdio. 1929. *Sandino ante el coloso.* Veracruz, Mexico: Editorial Veracruz.

Marcus, Bruce. 1985. *Nicaragua: The Sandinista People's Revolution, Speeches by Sandinista Leaders.* New York: Pathfinder.

Matagalpa, Juan. 1984. *Juan Matagalpa: Sandino, los Somoza y los nueve comandantes sandinistas.* [Tegucigalpa?]: Honduras Industrial.

McCarthy, D. J. 1967. "Prophet." In *Catholic Encyclopedia,* vol. 12. New York: McGraw-Hill.

Meyer, Jean. 1976. *The Cristero Rebellion: The Mexican People Between Church and State.* Trans. Richard Southern. Cambridge: Cambridge Univ. Press.

Meyer, Michael C., William L. Sherman, and Susan M. Deeds. 1999. *The Course of Mexican History.* 6th ed. New York: Oxford Univ. Press.

Mill, John Stuart. 1859. *On Liberty.* London: John W. Parker.

Millett, Richard. 1977. *Guardians of the Dynasty: A History of the U.S. Created Guardia Nacional de Nicaragua and the Somoza Family.* Maryknoll, N.Y.: Orbis.

Moncada, José María. 1985. *Nicaragua: Sangre en sus montañas.* San José, Calif.: Privately printed.

Navarro-Génie, Marco A. 2000. "Augusto 'César' Sandino: Prophet of the Segovias." In *Millennial Visions: Essays on Twentieth-Century Millenarianism,* ed. Martha F. Lee, 147–71. New York: Praeger.

Newland, Carlos. 1991. "La educación elemental en Hispanoamérica: Desde la independencia hasta la centralización de los sistemas educativos nacionales." *Hispanic American Historical Review* 71, no. 2: 335–64.

Nietzsche, Friedrich. 1966. *Beyond Good and Evil: Prelude to a Philosophy of the Future.* Trans. Walter Kaufmann. New York: Vintage.

Ortega Saavedra, Humberto. 1976. *50 años de lucha Sandinista.* Managua: Privately printed.

Paige, Jefferey M. 1997. *Coffee and Power: Revolution and the Rise of Democracy in Central America.* Cambridge. Mass.: Harvard Univ. Press.

Pérez-Brignoli, Héctor. 1989. *A Brief History of Central America.* Trans. Ricardo Sawrey and Susana Stettri. Berkeley: Univ. of California Press.

Pérez Valle, Eduardo. 1986. *El asesinato de Sandino.* Managua: Ministerio de Cultura.

Plutarch. 1982. *Selected Lives.* Trans. John Dryden. Franklin Center, Penn.: N.p. (Originally published in 1676.)

Portes Gil, Emilio. 1964. *Autobiografía de la revolución mexicana: Un tratado de interpretación histórica.* Mexico City: Instituto Mexicano de Cultura.

Quirk, Robert. 1962. *An Affair of Honor: Woodrow Wilson and the Occupation of Veracruz.* New York: Norton.

Redmond, R. X. 1967. "Prophecy (Theology of)." *Catholic Encyclopedia,* vol. 12. New York: McGraw-Hill.

Reed, Nelson. 1964. *The Caste War of Yucatán.* Stanford, Calif.: Stanford Univ. Press.

Rhodes, James M. 1980. *The Hitler Movement: A Modern Millenarian Movement.* Stanford, Calif.: Hoover Institution Press.

RIP-RIP. 1928. *El verdadero Sandino.* San Salvador: Tipografía La Unión.

Rius. 1986. *El hermano Sandino.* Mexico City: Grijalbo.

Rivera Bertrán, Enrique. 1930. Typed letter to Pedro José Zepeda, 9 June. Photocopy in possession of the author.

Rodó, José Enrique. 1957. *Ariel.* Mexico City: Editorial Novara. (Originally published in 1900.)

Román, José. 1979. *Maldito país.* Managua: Ediciones de El Pez y la Serpiente.

Rushdie, Salman. 1987. *The Jaguar Smile: A Nicaraguan Journey.* New York: Penguin.

Salvatierra, Sofonías. 1980. *Sandino o la tragedia de un pueblo.* 2nd ed. Managua: Talleres Litográficos Maltez.

———. 1986. Letter to Presidente Juan Bautista Sacasa, 11 Nov. 1934. *Boletín Archivo Nacional* 3: 46–51. Managua: Ministerio de Cultura.

Sandino, Augusto C. 1928a. "Carta del Invicto Defensor de la Soberanía de Nicaragua [29 Dec. 1927]." *Ariel* (Tegucigalpa) 4, no. 57: 1096.

———. 1928b. Letter to Froylán Turcios, 1 Apr. 1928. *Ariel* (Tegucigalpa) 4, no. 59: 1123.

———. 1929. Letter to Luis Araquistain, 31 July. *Amauta* (Lima), no. 20: 94–95.

———. 1930a. Typescript of letter to G. Gastón Lafarga, 4 Feb. Photocopy in possession of the author.

———. 1930b. Typescript of letter to Juan Segovia Escudero, 9 Mar. Photocopy in possession of the author.

———. 1930c. Typescript of letter to Francisco Vera, 23 Apr. Photocopy in possession of the author.

———. 1980. *Escritos literarios y documentos desconocidos.* Ed. Jorge Eduardo Arellano. Managua: Biblioteca Nacional de Nicaragua.

———. 1981. *El pensamiento vivo de Sandino.* Ed. Sergio Ramírez. 2nd ed., rev. 2 vol. Managua: Editorial Nueva Nicaragua.

———. 1990. *Sandino: The Testimony of a Nicaraguan Patriot, 1921–1934.* Ed. Sergio Ramírez, trans. R. E. Conrad. Princeton, N.J.: Princeton Univ. Press.

———. N.d. Autograph memorandum on accounting fragment. Photocopy in possession of the author.

Sandino, Sócrates. 1928. "La vida del General Sandino." *El Universal Ilustrado* (Mexico), 23 Feb.

Schlittler, Jaime. 1932. Typescript of letter to César Augusto Sandino, 24 Feb. Photocopy in possession of the author.

Schrauwers, Albert. 1993. *Awaiting the Millennium: The Children of Peace and the Village of Hope, 1812–1889.* Toronto: Toronto Univ. Press.

Schroeder, Michael J. 1993. " 'To Defend Our Nation's Honor': Toward a Social and Cultural History of the Sandino Rebellion in Nicaragua, 1927–1934." Ph.D. diss, Univ. of Michigan.

———. 1996. "Horse Thieves to Rebels to Dogs: Political Gang Violence and the State in the Western Segovias, Nicaragua, in the Time of Sandino, 1926–1934." *Journal of Latin American Studies* 28: 383–434.

Selser, Gregorio. 1960. *Sandino: General de hombres libres.* 2 vol. Havana: Imprenta Nacional de Cuba.

———. 1981. *Sandino: General of Free Men.* Trans. C. Belfrage. New York: Monthly Review Press.

———. 1983. *El pequeño ejército loco.* Managua: Editorial Nueva Nicaragua.

Sociedad Pro-Investigación de la Verdad Histórica sobre el Sandinismo. 1947. *La verdad histórica sobre el sandinismo.* Managua: Tipografía Atenas.

Somoza García, Anastasio. 1936. *El verdadero Sandino o el calvario de las Segovias.* Managua: Tipografía Robelo.

Stimson, Henry L. 1991. *American Policy in Nicaragua.* New York: Marcus Weiner.

Strong, Simon. 1992. *Shining Path: The World's Deadliest Revolutionary Force.* London: Harper Collins.

Talmon, Yonina. 1968. "Millenarism." *International Encyclopedia of the Social Sciences,* vol. 10. New York: Macmillan.

Tayacán, El. 1987. *Historia de la iglesia de los pobres en Nicaragua.* Managua: Privately printed.

Texeira, Diego de la, and Alfredo Matilda Rivas. 1978. *Sandino: Crónica de la guerra sandinista.* Managua: Privately printed.

Tirado López, Víctor. 1989. *Sandino y la doctrina de liberación.* Managua: Editorial Vanguardia.

Torres, Edelberto. 1984. *Sandino.* Mexico City: Editorial Katún.

Trincado, Joaquín. 1955. *Los cinco amores: ética y sociología.* Buenos Aires: Talleres Gráficos Preusche y Eggelin. (Originally published in 1922.)

Turcios, Froylán. 1928. "El héroe de la raza." *Ariel* (Tegucigalpa) 4, no. 59: 1111.

Vargas, Oscar-René. 1989a. *Elecciones presidenciales en Nicaragua, 1912–1932: Análysis político.* Managua: Talleres Gráficos Dilesa.

———. 1989b. "Sandino y la Costa Atlántica." *Nuevo Amanecer Cultural, Barricada* (Managua), 20 May, 3.

Vasconcelos, José. 1966. *La raza cósmica: Misión de la raza ibeoamericana.* Mexico City: Espasa-Calpe. (Originally published in 1925.)

———. 1990. Letter to José Angel Rodríguez, 30 June 1933. In Jorge Eduardo Arellano, "Sandino, Vasconcelos y el doctor Rodríguez," *La Prensa Literaria,* 22 Sept., 8.

Vayssière, Pierre. 1988. *Auguste César Sandino: Ou l'envers d'un mythe.* Toulouse: Centre National de Récherche Scientifique.

Velásquez Pereira, José Luis. 1992. *La formación del estado en Nicaragua: 1860–1930.* Managua: Fondo Editorial Banco Central de Nicaragua.

Vera, Francisco. 1932. Typescript of letter to Jaime Schlittler, 12 Feb. Photocopy in possession of the author.

Villanueva, Carlos. 1988. *Sandino en Yucatán 1929–1930.* Mexico City: Secretaría de Educación Pública.

Voegelin, Eric. 1952. *The New Science of Politics: An Introduction.* Chicago: Univ. of Chicago Press.

———. 1986. *The Political Religions.* Trans. T. J. DiNapoli and E. S. Easterly. New York: Edwin Mellen.

Vollmar, E. R. 1967. "Revivalism." In *Catholic Encyclopedia,* vol. 12. New York: McGraw-Hill.

Vondung, Klaus. 1992. "Millenarism, Hermeticism, and the Search for Universal Science." In *Science, Pseudo-Science, and Utopianism in Early Modern Thought,* ed. Stephen A. McKnight, 118–40. Columbia: Univ. of Missouri Press.

Wallace, Anthony F. C. 1956. "Revitalization Movements." *American Anthropologist* 58: 264–82.

Wallis, Ray, ed. 1982. *Millennialism and Charisma.* Belfast: Queen's Univ Press.

Weber, Eugene. 1999. *Apocalypses: Prophecies, Cults and Millennnial Beliefs Through the Ages.* Toronto: Random House.

Weber, Max. 1947. *The Theory of Social and Economic Organization.* Trans. A. M. Henderson and Talcott Parsons; ed. Talcott Parsons. New York: Free Press.

Woodward, Ralph Lee, Jr. 1985. *Central America: A Nation Divided.* 2nd ed. New York: Oxford Univ. Press.

Worsley, Peter. 1968. *The Trumpet Shall Sound: A Study of "Cargo" Cults in Melanesia.* New York: Schocken.

Wünderich, Volker. 1989. *Sandino en la costa: De las Segovias al litoral Atlántico.* Managua: Editorial Nueva Nicaragua.

————. 1995. *Sandino: Una biografía política.* Managua: Editorial Nueva Nicaragua.

Zepeda, Pedro José. 1930. Letter to Enrique Rivera Bertrán, 6 June. Photocopy in possession of the author.

# Index

Adamic race, 81

Adamites. *See* Bohemian Adamites

Adam-Moses, 144

Adas, Michael, 149, 154

*adelantos* (cash advances), 25–26

Africa, 145; millenarian movements of, 149

Aguado, Enoc, 42, 91

Alemán Bolaños, Gustavo, 118, 118n. 1, 132, 135, 158

Alexander, Alfonso, 105

*Alianza Popular Revolucionaria Americana* (APRA), 66–67, 74, 78, 85

All Souls Day, 26, 86

Altamirano, Pedro. *See* Pedrón

*Amauta* (review; Lima), xiv

anarchists, 17, *85*

Anglo-Saxon race, xx-xxi, 86, 147, 161, 162, 163

Anti-Imperialist League, 53, 64, 70–73

apocalypse, 16, 100, 105, 115, 142; signs of, 99–100

APRA. *See* Alianza Popular Revolucionaria Americana

Aráuz, Blanca, 31, 50, 90, 96–97, 123, 137–38

Archbishop Mora y del Río, 18

Archimedes, 58

*Ariel* (book), 52

*Ariel* (review; Tegucigalpa), xiv, 52

Aristotle, vii

Armageddon, Sandino's commitment to, 51

Army in Defense of the National Sovereignty of Nicaragua. *See Ejército Defensor de la Soberanía Nacional de Nicaragua* (EDSN)

Augustine, Saint, 164, 167, 171

*Autonomista* Army, 104,138

*Autonomista* (party), 133–34

Baldibia, Jesús, 104

Barahona, Humberto, 132–33, 135

Barahona, Lidia, 132–33

Barkun, Michael, 148–49, 160

Batista, Romao. *See* Father Cicero

Beals, Carleton, 7, 16, 20, 159

Belausteguigoitia, Ramón de, 7, 22, 22n.4, 31, 75, 80n. 6,101–2, 159, 166n. 3, 170

Bendaña, Alejandro, xxi, xxi n. 1, 94, 128n. 3

Benz, Ernest, 164

biblical prophesy, 142–43

biological determinism, 36, 131

Blavatsky, Helena, 83–84, 84n. 10

Bohemian Adamites, 98, 143–44, 169

*boleta* (registration card), 25

Bolívar, Simón, 40–41, 52, 56, 57, 59; Jamaica letter by, 40

Bolívar's Dream (plan), 57–61, 68, 130

Bonilla, Marco Antonio, 171–72

Borge, Tomás, 16

Branch Davidians, 16, *85*

brotherhood of mankind, 17, 18

Bryan-Chamorro Treaty, xx, 19, 40, 47, 123

cabalistic mysteries, 81

Cabo Gracias a Dios, 126

Calderón, Margarita (Sandino's mother), 4–6, 41–42, 77, 94, 150, 159

Calderón Sandino, Augusto Nicolás. *See* Sandino, Augusto